Ralph Maud

Charles Olson at the Harbor

Talonbooks

Talonbooks
P.O. Box 2076, Vancouver, British Columbia, Canada V6B 3S3
www.talonbooks.com

Typeset in Berkeley and printed and bound in Canada.

Second Printing: October 2008

The publisher gratefully acknowledges the financial support of the Canada Council for the Arts; the Government of Canada through the Book Publishing Industry Development Program; and the Province of British Columbia through the British Columbia Arts Council and the Book Publishing Tax Credit for our publishing activities.

With thanks to Wiesa Kujawa for computer help.

Library and Archives Canada Cataloguing in Publication

Maud, Ralph, date
    Charles Olson at the harbor / Ralph Maud.

Includes bibliographic references.
isbn 978-0-88922-576-3

    1. Olson, Charles, 1910–1970. 2. Poets, American—20th century—Biography
I. Title.

PS3529.L655Z74 2008   811'.54   C2008-901051-5

CHARLES OLSON AT THE HARBOR

Charles Olson in Washington D.C. c. 1943.
Kate Olson Archive.

Contents

Introduction

This is a reactive biography. From beginning to end, it takes on the one previous book-length biography, *Charles Olson: The Allegory of a Poet's Life* by Tom Clark, which, since the Norton edition of 1990, has stood squarely in the pathway of any attempt to follow it with another.

The situation I find myself in is somewhat akin to James Boswell's, as he describes it in the opening pages of *The Life of Samuel Johnson LL.D.* Boswell is compelled to refer to a preceding *Memoir* of Samuel Johnson by Sir John Hawkins, "a man, whom, during my long intimacy with Dr. Johnson, I never saw in his company, I think but once, and I am sure not above twice":

> Sir John Hawkins's ponderous labours, I must acknowledge, exhibit a *farrago*, of which a considerable portion is not devoid of entertainment to the lovers of literary gossip; but ... there is such an inaccuracy in the statement of facts, as in so solemn an authour is hardly excusable, and certainly makes his narrative very unsatisfactory. But what is still worse, there is throughout the whole of it a dark uncharitable cast, by which the most unfavourable construction is put upon almost every circumstance in the character and conduct of my illustrious friend. (*Oxford Standard Authors* p. 20)

By making some several corrections to Hawkins in his pages, Boswell hopes that Dr. Johnson might "by a true and fair delineation be vindicated" (p. 21).

In spite of my efforts during the ten years of editing the *Minutes of the Charles Olson Society* to reach Tom Clark with some information and reasoning that would give him pause, he has reissued *Charles Olson: The Allegory of a Poet's Life* unchanged, saying in the preface to the new printing that nothing has convinced him that his book "is at significant variance with truth" (North Atlantic paperback, 2000, p. xiii).

So I have decided that the stakes have been raised and that my complaints can now with honor be put into a book-length format where, having grown from righteous nitpicking through glorious indignation, they can be a castle of perseverance against the spread of Clark's misinformation.

The dominant mode of this approach is therefore more argumentative than descriptive. However, the weight of complaint cannot be uniformly sustained, and the narrative from time to time confronts Olson the man rather than his critic, especially when my personal acquaintance with the poet has given me stories to tell and the kind of insight that comes to someone from sitting with Olson at his kitchen table in Gloucester. Perhaps there are enough of these occasions to have this volume stand as the full-length biography of Charles Olson that I once intended to write.

1
Birth and Death

Tom Clark begins his biography naturally enough with Charles Olson's birth date, 27 December 1910, stressing that it is just after the winter solstice. He can then immediately connect to what he calls Olson's "fears of mortality" and "dread of death." I guess it's plausible—the darkest part of the year, obviously. But the sad old poet that Clark seems to want to parade before us in chains is a fiction. Of course Olson was not apart from humanity and its self-awarenesses, but Clark seems to think that there was something extraordinarily morbid in Olson's talking about his death in annual dinners with his sister-in-law, Jean Kaiser. I see it as admirable that he could appeal to her as the Wise Old Woman, to make his death a fact they could contemplate together. What a gift it is to have someone speak with love about the ultimate farewell. When once I was talking with Olson through the early hours and he came to the point of saying, "The world gives you so much, then it takes it away," I said I didn't want to talk about that. He said, "You don't?" Jean Kaiser was a wonderful person and could, I believe, help Olson feel that it was all right to die. Clark uses Jean's volunteered memories to bolster a cliché of his own manufacture—the poet as finished.

The end of his book brings us back to this theme and the winter solstice dinner of 1968, when, according to Clark, "the gnawing question of mortality was more on his mind than ever" (p. 342). "I knew then," Jean Kaiser told Clark, "that he was going to die. I could see it. I believe that he knew it too." Clark then feels free to pile on the pathos: "Olson's inner consciousness that the alchemy of creation was escaping him, and life itself along with it, was indeed now a source of much dread for him" (p. 342). Like so much of what Clark alleges about Olson, this at first might seem plausible, but on closer examination it turns out not to be true. I cite a letter written to Joyce Benson on 12 December 1968, when, far from chucking it all, Olson was in the midst of studying Sylvanus Smith's *Fisheries of Cape Ann*.

> Joyce: I'm lost in a bunch of vessels of olden time ... I am as usual
> "happy" at this time of year with southwest & west winds blowing
> in my windows—and consistent time, like on a long voyage, almost
> unbroken ... (Storrs unpublished letter)

It's true I felt the presence of something when, the summer before his
terminal illness, I went to see Olson in Gloucester on 7 June 1969; but he
talked vividly about many things, and when I wanted to say goodbye with
all the recognition of mortality that that entailed and I said, "It's very sad,"
Olson turned the tables on me and replied, "No, it isn't," again with full
recognition. I'm not sure I didn't repeat my statement, and he likewise.
There was a kind of a gap in time. Then he said only that I shouldn't send
my students to see him. He would reply to their letters; "but," he said, "my
breath is my own." As I was leaving, after the three-hour interruption, he
was turning back to the *Maximus* poem in progress on his kitchen table.

I do not, therefore, accept Clark's picture of the poet in decline, which
he appears to feel that he has clinched by quoting lines from a poem of
August 1968: "in loneliness & in such pain I <u>can't</u> /lift the bottom of the
alemb the gold-/making juices lie in" (p. 343). This is from a long and
beautiful poem beginning "I'm going to hate to leave this Earthly Paradise"
(*Maximus* III.197–201). It is the greatest poem (I think) of this later period,
or the one that gives the truest sense of Olson living out his life, a lot of it
in the late hours of the night as they pass into the early hours of the
morning. And on this night of 5–6 August 1968 at 2:25 A.M. he writes the
following lines after those Clark chose to cite to rest his case that the poet
was down and out. These, on the contrary, show us Charles Olson at the
harbor, focused and attentive, looking out and listening, the ecstasy arising
naturally from the accuracy of the particulars of the sights and sounds:

> ... while
> off-shore out the Harbor for the 1st
> of all the nights of life I've lived upon,
> around the Harbor I hear also
> even in the fair & clear near round
> & full moon August night the
> Groaner and the Whistling Buoy in their
> soft pelting of the land I love
>> As though I were my love & master Bach
> and say in hymn & prayer
> himself
>> God festen Berg

The passage ends "in hymn & celebration." Clark libels Olson by quoting only those lines that make him seem a sad, weakened Titan.

Now, returning to Clark's opening paragraphs, we are asked to entertain a further plausibility: if one dreads death, won't one seek the refuge of eternal life in some form or other? Olson, "a lapsed Catholic" (or so Clark pigeon-holes him), supposedly obtains consolation from the fact that time is really "a looping rubber band that never lost its elasticity" (p. 4). This loopy image, I believe, is Clark's; it's not in quotes. I don't think Olson ever talked about a "rubber band." Neither would Olson have accepted the phrase "eternal return," which Clark also wants to give him. Nor "mystical renewal." And the quote, "Eternity is more interesting than infinity," which is plucked from an unpublished letter to Robert Duncan eight years prior (8 February 1960), has much to do with Alfred North Whitehead and requires deeper digging. It can't possibly be used as evidence for Olson's trying to escape "death's finitude" (p. 4). What follows in the letter to Duncan is the exact opposite of that; it is the celebration of the eternity in the here and now:

> eternity is more interesting than infinity
> —like you and Ibn Araqui and Jess and I are
> and all whom we love, and what, are now

—which is an existentialism far from Clark's notion that Olson is trying to get back into religious "eternal life" by some other door.

Yes, it would be proper to begin a life of Olson by seeing how his Capricorn birth gave him a feeling for the winter solstice, if one then went on to do something as simple and direct as presenting Olson's poem called "Winter Solstice" (dated 8 December 1958, in *Collected Poems* p. 469).

> I'm going to get
> the hell as far
> south as I can to
> stay the hell out
> of the darkness. And
> when I turn (as
> I'll have to, the
> laws being
>
> what they are) I'll
> hesitate a day in
> order to scare the piss
> out of the useless

> ones who pine
> for less than
> the Great One who
>
> hides in
> the rose as
> the fire does
>
> in me

It was Robert Duncan, in his introduction to Olson's "Causal Mythology" lecture at Berkeley, who said, "I know where I'm going for the fire." But as we see from the above poem, although the fire is undoubtedly there, Olson doesn't quite take himself that seriously all the time.

2

Parents

A group photograph from the early 1900s shows seven young men out in their Sunday best, posed, some reclining, some standing. We are drawn to the tallest on the right, who, nattily dressed like the others, with hands in pockets, nevertheless projects a madcap edginess, hat tilted on the back of a full head of hair. Those who remember Karl Malden in his heyday will know the look, the earnest confrontation of the immediate event, almost comical even when not meant to be, but in the case of the Karl of this snapshot, very often deliberately so. There is another photograph of Olson's father, where he is standing between the rocks of a well-known Dogtown landmark called the "Whale's Jaw," and with his arms akimbo

Mary Olson (née Hines) in one of few known photographs of her.
Kate Olson Archive.

he is pretending he has separated the rocks by superhuman strength. This is the kind of slapstick that also gives us the cover photo of *The Post Office*, the small posthumous publication of three memories of the poet's child-hood: it is a formal studio portrait, Karl standing poker-faced in his official post office garb with his letter-bag slung in front and the baby Olson sitting happily in it like in a kangaroo pouch.

There are fewer photographs of Mary Teresa Olson (née Hines), nothing from her slim, younger days. Since she married late (aged thirty-five) Olson knew her only as round of face and body: "amniotic ... a cocoon of peace and ease around my nerves" (*The Post Office* p. 36). "They multiplied security, my mother and father were so balanced."

"Cocoon of peace ... so balanced"—very expressive phrases. Tom Clark chooses not to quote them. He has a different take on it all: "The temperamental differences between Karl and Mary would soon manifest

The Olson Family at Stage Fort Park, Gloucester, c. 1918.
Charles Olson Research Collection, Archives and Special Collections at the
Thomas J. Dodd Research Center, University of Connecticut Libraries.

themselves in the boy: his own ingrained 'laziness' and 'vacillation,' Olson
once claimed, had come from his mother, his 'physical and mental energy'
from his father" (Clark p. 5). Clark seems not able to stand to think of
Olson as happy and whole, not for one minute, not even if Olson said he
was. Clark has to get right away to a misperceived "shame and anger" (p. 6).
Already he cannot resist doing what many biographers fall into, that is,
quoting diary entries where their subjects are obviously off-guard, moody,
genuinely perplexed and often chiding themselves over-scrupulously. Clark
has here turned to a letter Olson wrote to Barbara Denny, a Worcester girl-
friend of some years, with whom he had broken up. With utmost chivalry,
the young poet puts himself in the wrong. A biographer can "prove" any
sort of malfeasance by picking out from such sources the worst of the
subject's self-reproaches. When we see defamatory adjectives dug up from
diaries and given prominence out of context throughout *The Allegory of a
Poet's Life*, we almost regret that Olson lived with a pen in his hand during
periods of severe self-examination.

For the record, I found the words "physical and mental energy" attached to his father in the stated source, the "May 6, 1934–1936" notebook at Storrs. I didn't find the words "laziness" or "vacillation," though they may be elsewhere in the thick notebook. What Olson does say in the same location is: "I think I have naturally a weak will—Mary T. gave me that along with life." This could imply that his mother had an "ingrained laziness and vacillation," but it doesn't exactly say so, and I don't believe it. I cite one fact: that she made sure her son went with her to mass every Sunday of his life until he left home for college. No laziness or vacillation there.

It is sad that the only substantial quote Clark selects from *The Post Office* has Olson calling his father "awkward, unable to cope with the failings of life" while at the same time "idealizing" him. If Clark had allowed himself to read *The Post Office*, especially the "Stocking Cap" story, with any openness of mind he would have felt in it such a glow of affection and security that he would have made space for much quotation to establish this serenity as the predominant mode of Olson's childhood. How depressing, then, when Clark summarizes the family closeness as "ambivalence" and goes on to stagger us with the following:

> And an early draft of his 1950 poem "ABCs: For Arthur Rimbaud" contains a revealing line he later deleted from the published version: "oh my washerwoman mother, oh my alcoholic dad."(p. 6)

Clark leaves the unsuspecting reader believing these depictions are true of Olson's parents, when they are not. Even if we didn't know the biographical fact of the matter, it is clear from the poem (though not clear to Clark apparently) that Olson is not talking about his own parents at all. The pertinent lines in the draft as sent to Frances Boldereff on 9 June 1950 are found on pages 370–71 of *Charles Olson and Frances Boldereff: A Modern Correspondence*:

> (REPELLENT, ILL., or whatever
> city, state, the LOVERS
> come from, our
> tenement boys (oh my washerwoman mother, oh
> my alcoholic dad)

One might have to go back to the poem's inception in a letter to Robert Creeley of the same date to determine exactly what Olson was getting at: that, while "form is never more than an extension of content," the content itself had better be good, not the posturings of naturalistic novelists, the kind of "tenement" writer Olson had never been, though born and raised in a tenement. It doesn't matter whether or not "Repellent, Ill." has a specific referent. The name is generic here, and Olson is going after those who play the false, though popular, notes of romantic complaint. The whining about "washerwomen" and "alcoholics" here comes from the mouths of obnoxious "tenement boys" conjured up within the poem to try to make a satirical thrust. Olson wasn't satisfied he had succeeded, and he ditched the lines in the final version (*Collected Poems* pp. 174–75). Clark makes it seem as though Olson first blurted out a truth about his parents and later thought better of it: this borders on slander.

"This ambivalent attitude toward his parents," says Clark, "carried over into Olson's adult relations with others" (p. 6). And then we get the even bigger lie: Olson as social climber and snob, albeit an "unconscious" one (p. 6). Oh my, the unconscious things we do! Is Tom Clark conscious of how much he reveals of his own self when he talks loosely of Olson "cultivating the rich and powerful" (p. 6)? Dreiser's *An American Tragedy* must have been one of Clark's favorite books in early manhood. It wasn't one of Olson's, so what is Clark doing pinning it on him? Clark reckons that it would be a favorite book for any "ambitious youth." Yes, but in Olson's case there is zero evidence. He owned several of Dreiser's novels, but not that one. In April 1939, way past Olson's "early manhood," Olson did attend to *An American Tragedy* in critiquing a screen adaptation of it that someone else was doing. (This person may actually have been the Harry Brown who was around Harvard at the time and is listed as the co-writer of the film adaptation, *A Place in the Sun,* of 1951.) Storrs contains two typescript pages of Olson's views, filed as Prose 172 under the opening words, "The mother acquires" (the screenplay he is commenting on is not extant). Rather than the social climbing aspects of the plot, Olson is interested in the mother's role:

> In our version, Clyde, in the death-cell, confesses to his mother that he did not kill Roberta, but that he wanted to do so. The mother, who clings to the ultra-Christian belief that a sin in thought is equivalent to a sin in deed, is deeply shocked. And, by reason of a sublimity quite the opposite to that of the mother in Gorky's story, this mother too becomes her son's betrayer.

Without expecting anything melodramatic, it would be good at this point to see in what sense Olson's mother may have "betrayed" him. Too strong a word, of course, but a full scale study would follow certain leads. For instance, the episode when Edward Dahlberg as a guest at their board in the early days was given left-overs (was it?) while Olson got the pork chops (or chicken, was it?). Olson in a letter of 23 April 1947 recalls Dahlberg's chiding him on this (*In Love, In Sorrow* p. 23). Dahlberg replies fulsomely (p. 26). Olson in the next letter refers to Dahlberg's "cursing my mother for the food she gave me" (p. 27). Dahlberg responds strongly: "Does one have to be clever to make you understand that it is base to sit at table and eat better food than you offer your guest?" (p. 30). It was a real row! Olson gave himself the last word, in *The Maximus Poems* (II.37):

> ... (as my life 'rotted', sd Edward Dahlberg
> on my own field, assaulting my mother
> because she gave me the pork chops—Edward
> glaring out of his one good eye to register
> his notice of the preference) "spoiling"
> me—la!

And Olson adds with a sigh:

> The which I do here record
> for eternity no less, lest it be lost, that
> a mother is a hard thing to get away from ...

And one can flash back to the trip Olson took with his father to Plymouth, Massachusetts, in 1920, for an example of not being able to get away:

> My mother was a Catholic and I was raised one. The problem was, in Plymouth, where I'd go to mass. Somewhere around the Cordage Co. we found a church my father and I decided must be Catholic. It had the right cross on it, I guess. I went in and he went on, to look over ropes. It wasn't very long when I was out, and so confused to be out so quickly I could not tell him, anymore than I could my mother afterwards, that I was sure I had been to a Catholic service. I knew only one thing, that when I had entered handbells were ringing as they are, in the mass, when communion is being prepared. I was sure this at least would satisfy my mother but, on the contrary, it made her only the more upset, for if it were that long after the Gospel that you went in, said she, with a voice that sounded as though she were wringing her hands, you did not hear Mass at all! (*The Post Office* pp. 34–35)

What one wonders at, perhaps more than Olson's bewilderment at the time, is that he should include this in a story twenty-eight years later when it is not at all integral to the main action. But, as Olson put it in an auto-biographical statement of November 1952: "I am still, at 40, hugely engaged with my parents" (*Collected Prose* p. 205). What he goes on to say about his mother modulates on the same theme:

> My mother was Mary Hines, and Yeats told me (on the grounds of my grandfather, who was the immigrant "born in Cork and brought up in Galway") that my mother's aunt must have been his "Mary Hines," the beloved of the blind poet Raftery and "the most beautiful woman in all Western Ireland." It was rough on my mother when I found this out at 18—my father and I never let her forget the fall from grace, that she was only the most beautiful woman in South Worcester, Mass.

One should remember that Olson chose the economy of staying with his mother in Oceanwood Cottage, Gloucester, for the months of August 1939 through February 1940 (and beyond that, after a break), when the award of a Guggenheim Fellowship put him to the most intense study of Melville. On 26 October 1939 he reports to Waldo Frank: "Yes I am still here ... I'm writing day and night"; and on 6 November 1939: "Though my mother and I are still here in our summer camp with no water and much cold, I dare not move until I have the first draft done." To F.O. Matthiessen 11 November 1939: "Yes, my mother and I are still here in this winter-fragile cottage, with more air inside than out when it blows from the north-west, and, now the city has decided to fear a freeze, the water is gone!" To William Carlos Williams 5 December 1939: "The Melville book spills day and night. I don't know what I've got—won't until spring—and maybe then I'll throw it all away. But I've been at it here for four months straight. I wanted to break its back before I moved." Olson's father had died five years before. Whether you look at it as serving the mother or using the mother, the effort to keep warm around the stove with blankets against the elements, this is archetypal cave stuff. No wonder that when he left for New York City in February after the Valentine's Day storm it was "with a leap ... an arabesque" (*Maximus* II.1).

Mary Olson died on 25 December 1950. Olson and his wife Connie had been ready to begin their journey to Yucatan via an 8 P.M. bus to New York City from Washington. Olson described the events in a letter to Robert Creeley of 21 December 1950: "one last thing, I must call my mother, to let her know, and, before doing that, just to make sure ... I'll call her doctor, first ... well, I call the guy, the moment the rates go down, 6:05, and WHISH there goes the trip, apparently: it seems her heart is in a state of failure, that is grave, that, Monday, he gave her digitalis ... SO: we leave here in the morning, for massachusetts, to give her what reinforcement

Constance Wilcock, later Connie Olson.
Kate Olson Archive.

we can." Five-and-a-half years after his mother's death, Olson wrote what must be among the greatest elegiac poems in the English language, "As the Dead Prey Upon Us" (*Collected Poems* pp. 388–95), based partly on dream and partly on a long-held wish to have his mother's presence cease. The title in a first draft was "To Alleviate the Dream" (MS at Storrs); in another draft, the "Mother Poem":

> … It was just then I went into my house
> and to my utter astonishment
> found my mother sitting there
>
> as she always had sat, as must she always
> forever sit there her head lolling
> into sleep. Awake, awake my mother
>
> what wind will lift you too
> forever from the tawdriness
> make you rich as all those souls
>
> crave crave crave
>
> to be rich?
>
> They are right. We must have
> what we want. We cannot afford
> not to. We have only one course:
>
> the nets which entangle us are flames
>
> > O souls, burn
> > alive, burn now

that you may forever
have peace, have

what you crave

O souls,
go into everything,
let not one knot pass
through your fingers ...

The "five hindrances" are from Buddhist thought (as Olson found it in his *Encyclopedia Britannica* 11th edition) and "the nets of being" remind one of the burning Nessus shirt of Hercules which he was unable to take off without removing his skin. As he puts it in "The Present is Prologue," Olson seeks his freedom from the parents who are "raging" in him by attention to "the phenomenological 'raging apart'" (*Collected Prose* p. 206). So, in the poem, the false "eternity" is conquered by work in the world:

... the nets of being
are only eternal if you sleep as your hands
ought to be busy. Method, method ...

Olson was a worker, and it was through methodology that he glimpsed his salvation.

Clark must see that this poem is a beautiful exemplum of Olson's work ethic, but he has to go off the poem to associate the mother with Olson's supposed sex guilt (p. 7). This leads into a world of amateur psychologizing where I do not intend to follow, even if Olson himself sometimes indulged. Clark quotes from one of Olson's letters: "What did my mother do or not do, that left her such a fixed image of woman in me?" (p. 7). An unanswerable question, but it's a commonplace phenomenon, and we do not need Clark to introduce a wise Solomon to point out that, because of his mother, "throughout his adult life he [Olson] was drawn to a series of female 'protectors,' her incarnations" (p. 7). Who is Norman Solomon?

Before leaving the Worcester of Olson's childhood I would like to offer two contrasting images. The one that Clark chooses is from the poem "The Thing Was Moving" (*Collected Poems* p. 263). The "thing" is the landfill that slowly approached the back of Olson's boyhood home, obliterating the brook and other old play-places. It is a terrifying image of the idyllic years coming to an end. Clark quotes lines which he summarizes as "the squalid small world of this junk-littered meadow-dump" (p. 7). What he does not quote from is the glorious Worcester poem, "An Ode on Nativity," which Olson read to great effect from the platform at the Berkeley Poetry Conference 1965, especially the following lines of nostalgic return:

> And she told us tales of my family
> I had not heard, how my grandfather
> rolled wild in the green grass
> on the banks of that same now underground river
> to cool himself from the steel mill's fires
> stripped down to his red underwear
>
> she was that gay, to have seen her daughter
> and that the two of us had had that car
> to take the Sisters downtown and drop them
> where they had to go
>
>   I had watched them
> swirl off in their black habits
> before I started the car again
> in the snow of that street, the same street
> my father had taken me to, to buy my first cap.

At that poignant memory Olson paused in his reading and said, as we have it recorded on tape, "Gee, I'm moved. Wow, I never wrote about Gloucester like this. Do you think I've been wrong all this time. I belong in—my subject is Worcester! Shit!" (*Mythologos* I.104). And the audience joined in the laughter at the poet's discovery of how easy it might have been to relax in the unexamined values of his home town. The meadow-dump image of "The Thing Was Moving" is thus not the whole story. The Worcester of "The Post Office" (father), "As the Dead Prey Upon Us" (mother) and "An Ode on Nativity" (himself) is going to persist as a bedrock value system even while Gloucester starts to create, beginning with summer holidays at age five, a new experience of sea and fishermen, the gradual awareness of a different sort of polis, one that would eventually sustain a modern epic, *The Maximus Poems*, in a way mere nostalgia would never have been able to do.

3
Early Gloucester

We don't know where Karl Olson got the idea of spending summers in Gloucester, but it was a good one. The fishing town, which also had excellent beaches, could be reached by interurban trolley cars from Worcester. He could leave his wife and boy there for the summer and come out for week-ends and his annual holiday. "Oceanwood," the cottage at Stage Fort Park in West Gloucester that they finally fixed on, was fairly primitive, but something to be proud of. Karl used the house nameplate emblem for his letterhead and envelopes.

Stage Fort in the summertime was a real community, witness the photograph in George Butterick's *Guide*, after page xxxii. Another group snapshot from the Kate Olson archive shows the young Olson in bathing costume looking out, next to his mother, who seems happy to be fully dressed.

Summer at Stage Fort Park.
Kate Olson Archive.

The letterhead used by Karl Olson (Charles J. Olson Sr.).
Kate Olson Archive.

> Did you know, she sd, growing up there,
> how rare it was. And it turned out later she meant exactly the long field
> drops down from Ravenswood where the land abrupts,
> this side of Fresh Water Cove, and throws out
> that wonder of my childhood.

Despite such passages from *The Maximus Poems* (I.10), Clark doesn't want to entice us into thinking Gloucester was Edenic. He tells the story of a day's fishing which produced only sculpins, "bloated, freckled bags of wind," which the grown-ups laughed at, reducing young Charles to tears. "It would take him some years," adds Clark, "to learn his fate was to mythologize the sea's heroes, not imitate them" (p. 10). Well, all right, it would take some years for him to learn lots of things, but meanwhile we do have evidence of the wondership that Gloucester was to the boy. It wasn't all tears.

There is a high school composition in the Storrs files, "Looking Across the Harbor," which tells a different story. In effect, it constitutes a contemporary gloss on the lovely lines from the "tansy" poem above. Here is the young Charles Olson writing about "Gloucester harbor, the beautiful!"

> The breakwater, a silver thread on the blue sea, extends from the narrow neck of land known as East Gloucester out into the ocean, protecting the city from the waves. This neck of land, during the summer, is a great mass of green foliage, here and there interrupted by a palatial residence and, at the beginning of the breakwater, by Eastern Point light, which stands out in vivid contrast with the rest of the landscape.

This high school composition ends:

> The surface of the harbor, itself, presents a delightful sight in the late afternoon sun. It and all the surroundings are clothed in a beautiful red hue which has a harmonious effect and recalls to mind the words of Champlain, when he first set eyes upon it, which were: "Le Beauport" (The Beautiful Harbor).

The French explorer Samuel de Champlain is here already cited, as he will be several times in *The Maximus Poems*, for instance [III.86], this extract approximately forty years later:

> ... it is like Champlain, water
> lends even a night sky no such infinity
> as space-search, no distance
> Night sky
> is an air
> of Heaven ...

We should also, in view of Olson's later storm poem, "Maximus at the Harbor," quote from the schoolboy essay his reference to "the treacherous reef of Norman's Woe."

The beauport has its darker side, which comes out in Olson's first play, written and performed in his junior year at Wesleyan University. Published in the *Wesleyan Cardinal* for June 1931 (and reprinted in *Minutes #34*), "The Fish Weir" ("weir" being the Gloucester name for a net) is a tragedy where the sensitive son of a boastful fisherman goes out in a dory during a blow. His mind is not really on the job, and he is taken down by the fishing net and drowned. Clark says the play has a "heavy sentimental weight" (p. 29). On the contrary, I feel it is a very realistic rendering. It has a worried mother who loves her son. When her son's dory mate returns without him "a low moan comes from her. She seems to speak as in a dream ... in low, broken tones" saying: "the ... sea ... took ... my ... boy?" One cannot say that this is overwriting. The father in anger throws the book his son had been reading "far out toward the sea." I don't understand Clark's applying the word "sentimental" to this.

Neither do I see it as "a family tragedy theme borrowed from his [Olson's] favorite dramatist of the moment, Eugene O'Neill" (p. 29). I don't believe Clark has any evidence that O'Neill had seriously entered Olson's consciousness at this time. The book that the youth had been reading is identified in the play as John Synge's *Riders to the Sea*. In a letter (*Selected Letters* p. 262) Olson says it was "via" Synge that he wrote the play. In this, his first literary act, Olson identifies himself with that earthiest of playwrights.

4
Olson's Public Speaking Triumph

"He became the school's premier public speaker" (Clark p. 12). Behind this summary statement lies an arduous apprenticeship worthy of a much closer look if we are to understand the development and honing of Olson's craft as a poet and his emerging ethos as a citizen of the polis. Storrs has many newspaper clippings of Olson participating in debate—even high school competition was news in Worcester, it seems. The final phases of the national oratory competition show the seventeen-year-old Olson going full throttle.

> Early April 1928: Worcester High schools 8th Annual Public Speaking Contest for the Worcester Evening Post cup won by the Classical High declamation team, Charles J. Olson Jr. and George Howarth. Subject: "The Heritage of American Patriotism."

> 4 May 1928: 19th Annual Lyford Interscholastic Prize Speaking Contest, Colby College. Second prize, Charles J. Olson Jr.: "The Heritage of American Patriotism."

> 7 May 1928: Worcester Telegram-Gazette Oratorical Contest prize-winner Charles J. Olson Jr.: "The Constitution—An Appreciation."

> 11 May 1928: 5th National & 3rd International Public Speaking Semi-final Contest, Troy, New York. Winner Charles J. Olson Jr.: "The Constitution—An Appreciation."

The *Worcester Telegram-Gazette* printed the text of the winning oration at Troy. It conforms to patriotic and high school rhetorical requirements and is of little interest in itself. It is the eye-witness report published with the text of the speech which establishes Olson vividly in our imagination:

> His performance was little short of marvelous, and he held the audience spellbound by the magnificence of his oratory, the splendid cadence of his voice as it rose and fell, and the perfect ease with

OLSON TAKES DEFEAT WITH EQUANIMITY

"Six Had to Lose," He Says—Guest at Dinner of John Hays Hammond

By Telegram Staff Correspondent

WASHINGTON, May 27—Charles J. Olson, The Telegram-Gazette National Oratorical contest entrant and winner of third place in last night's contest, is the dinner guest, tonight, of John Hays Hammond at his home in Washington, as are the six other finalists and the newspaper representatives who accompanied them to Washington. He will leave Washington at 12.10 tonight for New York and will reach Worcester tomorrow night on the train arriving at 8.53 daylight saving time.

The dinner tonight was the end of a busy day and the final gathering of the orators for the 1928 national contest, today all were the guests of the Washington Star on a sightseeing trip in private automobiles which lasted from 10 this morning until 5 this afternoon. Arlington, the grave of the Unknown Soldier, Lincoln memorial, Corcoran Art gallery, in fact, so many places were visited that the boys could hardly remember them all. One thing they did remember, however, the dinner of fried chicken and Virginia ham at a hotel in Alexandria.

Hard Fought Contest

Last night's contest in the opinion of officials was the hardest fought in the five years the national oratorical contest has taken place. All the orators were good, but there was no doubt in the minds of anyone who heard them that first, second and third places would be divided among Moore of Kentucky, Norquist of Missouri, and Olson; but there was a question how the honors would be distributed. These three, speaking second, fifth and last, were in a class by themselves and so

Continued on Page Ten

Worcester, Massachussetts, newspaper clipping. Kate Olson Archive.

which he stood before them. Here was a youthful master of the art of speaking, with the power to arouse and even electrify his hearers at one moment and to lull and sway them the next. An intensity of purpose and an intelligent appreciation of the subject in hand were added to his supreme vocal endowments.

He used gestures sparingly, but with all possible effect, the personification of ease and grace despite his unusual height. There was a total absence of self consciousness, and even when he was most intense and his speech most concise, the bond of under-standing which he had immediately established between himself and his hearers was not strained. He shifted from one position to another, and even walked about the stage a bit without losing his audience—the thousands of eyes and ears missed not the slightest sound nor movement.

Patently, it was no idle boast when, at the end of four hours on the plat-form at the Berkeley Poetry Conference, Olson stated: "I was at seventeen, by speech, the most powerful figure in the world" (*Muthologos* 1.153). Though it is true that he had a bad cold and came in third in the finals in Washington, D.C., Olson knew his own worth and at Berkeley thirty-seven years later he goes on to name the French contestant, Rene Ponthieu, the winner of the International line-up, "who was so inferior to me if I was in hell" (*Muthologos* 1.156)—supposing Dante was going to rank the contest-ants! In any case, as a finalist he had already won a paid trip to Europe.

"The brief trip yielded two memorable incidents," says Clark (p. 13). "One was a meeting in Ireland with the poet W.B. Yeats." This assumption about Olson has been around for some time, but it is clear that there was no visit to Ireland and no talk with Yeats at this time. We know the precise schedule as laid out by the organizers, and Olson wrote to one or another of his parents at every stop on the journey (letters in Storrs, published in *Minutes* #33). No Ireland. Olson actually met Yeats at the house of Bill Snow on one of Yeats's American tours (referred to in an unpublished letter to Snow 2 December 1959).

"The other big moment," declares Clark, "came during a stop in Cologne, when, on a dark rainy night near the cathedral, the young traveler received an offer from a street whore" (p. 13). Of course, this incident doesn't get into his letters home! I'm not denying the memorable-ness of such a challenge to his virginity—and Clark cites the later diaries to attest to it—but there were a thousand other tremendous impressions impinging on the young man that one thinks might be worthy of mention: Bodleian Library, Oxford; being shown round Stratford-on-Avon by the mayor; Paris on Bastille Day with dancing in the streets; *Venus de Milo* and *Winged Victory* in the Louvre; the Olympic Games in Amsterdam. And as to Olson's "big moment" with respect to Cologne Cathedral, with full awareness of the irony, I would like to quote the letter to his mother from Cologne (6 August 1928):

> Mother, you would have been thrilled by the sight of that far-famed cathedral—a massive structure towering aloft some 600 feet. I climbed and oh what a climb … as far as you can go—for the view of the city from the towers—the Rhine winding southward, the city spread about on its banks, the little midgets of people playing about at our feet. We all were tired and got to bed quite early.

Well, I guess Clark wins this one. Once she has been brought into the picture the street-walker cannot be forgotten. But I will try to bring us out of this single-minded fixation by listing the further romantic stopping places: Lucerne. Interlaken. Montreux. The Castle of Chillon by boat. Milan. Train, via Verona and Padua, to Venice. Then, what to Olson would count as the most memorable part of the trip: he got permission to leave the party for three days to go to Rome. He describes himself alone with his guidebook at the Roman Forum, the tomb of Ignacius Loyola, St. Peter's and the Vatican Museum, Raphael's *Transfiguration* and more. Then back with the party for embarkation 1 September 1928 to New York. All in all, Olson's ten weeks in Europe was equal to any Grand Tour a poet ever made, except perhaps for Byron who certainly would have acted differently on that dark night in Cologne.

Thus, Olson arrived at Wesleyan University in the fall of 1928 as a virginal freshman, but as a prize winning orator, and continued to excel in the latter category. Clark describes him as "progressing at full steam" (p. 20). I have no quarrel with this image; there seems to have been a great deal of steam involved—acting on the stage, debating and declaiming, sports, student newspaper editorials, ambitious student papers: it was a steam kettle, a drum.

He debated many times and lost only once. I doubt, however, that the defeat at Brown University on 20 February 1932 was quite as important as it is made out to seem (p. 20). There is a little of Tom Clark's fictional skill in the following account:

> Uneasy for days beforehand, he lost his nerve—and his train of thought—in the middle of his concluding remarks, faltered, and was defeated. Immediately afterwards he was overcome by feelings of humiliation, disappointment and anger far out of proportion to

the actual importance of the match. Instead of returning to Wesleyan with the team, he jumped into a taxi in Providence and ordered the driver to take him all the way back to his parents' home in Worcester, charging the $60 ride to his university.

Clark adds to the melodrama: "In his journal Charlie [sic] fretted at length over the Brown defeat and its causes" (p. 20). He quotes from a diary entry of ten months afterwards: "It is at once an aid and handicap that my style of debating depends on my mental exhilaration. I hate to prepare formal arguments, and frequently I speak muddleheadedly." But when Olson goes on, in lines Clark does not quote, he mentions Brown with resignation:

> But if the pistons of my mind are firing properly, as today, then logic and conviction and fluency are mine. Usually the exhilaration of a formal debate steps my mind up enough to ensure success—that Brown debate was once it did not.

I don't know that he mentions Brown again. It was Wilbert Snow, the debate coach, who told the story of the $60 taxi ride repeatedly.

The bigger disappointment of Olson's college career would have been not getting the Rhodes Scholarship. The *Selected Letters* volume gives the text of Olson's appeal to the "Gentlemen of the Committee" (a document in the Miscellaneous files at Storrs). It is a heart-felt expression of his situation, his strengths and weaknesses. Anyone might agree that it should have been the first draft and that the final letter should have been more urbane, as John W. Wells's undoubtedly was. Olson was Phi Beta Kappa, he got the Rich Prize for oration and the Briggs Prize for general ability (as reported in the *New York Times* of 21 June 1932), but he was not class president. John W. Wells was; and Wells got the Rhodes. Mary Olson carried her son's Phi Beta Kappa key in her purse for the rest of her life (a detail we owe to Clark, though we would like to know the source). To have had her son at Oxford would have been something bigger than a purse could hold.

This does not mean that John Wells was Olson's life-long nemesis as Clark implies:

> Olson would follow with jealous interest the career of this symbolic rival; even at a subsequent time when he'd long since left both politics and academia behind, the mere mention of the name Jack Wells, reminder of his desperate struggle to impress during his undergraduate years at Wesleyan, could pitch him into momentary "sickness." (p. 21)

I don't know where Clark got this information. The word "sickness" he takes from a letter to Connie of 15 November 1952: "Maybe one reason why Wesleyan, *to this day*, gives me a sickness, is, that right there, fall 1928, the dream was broken: I had to deal with others. And actually, didn't know *how to begin!*" (*Selected Letters* p. 176). Two points need to be made about this: strictly speaking, Olson is talking about his freshman year and general threats. John W. Wells individually is not mentioned, not here, not in the whole letter, not in the whole of the *Selected Letters*. One of the Storrs notebooks records that Wells, or a Wells type, made an appearance in a dream of Thursday 2 September 1954 (Clark p. 247), but Robert Richman of the Institute of Contemporary Arts, Washington, made an appearance the following Wednesday, so I can't make too much of that. I doubt that Wells "loomed" in Olson's imagination "as a secret symbolic rival" (Clark p. 42). At Berkeley, in the intermission, talking casually about politics, Olson mentions that he had inscribed a poem to Jack Wells, "who was Rockefeller's national political manager last year" (*Muthologos* 1.124). The poem, "The Condition of Light from the Sun" of February 1964, which got included in the posthumous *Maximus Poems Volume Three* (III.44), had a second dedicatee, Alan Cranston, who hired Olson in Washington for the Office of War Information and was then a Democratic Senator from California. Olson was balancing Democrat and Republican. There may have been some vestigial jealousy: Olson appends to Wells's name in the dedication to the poem the identifying parentheses: "Oxon. 1934."

The other point to make about Olson on Wesleyan University in the letter to Connie of 15 November 1952 is that the remarks could have come from almost anybody entering college:

> I go back to that biz, of 17; and faced with others for the first time, and how only two ways seemed available: (1) to "show 'em," by prizes, positions, etc, which got done; & (2) sexuality—which didn't.

One can easily comb Olson's reflective letters and confessional diaries and find wording which evokes visions of a disabling crisis. But this all seems to be fairly normal stuff.

5
Melville Beginnings

When it comes to Olson's M.A. thesis, Clark says: "Wilbert Snow suggested a long paper on a subject of mutual interest, Herman Melville, and agreed to serve as advisor" (p. 22). But Clark got his version from Snow, and it falsely gives Olson a very static role. Snow was actually away on leave the term Olson returned to Wesleyan as a graduate student. Olson wrote to him around 16 October 1932 (letter in the archives at Wesleyan):

> … Frankly, however, I miss you. There are no talks over "cokes." The inspiration of your intense interest is missing. Above all I wanted to work on my Master's thesis with you.

It seems that the topic had not been broached before, for Olson goes on:

> This summer I got acquainted with a person by the name of Herman Melville, introduced to me through a story called "Moby Dick" and some short "Piazza Tales." Now I burn to know, to possess the man completely. With Woodbridge's rather enthusiastic approval I have decided to do my thesis on him … He accepted the idea of Cowie acting until you return—presuming, of course, that you are willing to work the thesis on Melville out with me. You are, aren't you, Bill?

Snow was willing, of course; and Clark retells Snow's amusing stories of Olson's way of meeting deadlines. What Clark fails to do, however, is to communicate to us what a magnificent piece of work "The Growth of Herman Melville, Prose Writer and Poetic Thinker" was. He quotes Olson's opening note that the thesis contains "the first complete bibliography of Herman Melville ever attempted," but he doesn't reveal that this bibliography included not only Melville's books and periodical contributions, but all known letters and unpublished works as well. Also there is a very impressive listing of articles and reviews on Melville, thirty pages in all before we get to chapter one and its epigraph, "Call me Ishmael."

The thesis is a sustained analysis of Melville's novels one by one chronologically. *Typee*: "Critically, the book is interesting in its promise, not in its realization. Immaturity writes itself on every page. Yet this very quality adds to the romantic effect. The rare passages of saccharine sentiment seem to taste right—as sugar with cream" (pp. 18–19). *Omoo*: "The book has a healthy glow like the tanned cheek of a sailor, deeper than the boyish flush of *Typee*. Melville is taking hold with a stronger hand; he has aplomb" (p. 43). And so on. But small quotations do not give the right impression. There is such a thoroughness of analysis that one is persuaded that this young scholar has engaged himself fully with what each novel offers. One more quote; Olson aged twenty-three on *Moby-Dick*:

> It stands as the peak of Melville's work, to which all that has gone before inevitably leads, from which all that follows moves. This was that "undiscovered prime thing" he hoped might be locked within him. There is nothing else in Melville, little else in American literature and thought, that approaches it.
>
> It defies a label. To judge it a novel is possible; but it is like measuring Gibraltar with a foot-rule. There is point in declaring it a dramatic tragedy. It is most properly a prose epic, for here are the proportions of *The Iliad* and *Paradise Lost* and *The Mahabharata*. And that it is prose it is no less epic—Milton regarded the Book of Job as a "brief model" for the epic. *Moby-Dick* is close to being the most ancient epic of the English-speaking peoples. As Van Wyck Brooks observes, "Grendel in *Beowulf* might almost be described as the prototype of the White Whale."
>
> *Moby-Dick* is an integrated whole, an artistic plotting that partakes of Shakespeare's highest skill. There is the same ingenious planting of the seeds of the conclusion. In many ways the book is related most revealingly to the Elizabethan plays. Only the Russian novels of the nineteenth century are of sufficient magnitude in construction to be compared with it.

At that time there were only three books on Melville in existence: Raymond Weaver (1921), John Freeman (1926) and Louis Mumford (1929). I believe that if "The Growth of Herman Melville, Prose Writer and Poetic Thinker" had been published it would have stood up well beside these other pioneer works. It is far superior to them in one way—the treatment of Melville's literary predecessors and sources. Starting with Melville's boyhood books, Olson at every stage says, "It is pertinent to ask what his reading was in these years" (p. 13). From Melville's earliest pieces we see that Burton's *Anatomy of Melancholy* figures highly: "This man should brood beneath the lintel of Melville's door … Shakespeare, Scott, Byron, Milton, and Coleridge are alluded to or quoted. Much classical mythology and geography are marshaled" (pp. 9–10).

Melville's books—this is the task that we see Olson dedicating himself to in the academic year following his M.A., 1933–34, when he was a free-lance researcher, with a little money found for him by Wilbert Snow. In his thesis he quotes the letter to Duyckinck in which Melville tells of having found a Shakespeare with large enough print for him to read with ease: "Dolt and ass that I am I have lived more than 29 years, & until a few days ago never made a close acquaintance with the divine William … But chancing to fall in with this glorious edition, I now exult over it page after page" (p. 49). Little could Olson have expected to discover this same seven-volume Shakespeare, with Melville's own marginalia; but in a triumph beyond any young scholar's dreams, he did.

The story of Olson's visiting one of Melville's granddaughters and coming away with the Shakespeare and many more Melville books is one that Clark tells well (pp. 24–25). He also tells of Olson following a book-seller's trail to the Brooklyn Public Library and finding Melville books there by simply asking for likely titles from the stacks and noting the writing in them. But he tells it in a very matter-of-fact way compared with the way I heard it. On 15 June 1965, practically our last evening in Buffalo, my wife and I had Olson over to dinner and he told in hushed tones about open-ing a copy of Thomas Warton's *History of English Poetry* and finding Melville's unmistakable marginal comments. He hid from us the exact location of this as yet untapped cache, dangling the hook, mainly for the benefit of our guest George Hochfield, a scholar in American Literature. Olson was still looking for someone to take up the Brooklyn Public Library task, the thing that Merton Sealts had failed to do. (Sealts in *Pursuing Melville* p. 151 reports that Olson phoned him later that night to see how he was.)

Clark does not mention the late Merton Sealts, scholar and gentleman, beyond his first (and, as it turned out, only) meeting with Olson in 1941 (p. 69), but their relationship is very illuminating. When Sealts showed initiative in this area, Olson handed the Melville books project over to him, and helped him with many specific questions. He got him to go over to Brooklyn but apparently the librarians put up obstacles, and Sealts never succeeded in doing a proper search. This was disappointing to Olson; but more disappointing was the fact that, when Sealts's first "Check-list of Books Owned and Borrowed" came out in *Harvard Library Bulletin* of May

1950, Olson wasn't given any credit for being on to it first. Sealts, in *Pursuing Melville*, quotes from Olson's letter of 2 June 1950, adding that "his hot words scorched then, thirty years ago, and they scorch now as I read them over":

> It is such a valuable thing you have done, and so you will the more measure my valuing of you, if i raise up, how irked i am, that you too play the scholar's game, the academic back-scratch—& leave things that you know, unsaid ... it is an irony that, to this date, (with even a Sealts' job out, specifically on the reading, and the books) it should still be only one F. Barron Freeman (and he, fr no personal cause whatsoever) who, in print, has had the accuracy to state Olson's "sole" relationship to the deposit of mss in The Harvard Library, let alone that which would seem, would it not, of much more importance, the same's relation to the use of the path of Melville's reading to understanding of him. (p. 108)

A few days later, in a letter of 14 June 1950, Olson wrote his "beef" to Jay Leyda:

> Sealts knows, so I can speak of it to you, though he is a very sick boy, and I see no reason why it should be added, now, to his burden. But I was deeply wounded that, in his Check-list, one would never gather that it was I who
> (1) had the idea of such a list, in the first place
> (2) was the first to reconstruct the library
> (3) by the Osborne books, caused Harvard to buy the Shakespeare, was, as a matter of fact, agent (with DeLacey) of the sale, the 1st Harvard purchase ($250!)
> (4) spent weeks, spring, 1934, in NY, flushing the story of the sale of the books (it was Anderson, and thru him, I who got Wegelin out of NJ, and yet, in his article, you would not know who provoked his memories!) ((Saw Farnell myself (the son of AB), and started the Brooklyn business.))
> & (5) who, in Twice A Year, 1938, 1st used in print the methodology of, M's markings (*Selected Letters* p. 114)

And to turn back to the letter to Sealts for a summary:

> A man's simplest wish, if he is an honest worker, is not coups, or the riding on the back of other men, but simply this—that the time I gave to such labors as you, more than anyone else, has carried on, should, by you, of all people, not be slurred, or washed away in the general seas. For a man's hours are his fate.

The strange thing is that when the final *Melville's Reading* came out in book form from University of Wisconsin Press in 1966 it was clear that Sealts had not taken any steps to amend matters. His formal scholarship seems not to have allowed Olson in. Olson was sent the book; he greeted it with, I suppose, a sigh, certainly silence.

6
Clark University, Worcester, 1934–1936

Clark describes Olson's first teaching job as "the humdrum grind of academia" (p. 26), "two years of treading water" (p. 26) and "drone duties in the assembly line" (p. 28). We know that a truly intelligent person is never bored, but these years were a severe test of that hypothesis. Olson's Wesleyan mentor, Wilbert Snow, in a letter of 21 September 1934 (at Storrs), told him his program at Clark University was "the most formidable one I have heard about in ten years. You are going to kill yourself." It was imperative to reduce the ninety-five freshman themes from twice a week to once a week. The university "must be extremely hard up when it asks one man to do three men's work."

There is no evidence that Olson tried to dodge any of the drudgery he had committed himself to. On the back page of *Minutes* #44, guest-edited by Worcester resident Jim Fay, there is a reproduction of a page of grades, with one A– (manuscript at Storrs). Naturally he was put in charge of the debate team; he supervised the theatre group. Specifics are sparse. Clark refers to "occasional speeches at campus rallies" (p. 36). I know of only one, as reported in *Clark News* 13 November 1935 under the headline "Speakers Forceful at Poorly Attended Anti-War Meeting Friday" (reprinted in the Olson issue of *Maps*):

> Probably the outstanding contribution of the day was the speech delivered by Professor Charles Olson, in which he pointed out the inherent barbarism in man, the emotional forces that drove men into battle—ending with the warning that only by substituting a cause with as great an emotional appeal as war, only by fighting war with the fanaticism of religious maniacs, could the peacemakers hope to avert war, even temporarily.

Another tangentially illuminating document is a mild reprimand from the Dean of Students during the time Olson was the official proctor of Estabrook Hall dormitory:

November 6, 1935

Dear Mr. Olson:

From the stories that have come to me I fear that the boys are
running a little wild, perhaps getting away from you at the dormitory, or running wild whenever you are not there in the evening. I
know they have done some damage to the building and made so
much noise, especially with the piano, late at night that complaints
are coming from those who cannot rest. I think you could put a
stop to the boisterous noise; perhaps the use of the piano should
stop at ten o'clock.

I know it is a lovely theory to have self-government and to count
upon a committee of the house group to prevent disturbances or
disorder that really infringe upon the rights of others, but the
theory does not always work unless there is someone to enforce it.
I know you may find it rather difficult to be there some of the time
now with your mother so much alone, but I hope you can make
some arrangement so that there are not complaints coming to me
about it.

Cordially yours

(unsigned carbon copy at Clark University)

The reference to Olson's mother being "so much alone" is an acknowledgement that she was newly a widow, Olson's father having died during
the summer of 1935—an event that Clark deals with (p. 28ff); as also
Olson's Worcester girl-friend, Barbara Denny (p. 17ff). Not happy subjects.

Clark does, however, neglect one event which must have given Olson
a tremendous boost, ensuring him something of a celebrity status on his
arrival at Clark University gates. On the week-end of 5–6 October 1934
Olson was an invited speaker, along with the famous Lewis Mumford, at
the New England Conference of the American Association of Librarians at
the Berkshire Museum, Pittsfield, Massachusetts. The text of Olson's after-
dinner talk, which was obviously written an hour before the event (or
during the dinner itself maybe!) is preserved at Storrs, a section from it
published in *OLSON #2.* "God deliver Melville," said Olson with some
urbanity, "from what the Concord group have suffered until Emerson has
acquired an odor of lavender and old lace ... Melville is abroad in these
hills more intimately than Emerson is in Concord ..." And he adds to this
theme something that will echo seventeen years later in his poem "Letter
for Melville 1951": "Melville's banquets will not be monuments. He will
keep himself vital." But, because this is a light-hearted scene, when he says

Olson swordfishing, July 1936.
Kate Olson Archive.

that Melville's vitality has delivered him from the scholars, he is making fun of himself as the one person present who might most qualify for the epithet "the pale usher." It is sadly in keeping with Clark's jaundiced view of things that this is the one thing he quotes, using it as evidence that even Olson's Melville research files "had become a burden to him" at this time (p. 26). And that's all we get from Clark about this special occasion. He doesn't say that Olson added something to his "pale usher" comment: "The dust I've stirred has minded me more of my sinus, however, than my mortality." Just what his late father would have said! A little pleasantry when the world of scholarship was new.

The other extraordinary event, two years later, as a sort of book-end to his time at Clark University, when Olson had already been accepted into Harvard graduate school and other doors were opening, was a three-week swordfishing voyage out of Gloucester on the *Doris M. Hawes*. Olson signed on as a deck-hand, "as close as you can come to old American whaling" (*Selected Letters* p. 16). Clark deals with this fully, drawing on

Olson's own journals as published by George Butterick in *OLSON* #7. An additional sense of the adventure can be obtained from two letters to his Worcester friend, Anne Brosshard, which apparently Clark had not seen. The first of these, 6 July 1936, can be found in *Selected Letters* (pp. 16–17); the second is Olson's report back to Anne Brosshard soon after his return:

> A full three weeks fore and aft, fore and aft, yes, on and under the plankings of a deck, sleeping in the peak of the fo'c'sle on a flat hard, pillowless mattress, walking the deck with legs which became prehensile, climbing the rigging with a body become all grip, to a masthead where the suspension is after five hours more than a gull-like clinging of the body to a wooden crosstree 75 ft from a wooden deck, when slowly, subtly, the body has slid away and I am extended infinitely, mystically in a sway over sea in air.

The sea was not, finally—or even conceivably—Olson's trade. But in three weeks he did manage to get it out of his system efficiently. With that, he was ready for his *vita nuova*.

7
Twice A Year

I have little quarrel with Clark's treatment of Olson and Harvard, Olson and the Ballet Russe de Monte Carlo, Olson and the Metcalf family. Documents are sparse, and Clark's interview with John Finch is undoubtedly definitive for those years. I suspect, however, that Clark is belittling Olson's serious political nature when he sums up the Spanish Civil War question: "His self-described 'Guerre Civile crisis,' triggered by the enlistment of a Harvard friend in the Abraham Lincoln Brigade, lasted only until the next Dietrich movie" (p. 43). I imagine that more evidence for Olson's concern will be forthcoming at some time in the future.

What we do have a full account of, from the correspondences with Edward Dahlberg and Dorothy Norman (though not from Clark), is the story of Olson's first important publication, "Lear and Moby Dick," in the inaugural issue of *Twice A Year* (Fall–Winter 1938), which is what Olson did instead of going to Spain. It began as a term paper on Shakespeare and Melville for Prof. F.O. Matthiessen; proving a great challenge, it was not finished by the end of the 1936–37 academic year. Olson wrote to "Matty" while working on it during the summer in Gloucester, asking to submit it in September (a draft of the letter exists at Storrs, undated, but probably about 8 August 1937):

> My plan has been to get Shakespeare in suspension in my mind and to reread Melville from *White Jacket* on ... To get a sharper focus I've written sections on plays while they, the criticism on them and Melville's notes were fresh in my mind; in this form the Timon and Lear are done ... I did want to do more than just transcribe the annotations.

This is typical Olson overkill on a problem; but one thing is clear from this description: "Lear and Moby Dick" has already been conceived in its essentials.

Presumably it was submitted to Matty's satisfaction on Olson's return to Harvard. Edward Dahlberg, who was recruiting writers for the proposed magazine *Twice A Year* saw it about the same time. It is referred to as "your piece on Melville" in a letter of 27 October 1937. Dahlberg had met Olson in Gloucester that summer and been impressed enough to have him meet the editor and owner Dorothy Norman. Writing to Olson on 24 November Norman summarizes the wide-ranging discussion (letter at Yale):

> You were going to see Murdock about the Peirce material; you were going to write to Massine also. As to Whitehead, I wonder what the chances are of getting him to give us anything. You mentioned Frances Rogers. Did you mean that I should get in touch with her. And you said Ellery Sedgwick was sending us his paper.

It appears that Olson had been beating everybody else's drum but his own, for she adds simply: "And you are going to send us anything of yours, I hope."

It was to subeditor Dahlberg that Olson sent what he had done by the end of November, knowing that there would be useful criticism. He was not disappointed. A letter from Dahlberg of 2 December 1937 (at Yale) indicates that he had read it twice: "upon second reading, I find your Melville essay even more impressive, particularly the latter part which deals with Moby Dick." He wants Olson to make this latter part ("the best piece of imaginative criticism on Moby Dick that I have every read any-where") the whole theme of the essay, indicating where Olson can tighten up the whole piece: "don't delay, as we need it" (*In Love, In Sorrow* p. 7).

Then Olson got sick the whole month of December, sick in the way Clark describes as a "phobia" (p. 48) but Olson called "a hideous trauma of my whole system" (*In Love, In Sorrow* p. 3): "It is as though I had slept away a month: actually I have slept many hours, forced to bed, neglecting everything. I seem to have awoke only yesterday" (letter 22 December 1937). Anyway, he got the revision to Dahlberg by mid-February, after asking Matthiessen's view of it at the last minute. In a letter of 26 February 1938 (carbon copy at Yale) Dorothy Norman says: "The essay is really beautiful ... We are going over it again carefully, and then we are planning to send it to you, or confer about the slight suggestions." But it is several weeks before her editorial work gets done. On 13 April 1938 she sends Olson an advance, which she thought "might be welcome meanwhile." On 5 May 1938 she suggests they meet at her summer place at Woods Hole after 10 June to discuss the details. This proves that, contrary to Clark's account, the delay was not Olson's. It is quite unfair to say that "as the months went by, Dahlberg simmered with impatience—coaxing, cajoling, complaining of his 'nefarious silence' ... Still Charles stalled" (p. 48). Not true; and we should point out that the "nefarious silence" complaint was in a 9 February 1938 letter, previous to all this delay caused by Dorothy Norman. At the end of June, Norman writes that she is ready for a meeting, but by then Olson has decided to take advantage of a lift to Kansas City from the classicist Gerald Else, a fellow resident of Winthrop House (as related in a letter to Anne Brosshard 27 June 1938 at Storrs). It wasn't a matter of perversely going down to the bus station (as Clark says p. 49) when he should have been doing his duty. No, in the absence of activity on the *Twice A Year* front, Olson took up an offer he couldn't refuse. He was particularly looking forward to seeing his really good friend Ephraim Doner, who had just gone out to Carmel, California. He tells Anne Brosshard he's planning to go "finally to my lodestone, San Francisco: for, say, 10 days. Back by the 1st of August. All under $125, unless I fail myself."

Olson more or less kept to this schedule, writing to Dorothy Norman from Gloucester on 14 August 1938 (letter at Yale): "yes, here, at last, and quickly and deeply settled into this life I love." Reading these optimistic words, I find it unnerving to hear this homecoming described by Clark quite differently: "He arrived back in Gloucester a dusty, weary and still unfulfilled voyager, more concerned than ever about 'the persistence of failure' in his life" (p. 49). Where did Clark get that from? The phrase "the persistence of failure" Clark culls from an earlier letter to Norman written while Olson was still traveling. It is a letter on the stationery of the Keystone Hotel, San Francisco, dated at the top 27 July 1938: "I begin to suspect I never did write you the note I intended to when I left Gloucester the 1st." That's as far as he gets with that. Then, further down the page, under the dateline "Detroit, Sunday," he re-begins: "I'll just continue this to prove the persistence and the failure," saying he will write properly the moment he reaches Gloucester. It's "persistence" *and* "failure." He's persisting in trying to write some kind of a letter on the move, but acknowledging that he is failing in doing so. It's specifically this, and not a comment on the state of his whole existence. Clark distorts the phrase and offers a totally false picture of Olson arriving back with low morale, ignoring the contrary evidence of the 14 August letter to Dorothy Norman, where he reiterates: "In Gloucester I find location for my self, and all that is centrifugal ties in. I am at work on a new book I worked my way through in thought as I indolently wound back from

California by Greyhound." He is also "hungry" to see "Lear and Moby Dick" get into print and hopes she can send the manuscript and her suggestions by mail, as he is not really ready to travel again right away. He is, however, ready to finish up the essay "instantly": "I've already been over my carbon of it and prepared for your suggestions."

They meet in Boston for their editorial discussion. But there is a fly in the ointment: Dahlberg has come along, too, apparently with the intention of issuing an ultimatum on something or other, as was his wont. "Despite the fact that we were both so very much upset by what happened the other day," Norman writes to Olson on 29 August 1938 (letter at Yale), "I did feel something very fine about our talk ... I like what you have done. I look forward to hearing from you, and I do hope that Edward understood the spirit of the letter that I wrote to him."

Then Olson had to attend to "something personal and important I wished to do and had to do." In this letter of 6 September to Norman, explaining himself, he is not at all detailed. Clark implies he's malingering by "attributing his last-minute delaying to an urgent 'crisis'" (p. 50); but in a letter to Norman headed "Sunday" and presumably 25 September 1938 Olson is emphatic about his reasons, if still secretive:

> I am rushing this note to you as I pass through Boston this night of Dis, belching rain upon my already sodden spirit. I have for the past ten days, almost since I wrote to you, been cast into a family turmoil, both emotional and financial, which I alone and I completely had to handle. Please understand. It was one of those personal and intimate things which demand all your attention instantly like death. I have been on the roads seeing people and wasting myself ... Thursday I got back to Gloucester planning to answer your card when another telegram and I had to leave. Today it ended. I have just driven 200 miles in this horrible rain and stopped here to get this off to you special delivery, so that you will know. I leave immediately for Gloucester and shall work tonight and tomorrow, and if necessary all the next night. I recognize how questioning you must have been, but please understand this was one of the most critical and demanding ten days of my life.

Norman sends him a quietening telegram, and Olson writes the next evening:

> I think it [the telegram] propelled me into a fruitful day for I have been at the essay now eight hours and shall carry on until it is done ... I have made all suggested changes and am now at work rearranging those longer and incoherent passages.

He says he will bring the finished piece by train the following day or the day after that. And apparently that is what happened, for Olson writes to Norman from Harvard on "Friday night" (that would be 30 September 1937), having received a further telegram from her which eased his mind. So the essay got to the printer on time. He writes an autobiographical squib for her and raises the question of a completion check, being "in the hard time of the year financially." Norman obliges in a letter of 8 October 1938. (The total for the essay was $86.62, it seems.)

I have gone through these stages methodically because Clark wants to see it all as dementia: "a 'crazy, not human' writing binge—seventy-two manic hours at the typewriter without food or sleep, talking to himself, sustained only by a carton of Philip Morris and a quart bottle of Vat 69— produced the essay 'Lear and Moby Dick'" (p. 50). Admittedly, Olson himself supplied some of the exaggeration later in a cited letter to Creeley of 25 October 1950: "wrote 1st piece, Lear–MD, 72 hrs straight, and two quarts of Vat 69 (then). No food. Nothing. Talkin to myself." OK, Olson is boasting to his pal. Clark is inaccurate: it was two quarts of Vat 69, not one! But we should stress that Olson is talking about the final revision process. It wasn't the actual writing of the piece, but only the last extreme measures to get it right.

And what are we to make of Clark's prolongation of Olson's supposed franticness? "Throughout October he pestered Norman with late corrections, continuing to fret even as the magazine went to press. The first copies had already been printed when he was stricken with sudden doubts over his punctuation, demanding that Norman make further small changes by hand in the published volume. (The patient editor balked at this last request.)" (p. 50). Clark gets some of this via John Cech's *Charles Olson and Edward Dahlberg: A Portrait of a Friendship*, where Cech writes up bits from an interview with Dorothy Norman, thirty-five years after the event. It makes a good story. But the truth of the matter obtainable from letters is much more pedestrian. Olson wrote to Norman on "Wednesday afternoon" (presumably 19 October 1938) on receiving galley proofs, which he termed "almost impeccable":

> You say something about pageproof: does that mean you might still catch a slip or two. On that chance I'll list one major slip and a couple of small ones and pray you can get the printer to correct them.

He actually lists six in all and says, with a joviality beyond anything Clark allows him, "That covers it and God bless you!" Norman replied (21 October

1938 carbon copy at Yale) that the slips cannot be corrected, "firstly, because it is too late, and secondly, because the thing reads perfectly." We deduce from Norman's letter to Olson of 1 November 1938 some further talk of a comma: "Putting the comma in looks pretty awful because of the space. I am putting it in only certain copies ... going to the people you know." It had not been a *contretemps*. Norman ends the letter: "It was so fine to see you." There was only one change talked about after the printing (not "changes"), and Norman did not altogether "balk" at Olson's request.

We cannot leave this Harvard period without looking at the question of Olson's abandoning his Ph.D. Clark says: "Throwing over his doctoral work was the most momentous act of Olson's first thirty years" (p. 51). Since Olson left Harvard to do independent research on Melville with a Guggenheim Fellowship there doesn't seem to be any irreversible break whatsoever. But Clark wants to make it seem that Olson made a foolish mistake he later regrets: "Eight years later, when he had finally written his Melville book, he asked Harvard to award him a doctorate retroactively. The university's refusal remained a sore point with him for good" (p. 51). This is all wrong. It is the result of Clark's misreading of a questionnaire that Olson filled in for a sociology researcher at the State University of New York, Buffalo, on 22 September 1964, reproduced in *Minutes* #13. Clark thinks that in the blank under "highest degree" Olson wrote, "'Ph D' ... asked for ... but not offered" (the dots are in Clark's quote). Actually, Olson ticked the space for "Master's," then wrote: "plus 'Ph D' Harvard— without *Call Me Ishmael* (Reynal & Hitchcock 1947), asked for but not offered." What this means is that Olson's Ph.D. from Harvard remained in limbo because he didn't submit *Call Me Ishmael* when asked to do so. It was he who didn't offer it, when to do so would have got him the degree. This interpretation of the document in question, totally contrary to Clark's, is confirmed by Olson in writing to George Bowering in a letter of 7 March 1963. Olson was due to teach at the University of British Columbia the following summer and they were wanting to know if it were true that he had a Ph.D. (This letter now at Storrs is included in full in *Selected Letters* pp. 289–93.)

> ... when it came to the degree—and I was "offered" it one day years later on the steps of Harvard's library, by Murdoch in Merk's presence—and this will tell you—for Call Me Ishmael (that is, as the "acceptable" dissertation—not bad, Harvard University)—I sd, bumptiously and with stupid impossible confidence, no.

In short, it was Olson who was offered the degree informally by two professors who could have made it happen if he had submitted *Call Me Ishmael*; and it was Olson who decided not to.

8
Connie—the Courtship

Did Charles and Connie sleep together the first day they met, as Clark suggests (p. 66)? Connie's mother certainly feared it. Olson's invitation for the Memorial Day 1940 week-end had been to Connie's sister Jane, who wasn't about to go. When Connie said she would go in her sister's place, having seen Olson once, but not having met him, her mother immediately forbade it, according to Jane Atherton's account in *Minutes* #31/32, which gives us most of our information on these matters and was also Clark's source. "Mom, you don't have to worry," Jane describes herself saying. "Charles's mother will be there, she has other roomers, and really Charles is a gentleman" (p. 9). But the mother didn't like Connie's determination and was equally relentless. Clark calls the mother's protestations "mild" (p. 65). But that is not how his source describes them. Connie's act is more than simply opposing a mild mother; it is strong beyond all reason. Fate seems to have been at work. But did fate throw them into each other's arms the first night?

Jane Atherton says that on her sister's return after the week-end, Connie was "thoughtful" and "had not much to say" (*Minutes* #31/32 p.9). In a novel this would be a give-away; but Connie didn't confess anything to her sister, neither then nor at any time afterwards, so the word "thoughtful" doesn't seem to be quite enough proof. When Olson is telling Creeley about his meeting with Connie in a letter of 1 October 1951, he talks of "what was, for me, always, the joy, the bones":

> ... her legs ... went for them (it was crazy, really, the way, we went into it, her self, revealed, from under a demure dress, in a bathing suit I still keep looking for the duplicate of, with a skirt, blue, and there we were in Rockport, not at the sea, but in front of a house with a stone wall, and she took to jumping down for me to catch her where I stood in the grass. What a flirt, eh. It sounds so. But, for her, or me, not so easy. The thing was, it happened that time,

fast—and it was what? play, sure, but to be able to play, that takes a change, a shift of base, eh. Anyhow, I was caught, just, the damned delicate strength, or the directness, of, from what clearly she was, coming straight. (*CO/RC* 7 pp. 219–20)

This is a description of a day of physical attraction, which could have got them into bed.

Jane Atherton tells of the subsequent scene when Olson was visiting the family for the first time while they were in a vacation house in Barnstable on Cape Cod (August 1940, it would be):

> One day, in sweeping out Charles's room, mother found a package of condoms. She was shocked. Now she had a reason for asking Charles to leave. Until then she had no idea how long Charles planned to stay, and Connie had remained silent when the question was brought up. Mother confronted Charles with the evidence.
>
> He was plainly embarrassed, and apologized profusely for the ugly intrusion into our family life. He assured her that he had not seduced her daughter, but it was plain that the intent was there. Mother did not have to ask him to leave. He voluntarily packed up his belongings and left the house immediately.
>
> Connie was at the beach. When she returned, Charles was gone. Mother showed her the evidence, and Connie, white-faced, turned from her and ran up the road after Charles. The train for Boston had not yet arrived. What went on between the two of them as they sat in the station waiting room I don't know. But farewells were said and assurances of further meetings made. (p. 9)

He denied it to Connie's mother, for he was always chivalrous. What was the truth? There is another place where Olson is relating the sequence of events between them to the one person who would know, that is, Connie. In an undated letter (Clark thinks 1946, whereas I think 1941) Olson shares with Connie the memory of "that graveyard at Barnstable and the voices below us," and then "the bed at Ipswich when quickly we were in each other's arms two Buddhas of desire" (unpublished letter at Storrs). Clark says that this was the first evening in Gloucester on the very first visit; "once his mother was safely asleep, he slipped into Connie's bed in Oceanwood's sea-facing guest room. They spent the night in each other's arms" (p. 66) and adds the image of the two Buddhas of desire, but suppresses the mention of Ipswich as where this happened. Ipswich is near Gloucester, but it isn't Gloucester, and definitely not Oceanwood cottage. And it is apparently after Barnstable.

The condom story takes some of the fairy tale flavor out of this romance. And more than that. When Olson and Connie finally left for New York after Labor Day 1941, the first thing they had to face together as common-law man and wife was an abortion. Jane Atherton writes of this:

> We knew that Connie had a successful abortion. She wrote the news to mother, but did not mention her emotions or the physical ordeal. She said that she and Charles were both job-hunting. Later, Connie would tell me with bitterness of Charles's refusal to let her have children. She said he did not want to put down roots, and any suggestion of settling in one place to establish a home and family was anathema to him. (*Minutes* #31/32 p.17)

Tom Clark tells it this way:

> Connie's medical procedure, performed in New York, proved unexpectedly trying, a source of serious problems in later years. But Charlie nursed her back to health, and once she was well, she returned his solicitude redoubled, adopting the role of quiet, self-effacing and adoring mate. Up early every morning, she combed the 8th Street produce markets for fresh fruit to prepare "ambrosial" breakfasts for him. He lounged in bed till late, then read and wrote in his cozy office alcove. After dinner he and Connie strolled the Village streets together in the soft autumn twilight, an obviously happy young couple. He introduced her to friends as his wife. (p. 73)

Obviously, Olson doesn't deserve Connie!

Don't worry, he himself knew he was living with a goddess. That "ambrosia" was Olson's word for what he was being served. It is from a letter to Connie of 4 November 1952 (Storrs, unpublished), which asserts that it wasn't really Olson's "solicitude" that healed; it was his strength in himself and his seeming heroic action in the world, the world of politics, especially. That, at least, is Olson's guess (as opposed to his biographer's). In the letter, he thinks it was the trips he took to the Chicago convention, for instance, that gave him "the lineaments of an individual … as though I am another man in the world of men." And then the hero returns from his expeditions: "very much a question whether those mornings Charles St when you made me those ambrosia and nectar bowls wasn't our perfect union!" Then comes the Homeric comparison: " … when I was discharging in the world, and you were sending me out into it like Ulysses armed with Kalypso food." This specific allegory of a poet's life is something Clark missed, or suppressed in his own mind, not wanting to accept the young Olson (or, in fact, Olson at any age) as heroic. This motif is picked up in

The Maximus Poems in "On first Looking out through Juan de la Cosa's Eyes" of 10 May 1953, where he brings Ulysses and Calypso into the poem (I.78):

> (You could go any coast
> in such a raft as she taught,
> as she taught him [me], favoring him [me]
>
> with cedar, & much niceties. It was only because the gods willed
> that he could leave her, go away, determined though he [I] had been
> the whole time
> not to eat her food, not to wear gods' clothes,
> to stick to what men [I] eat
>
> And wore [wear]

The square brackets are the additions Olson made when he read this passage at Berkeley. He is making sure we read this as autobiography, and understand what "ambrosia" could mean in the world of a Greenwich Village courtship.

It was a long courtship, since they never actually married. It survived a Circe (see later chapters on Frances Boldereff); it survived until the time the above *Maximus* poem was written. Maybe until the end. For Connie came to Charles's deathbed, flying from Europe, as Jane Atherton describes:

> Because of the time difference it was two in the morning when the call was returned. Kate was sleeping in an attic bedroom and I had hoped she would not hear the call. But she did, and flew down the stairs. I had time only to tell Connie that Charles's illness was very serious. Kate then took over the telephone. Connie told her that she would fly to New York on the first available plane. The next day Kate left for New York to meet her mother and the two went directly to the Cornell Medical Center.
>
> There were many telephone calls to Scituate, Connie or Janet telling us of test results, each call sadder and more negative. Then it was over. Charles died at quarter of two on the morning of January 10. Connie was there. She had been with him every day, comforting him, nursing him and encouraging him as she had done years before.
>
> When she came to Scituate en route to the funeral in Gloucester she told me of their closeness as he slipped into unconsciousness, returning to her again for a few seconds, this repeated many times until the last when she knew he would open his eyes no more.
>
> "Oh, Charlie me boy, oh Charlie me boy," she continued to whisper. (p. 41)

9
The War, and the War of Words

Olson's propaganda work for the Office of War Information, Washington D.C., beginning in September 1941, can best be seen as a natural, patriotic extension of his high school and college forensics, what Clark calls his "highly developed powers of persuasion" (p. 78): "he threw himself with a passion into the task of interpreting and 'promoting' the war for the benefit of the millions of immigrant citizens who were being counted on to populate the trenches and assembly lines." Clark couldn't have been clearer if he'd said Olson was priming American immigrants for cannon fodder.

However, if Clark has read Olson's press releases and radio speeches, he has done more than I have. I don't know where they are. The two items that are known to have been published in the war years do not bear out the assertion that Olson was "promoting" the war, even if his ostensible job was to do so. I don't know if Olson would claim every word of the pamphlet *Spanish Speaking Americans in the War* (1943), but one page is certainly his.

Olson calls the battle of Bataan in the Philippines (April 1942, not 1943 as Clark has it) a "tragedy." True, he also uses the word "glory," but it is followed closely by "grief." The whole page speaks to the pity of war. Clark refers to it as follows:

> On one especially effective page, balancing bold-type stanzas of an Olson documentary poem faced one another above the starkly expressive photo image of a dark-veiled woman at a sun-bleached grave.

> | | |
> |---|---|
> | *Bataan—* | *Tejuan—* |
> | *old Spain's sun* | *along white mud* |
> | *dries copper skin* | *black women lean,* |
> | *of Coronado child* | *cry, moan:* |
> | *holed up and killed* | *"Bataan, battalion,"* |
> | | *"Bataan,"* |
> | | *"Bataan"*   (p. 78) |

52

BATAAN was a National Guard tragedy. The first soldiers ready, they were the first to go. Unlike the regular army, the Guards were home town units, local soldiers, local leaders. The threat of war was too great to allow time to regroup them. They went to the Philippines as they were. The 200th and 515th Coast Artillery of New Mexico were sent because they could talk Spanish and above all because they were the crack anti-aircraft units the Filipino people needed.

On April 9th, it was over. The glory of Bataan is the nation's but the grief is in the homes of the small towns of America—from Harrodsburg, Kentucky to Salinas, California, on the faces of this New Mexican mother, these Kentucky parents. New Mexico gave the fullest measure of devotion—one quarter of the 9,000 men from the mainland lost.

Whoever has a copy of *Spanish Speaking Americans in the War* with Olson's poem appearing in the manner Clark describes owns a great rarity, printed before the poem was censored out. In the copies I have seen there is just a large blank of sky. Olson told the story to Edward Van Aelstyn, editor of the campus *Northwest Review*, when asked to respond to the censorship going on at the University of Oregon:

> During World War II Ben Shahn & I did a pamphlet together for the U.S. Govt. It was *before* I was Foreign Nationality Director of the Democratic National Committee, & was then the same for the Office of War Information.—Mr Rockefeller (the present New York governor then Coordinator of Inter American Affairs) agreed to print this booklet (with photographs edited by Shahn) to spread it throughout Latin America—though its title was "Spanish Speaking Americans and the War" & was directly addressed to a very unpleasant fact: that at Bataan an enormous number of the dead had been from one anti-Aircraft battalion from two small towns in New Mexico, therefore almost all "Spanish" names therefore almost a resentment throughout etc
>
> OK. A fine photograph in *black* emphasis from the Life photographer—? Brown (cf mast-head) so interested me I wrote a poem
>
> > Bataan
> > Shahn
> > etc
> > & *black* women lean
>
> & Shahn went home to New Jersey & came back with this poem set in the New Mexico sky over sd woman visiting tomb in cemetery etc.
>
> Thereon enter the "Don't Hurt Everybody Man"—Phileo Nash (since himself almost governor of Wisconsin etc): who told Rockefeller "black" would insult the Spanish Speaking American of the Southwest—& of course South America! (*Selected Letters* p. 308)

As it transpired, the *Northwest Review* was no more able to resist the censorship than Olson and Shahn had been.

It is important to have this Bataan affair in mind when we consider how Olson and his immediate superior in OWI, his friend Constantine Poulos, came to feel they had to resign. According to a *New York Times* report, datelined 18 May 1944, Olson and Poulos "charged that censorship ... had 'hamstrung' the division" (quoted by Clark p. 85). What Clark does not quote is the statement by Olson that their superiors "had prevented them from functioning to offset Axis propaganda aimed at creating dissention among America's 35,000,000 citizens of foreign ancestry." We need this information to understand the background to the second publication we have to examine from the war years. Apparently, what Olson published in *Survey Graphic* (August 1944) as "People v. The Fascist, U.S. (1944)" was something he had been working on, with resistance from above, for quite a while. Clark wants to see it as a hasty "counter-attack" in the heat of the 1944 election. I do not think it is "a thinly veiled reference to the discriminatory tone of Republican campaign rhetoric" (Clark p. 87). The references are consistently to fascists and the racist "divide and conquer" of Nazi fifth-columnists inside wartime U.S.A.; example, a "Jew-baiting agitator, Joe McWilliams" (*Survey Graphic* p. 356). What Olson is pro-posing is that groups of people directly affected by this racism be able to sue in the courts for libel. He is asking for what amounts to a forerunner of today's hate laws, using class action civil law suits. He sees it as neces-sary in the war of ideas. Olson relied a great deal on articles written by his friend David Riesman (he kept the offprints and they are there at Storrs), but clearly Olson the champion orator has finally found something solid, something other than high school rhetoric, to which to attach his love of the U.S. Constitution.

Being able to publish this piece unfettered was an immediate benefit derived from Olson's leaving government bureaucracy. Another was earning quick money as a lobbyist on behalf of Polish Government interests, urged to it by Oscar Lange, later Poland's ambassador to the United Nations, through a mutual friend, Adam Kulikowski, of the OWI. And then he made a quick change to paid electioneering agent for the Democratic Party. Part of Olson's duties was organizing the "Everybody for Roosevelt" rally in Madison Square Gardens in November 1944, where not only was he "busy shepherding the entertainers backstage" (Clark p. 89) but actually introduced in the spotlight none other than the young Frank Sinatra.

For someone as successful a back-room politician as Olson, the normal expectation is that one would go with the crowd and take one's reward. Olson did not do this, and it behooves us to examine why. Clark is good on this, quoting the poem "The K" as Olson's declaration of independence, and also an illuminating letter to Ruth Benedict of 12 January 1945, where Olson says that a creative individual has no chance in America to be "central to social action" like Yeats was in Ireland. He will have to go it alone for a while, "working down to the word where it lies in the blood"

Advertisement in the *New York Times*.

(quoted by Clark p. 95). We can add to Clark's evidence a later letter to Creeley (*CO/RC* 1.27) with the summary:

c. 1917 the scientist was done as leader ...
c. 1945, august, the political activist likewise done.

Who was left was the poet: "the only one who, since the beginning of the species, had spent 40 hrs a day on the problem, what is the reach of man's imagination."

These perceptions were the intellectual thrust; we still have to look around for the conditions that provided Olson with the heart to leave the path of career politician and stride off into the profession of writer. What did it, I believe, was another synchronicity. In Key West, the Olsons were offered accommodation in the poolside bungalow of the Hemingway house. Pauline Hemingway had kept the big house going, after her husband's departure, as a home for their two sons, and this adjacent living space became the Olsons' in exchange for a little help with the boys. The result was that Olson worked daily at Hemingway's desk, the desk at which *For Whom the Bell Tolls* had not long ago been written, and surrounded by the books that had been left largely as Hemingway had had them.

I relish this picture. Clark has, it seems, no interest in allowing that a mantle might have fallen from Hemingway to Olson; he has nothing on what it must have meant to Olson to be, if not possessed by, at least possessed of, Hemingway's spirit. Clark only quotes Olson in an early notebook dismissing *Winner Take Nothing* as the work of a "castrated ex-winner" (quoted p. 16). I didn't see that phrase in the notebook; presumably it is there. But what is certainly there is a whole essay on Hemingway under the date 26 October 1932. It springs from the latest publication, *Death in the Afternoon*, but shows Olson's familiarity with everything Hemingway had written up to then. This essay was printed in the *Wesleyan Cardinal* (February 1933) and reprinted in *Minutes* #12, and proves Olson knew his Hemingway early. And now here he was in a real writer's den.

One can see it as a tourist today. The place itself is beautiful, looking out on the pool and palm trees. A successful writer had created this space. As Olson worked there day after day I imagine him saying to himself: "I can do this too." Clark notes that "Hemingway's large shadow" lingered everywhere, but he does not consider that it could be an awakening for Olson. He has him listless: "A restless sense of false peace seemed to pervade the place" (p. 90). The intellectual fireworks of Olson's two Key West notebooks refute Clark's view.

Present-day postcards of the Hemingway House, Key West, Florida.

We know for sure one momentous thing that happened. Olson took down from Hemingway's bookshelves his copy of Pound's *Personae*. We know from a later statement that this was Olson's first introduction to Pound. But he soon caught up. The *Cantos* must have been there, too, for he writes a piece in his "Key West II" notebook in early February 1945 that tries to understand the appeal of Pound as it moves him away from his old loyalty to Yeats. We have the typescript "Joyce, Pound, and W.B. Yeats," prepared for publication 30 April 1945 from the notebook draft (Storrs Prose #12). By placing these men in relation to each other he is preparing his own stance. This is the war of ideas in his new chosen civic arena.

> Yeats left himself uncompleted. For years now I have felt it, beneath all his beauty, all his power. It has to do with his failure to give himself up to a large piece of work to which all of him might have been brought to bear. The shame is, he had it in his hand, as early as 1917, in A Vision. He had twenty years to take it up, shape it, and make it poetically and dramatically what it inherently is—another Finnegan's Wake, another Hundred Cantos, more than either.
>
> In the narrows of our own day we think of Joyce and Pound as beginners. They look so, they so revolutionize language and forms and approaches. But the truth is they are enders, no less great, greater indeed as enders.

In this unpublished essay Olson seems to be opening up a space for himself as the future author of a modern epic poem.

10
Olson and Pound

The records of the relationship between these two poets will be combed through many times in the future. Catherine Seelye's book *Charles Olson & Ezra Pound: An Encounter at St. Elizabeths* (1975) was a good start, presenting Olson's notes made after each of his visits to Pound. Clark, of course, has much to say on the subject. My purpose here is to test these two accounts against the material in the "Pound" file at Storrs, including Pound's letters to Olson, and also Olson's letters to Pound, now at the Lilly Library, Indiana University.

About the same time as Olson was drafting "Joyce, Pound and W.B. Yeats" in his notebook (Storrs OS #56), he was also puzzling out ideas about Pound's treason, and how to separate the man and his work. These pages headed "February 1" (1945) contain crossings out and rephrasings consistent with its being a first draft—but a first draft of what? Clark quotes from the piece, saying that it is the text of a letter to Francis Biddle, U.S. Attorney General (p. 98). I doubt this. The tone is not right for someone approaching a person of power to try to "save" Pound's skin. I believe the direct address to "Mr Biddle" here is as much a rhetorical device as the address to "Mr American."

> Yeats who knew Pound, both of him, could not agree with his politics or his economics any more than the Attorney General of the U.S. Yeats called him a revolutionary simpleton. And Yeats knew of what politics he spoke, for he was an Irishman, by nature and act a revolutionist as well as a Senator of the Irish Free State, a thing Pound or I or no other poet could be in these United States.
>
> A revolutionary simpleton. Why not let that stand, Mr Biddle? Do you, Mr American, not agree about that "crackpot" Pound, all poets? aren't they all simpletons? So you and Yeats agree.

Besides the tone, one other thing makes me doubt that this was a letter to

Biddle. An Olson letter to Malcolm Cowley of 26 April 1945 says that he "might be able to front for it [Pound's case] with the Justice Department" (*Selected Letters* p. 41). That seems to rule out his already having done so.

I prefer to think of this notebook entry, with its continual reference to Yeats's viewpoint, as the inception of what became, after much reframing, the essay "This Is Yeats Speaking." This was finished the day Pound arrived in the U.S. from Italy, 18 November 1945, and was first submitted through Harry Levin to *Foreground* at Harvard, then hand-delivered on 29 November 1945 to Philip Rahv of *Partisan Review*, where it was published in the Winter 1946 issue.

Clark summarizes "This Is Yeats Speaking" on pages 107–108, and I would add only one point, to make clear what Olson emphasizes more in the drafts (Seelye pp. 16–17): that Pound should be tried by "the only men who conceivably can recognize and judge him, his fellow writers ... Shall the State do what men, whose business it is to come by truth, do not do?" So an account of the thrust of this essay should stress not only the reflective tone Olson uses the voice of Yeats for, but also the aggrieved tone in which he has Yeats say: "You have allowed this to happen without a trial of your own" (Seelye p. 30).

There are a couple of evidences of Olson's work on Pound not previously revealed. One is a typescript page (in Box 51 at Storrs), which can be dated around the end of May 1945. It is simply terse one-line summaries for each of Pound's cantos, with a list of the "Archetypal Persons" of the poem (Confucius, Malatesta, Adams, etc.) and notes on "themes." Olson, with some deliberation, was preparing himself. Also, according to the "Washington Spring 1945" notebook at Storrs, Olson also did a close reading of Pound's *Jefferson and/or Mussolini*. It is from this volume (pp. 112–13) that Olson "steals" a poem, as he put it to Pound later (Seelye p. 69). Seelye prints the poem "A Translation" in her notes (p. 128). It is the AXE TREE SUN section of "2 Propositions and 3 Proofs" (*Collected Poems* pp. 36–37). Clark refers to the poem as "a Chinese inscription rifled directly from 'Canto XIII'" (p. 108). Canto XIII is an error. This is an error Seelye also makes. A comparison with the cited pages of *Jefferson and/or Mussolini* would clearly reveal its source.

Clark wrote of Olson at this time: "He persuaded Dorothy Norman to assign him to cover the Pound legal proceedings as a *Twice A Year* reporter. Turning himself into a journalist was no part of his intent; he merely wanted a press credential to get him into Judge Bolitha J. Laws' district courtroom as a spectator" (p. 108). It seems to me an unwarranted assumption on Clark's part that Olson wanted to be merely a "curious onlooker." All the verse and prose on Pound, leading up to "This Is Yeats Speaking," testifies to Olson's wish to express himself seriously on the events as they would unfold. I would like to place on the table Olson's letter to Dorothy Norman of 19 November 1945 (at Yale):

> Pound's return to the U.S. last night came sooner than I was advised it would. And the new indictment may go to the Grand Jury at any moment. Thus the haste.
>
> I have had in mind to free lance the case, observe, gather, comment—if the knot of it reveals a space from which to unravel. I believe the record of it at least is an important document. The press smells the scent: POET Ezra Pound. He talks loud himself. It's the first treason since Benedict Arnold!
>
> I would like to give it as much time as I can afford.

One might add that, of course, this proposal depended on the fact that Olson was living in Washington D.C. He could not have afforded to travel from elsewhere and would not have felt it his duty to do so. But Fate had him placed in Pound's direct path, and Olson took his cue from that.

Seelye did not attempt to pin down all of Olson's visits to Pound. The following account will try, for the record, to fill in the gaps. The visits lasted from January 1946 to February 1948, with a long hiatus because of Olson's nine-month trip to the West Coast.

(1) Friday 4 January 1946. "First Canto, January 5, 1946" (Seelye pp. 35–41).

After this first visit Olson "wrote James Laughlin to convey Pound's request for a copy of *Cantos 50–61* to present to one of the doctors at St. Elizabeths ..." (Clark p. 110). There is no such title as "Cantos 50–61." It was *Cantos LII–LXXI* (New Directions 1940). He then goes on to cast Olson in rather a bad light: he claims it was "a service less than entirely unselfish, since Olson also attempted to use the opportunity to forward his own literary interest, offering the publisher his Melville book, on which he still hadn't received a decision from Harcourt" (p. 110). But Laughlin in his letter of 29 December 1945, which had started the whole thing, had asked: "Whatever happened to your book on Melville?" Olson can't really be considered pushy if he answers the question asked: "You ask about the Melville thing. I got back to it last June, and it's done. I'm just now adding the last stuff, Melville's own notes in his copy of the Essex. Picked them up last month. It turns out to be a little book, critical, with a few twists here and there. I should be delighted, of course, if you'd be interested in it. I could send it to you in about a week" (letter in Laughlin archive). Clark makes it sound as though Olson had committed an indiscretion: "Laughlin politely passed." But Laughlin was just away skiing.

(2) Tuesday 15 January 1946. "Canto 2" (Seelye pp. 42–49).

According to Clark, Olson is supposed to have had some "sober thoughts" between his first and second visits because of "an unsettling encounter with Michael Greenberg, a State Department Far Eastern policy adviser he'd gotten to know in his last months at the OWI. Greenberg had read "This Is Yeats Speaking," just out in the Winter 1946 issue of *Partisan Review* ..." (p. 110). The fact is that the *Partisan Review* had not yet come out by the time of the second visit 15 January 1946. Even on 29 January 1946 Olson is not at all sure when "This Is Yeats Speaking" will appear (letter to Philip Rahv of that date). The discussion with Greenberg took place long before, and Olson in "Canto 2" describes himself as prompted to remember back to "Greenberg's analysis, that my demand for a judgment of Pound by the writers as a writer must not be misunderstood, that two other things must simultaneously go on, his trial for treason, a judgment of him as fascist, as well as a total picture of what he was and how he came to be what he is" (Seelye pp. 45–46). Clark's picture of Olson making his second visit with this "warning" still "reverberating in his mind" is pure fantasy.

(3) Thursday 24 January 1946. Third visit, as described in "Canto 3, January 24, 1946, 3:10–3:30" (Seelye pp. 50–60).

At Pound's suggestion, Olson wrote to the attorney Julien Cornell asking for access to Pound's broadcasts (letter 26 January 1946 draft at Storrs).

(4) Tuesday 29 January 1946. Fourth visit, described in "Canto 4, January 29, 2:55–3:15" (Seelye pp. 61–67).

Pound signed copies of his books, which Olson had brought with him: *Eleven New Cantos* and *Guide to Kulchur*.

(5) Thursday 7 February 1946. Fifth visit, as described in "Canto 5, February 7, 1946, 3:15–3:30" (Seelye pp. 68–71).

Olson was accompanied by Connie. Note: the word "recording" in the last paragraph of Seelye (p. 71) should be "rereading" as per manuscript. We should not go looking for tape recordings; they do not exist.

(6) Thursday 14 February 1946. Sixth visit, as described in "Canto VI, February 14, 2:30–2:45" (Seelye pp. 72–77).

Olson used his notebook "Washington Fall 1945 II–Spring 1946" to copy down passages from the typescript of Pisan cantos 74 and 75, which Pound had given to Olson to give to Laughlin. (Note: the miscellaneous notes in Seelye at the top of pages 109–110 also belong to this visit.)

(7) Tuesday 19 March 1946. Seventh visit, notes typed up as "Canto 3 March 19, 1946" (Seelye supplies title "Canto [7]" on pp. 78–84).

(8) Tuesday 26 March 1946. Eighth visit. The notes for this visit were not typed up as a "canto"; they are found on the back of an envelope post-marked from New York City 21 March 1946 in the "Pound" file at Storrs. They have been transcribed in part by Seelye in the miscellaneous notes, pages 107–108, beginning with "sewers of Freud" and ending with "in all that time."

(9) Tuesday 30 April 1946 Ninth visit. The notes for this visit were made in the "Washington Fall 1945 II–Spring 1946" notebook, and typed up with the heading "POUND: April 30 (after five weeks): 20 minutes" (Seelye pp. 85–86).

Olson has been away in New York and Gloucester. The miscellaneous notes on Seelye page 108 (lower half of page) pertain to this visit.

During the April 1946 trip to New York to sign the contract for *Call Me Ishmael*, Clark has Olson making "the round of foundation offices" (p. 112) and writing a letter home to Connie, which Clark deliberately paraphrases to make Olson look pathetic in his struggles to earn a living as a writer. But Clark has the date wrong. This letter to Connie is actually from March 1941, five years before. Connie accompanied Olson to New York in April 1946.

In response to Pound's questioning, Olson on the 14 February visit had mentioned *Call Me Ishmael*, but Olson didn't bring the manuscript right away: it wasn't on the 19 March visit, but on the 26 March visit. By the 30 April visit, Pound has read it. And though he is known to have damned it with faint praise (e.g. to D.G. Bridson in a BBC interview, transcribed in *New Directions* #17: "There was a guy who did a book on Melville, and I was so glad to see a short book that saved me the trouble of reading Melville that I recommended it to the Reverent Eliot"), to Olson in person he said: "Don't touch the form as is, this book and Ron Duncan's the only two book we have" (Seelye p. 86).

(10) Tuesday 14 May 1946. Tenth visit. No notes appear to exist.

Olson had sent Pound the poem "Auctour" with the message: "Sunday May 12 Dear E.P.: Will be over Tuesday Yrs Charles Olson." (See *A Nation of Nothing But Poetry* p. 177; Seelye p. 135 prints the poem and message, but not the date.) An unsent letter also dated 12 May exists at Storrs, which indicates that Olson was intending to send ahead of time his review of Ronald Duncan's *Journal of a Husbandman*; he presumably took the review with him instead—the manuscript has Pound's annotations on it. An Olson letter to George Leite dated 14 May 1946 (at Buffalo) indicates what was discussed on this visit.

(11) Tuesday 21 May 1946. Eleventh visit. Not in Seelye, no written notes.

Olson had sent a note to Pound: "Will be over Tuesday. Will try to make it around 1:30." This message is in the Storrs collection because Pound used it for a message of his own, dated by him 21 May 1946 (envelope postmarked 23 May 1946), which reads: "Don't bring back shirt till I ask for it." This implies that on a visit of that date Olson had been given an errand involving his taking away one of Pound's shirts! The first draft of "ABCs," dated in the *Collected Poems* (p. 652) as May 1946 may have been a consequence of this visit.

(12) Tuesday 18 June 1946. Twelfth visit, written up with the heading "June 18, 1946: with EP from 1:20–1:45" (Seelye pp. 87–91).

Olson and Connie had come up from their summer cottage at Enniscorthy, Virginia, to Washington for a few days, mainly to see Pound.

On Saturday 29 June 1946 Olson attempted a visit, but was refused entry by an officious guard, since it was not a regular visiting day. Pound had written 17 June 1946 asking Olson if he still wanted magazines saved for him; Olson replied on 26 June 1946 that he had to be in Washington for a conference that next week-end, and would try to see him to get the magazines. In a letter of 6 July 1946 to Pound, Olson explained that he had tried. (He did not get back into the city for the rest of the summer.)

Pound certainly led Olson in Poundian directions: Confucius, Fenellosa, Frobenius and Fox; but I do not think that Olson more than sniffed at Remy de Gourmont and Henry James, the authors Clark says Pound led him to (p. 116). It is also beyond belief that "under Pound's tutelage he also embarked on a serious study of the rhythmic cadences of Greek poetry" (p. 116); his meetings with Pound were sometimes less than half an hour, and filled with Pound's gossip and opinions. Olson tried to get in on the

Rudd Fleming translation sessions, which resulted in the posthumous *Elektra* (New Directions 1988), but he was not invited. Michael Lekakis is the one we know Olson turned to for a sense of ancient Greek recitation.

Clark is also in error when he says it was "on Pound's advice" that Olson read Victor Berard and Jane Harrison (p. 116). It was Edward Dahlberg who in a letter of 5 April 1949 brought Berard to Olson's attention; the same for Jane Harrison (see *Olson's Reading* p. 30), except much earlier. Clark must have noted the names Berard and Harrison in Olson's "1946 Summer Field Book, Enniscorthy" (Storrs #38), assuming that these Odyssey notes were the result of a talk with Pound, not noticing that these particular notes are in fact later, dated "1949."

(13) Sunday 22 September 1946 Thirteenth visit. The "Enniscorthy—June 1946" notebook contains what must be notes on this visit; though undated, they come after an entry dated 18 August 1946. They are transcribed in part in Seelye pp. 110–111 beginning with "Little magazines" and ending with "4 books."

Pound wrote a letter of 25 September 1946, which indicates that they had again been discussing the "New Loeb" series of cheap classics. Olson wrote a postcard to Dorothy Pound dated 26 September 1946, which indicates that Connie was present, and includes the sentence: "It was a lovely afternoon Sunday, definitely SUN AXE TREE!"

(14) Sunday 20 October 1946. Fourteenth visit.

Olson wrote to Dorothy Pound 16 October 1946: "I want now to come over Sunday to see you both. I shall try to get there around 11:30." There appear to be no notes identifiable as being from this meeting.

(15) Thursday 14 November 1946. Fifteenth visit.

Olson had written to Pound: "Expect now to be able to make it tomorrow. I had too much of a cold to get over." This is dated only "Wednesday"; the conjecture is that this is the same cold as referred to in a letter to Caresse Crosby of 14 November 1946: "been bound to the house with a cold, or I would have been over to see you." There are notes in the "BOOK" notebook made on a visit to St. Elizabeths with material of around November 1946.

On Wednesday 4 December 1946 Dorothy and Omar Pound joined Olson and Connie for a supper and a show, according to a letter to Dorothy Pound of 30 November 1946.

(16) Tuesday 17 December 1946. Sixteenth visit. The notes for this visit are probably those found in Olson's notebook of this time, the "Verse & Geometry plus EP" notebook; they are transcribed in part in Seelye (section beginning "Briarcliffe" p. 110).

Olson wrote Pound 15 December 1946: "I expect now to get over Tuesday, and will bring back little Hoffman's big book" (possibly Ross J.S. Hoffman's *Medieval History* is meant).

(17) Sunday 23 February 1947. Seventeenth visit (Pound now in Chestnut Ward).

A letter from Olson to Pound of 18 February indicates that he has not been to St. Elizabeths since before Christmas, having been confined to his bed with a glandular problem of the neck. A letter to Harvey Breit of 1 March 1947 says, "I got out for the first time in a month Sunday, and had a gab with Poundie." The "1947 February–December 2" notebook contains a list of names jotted down during this visit, when a Committee of Correspondence was being discussed. We know that Olson wrote to one of them, John Berryman, the next day (a letter of 24 February at University of Minnesota).

(18) Sunday 16 March 1947. Eighteenth visit. The "1947 February–December 2" notebook has an entry dated 16 March 1947: "1 hr conversation EP, C, O and myself," i.e. Omar Pound and Connie were present. The notes that follow in the notebook appear in Seelye (bottom p. 111 to top p. 113). (Note: "kafka-theory" on page 112 should be "knife-theory and"; "Lewis" further down the page is "Denis"; and top of page 113 "reaching" should be "remarking on.")

This is the occasion that prompted Pound's remark in a letter of 20 March: "Been fighting against pic-nic lunches for years." The Committee of Correspondence was again discussed, for Olson wrote a further letter to John Berryman on 19 March 1947.

About Pound's urging Olson to rally support for a Committee of Correspondence, Clark says: "some of his letters, most notably those to Berryman, went ignored" (p. 117). On the contrary, Ray West, the only other person Olson wrote to in this regard, answered his letters. And so did Berryman! In response to Olson's first letter (24 February 1947), Berryman replied directly to Pound. To Olson's second letter (19 March 1947), he replied in a postcard to Olson that he didn't want to cooperate in something just to gratify Pound (card dated 22 March 1947, postmarked 29 March 1947, at Storrs).

Clark suggests that "the Pound connection" was the "opening stake at the gaming tables of literary careering," quoting one of the Committee of Correspondence letters out of context: "the Olson hand is little played as yet" (p. 117). What Olson meant by saying that his "hand is little played as yet" was that he had not really published enough. "I would lead," he says in the letter, "have any man lead, with his work." And now he can lead, with *Call Me Ishmael* "out this month" and "poems coming up soon from Black Sun Press" (letter to Berryman 24 February 1947 at the University of Minnesota Library). Clark presents it as Olson's "admission" that he is participating in career games. Quite the opposite: he intends to be judged by his own work alone, and will not presume a status ahead of its appearance.

(19) Sunday 23 March 1947. Nineteenth visit.

Olson's copy of the New Directions edition of *Confucius* was inscribed to him by Pound with the date 20 March 1947 (publication date). Olson wrote to Pound: "Read several pages of UNWAVERING AXIS (alias UNWOBBLING PIVOT) yesterday afternoon, and want to tell you it is beautiful, and an historic act." The letter is dated only "Monday"; but it refers to a Sunday meeting on which he received the *Confucius*, presumably 23 March 1947.

(20) Tuesday 15 April 1947. Twentieth visit.

Pound wrote to Wyndham Lewis in a letter begun on 17 April 1947 but continued and mailed a few days later: "a pseudo Sweed wuz mentionin' Lion & Fox as about the only ecc. & at least the Sweed's 'awake'" (ed. Timothy Materer *Pound/Lewis* p. 236).

(21) Sunday 18 May 1947. Twenty-first visit.

Olson had sent Pound Edward Dahlberg's *Do These Bones Live*; a Pound postcard of 16 May 1947 asks if he should bring the Dahlberg downstairs for Olson "on Sunday." Olson wrote to James Laughlin on 18 May 1947: "EP is now Grandpa, Mary begot it in the ruined castle. It gave Eppie a boost, and talk as tho I was being handed seegars, fine Havana seegars. But he still goes up and down, tho not down as down was in Howard Hall … one visits for two, three hours and P, with that troublesome cerebellum rested against the back of a blue easy chair, spins out the speech, de dove sta memora. It's often wonderful."

(22) Thursday 29 May 1947. Twenty-second visit. The "1947 February –December 2" notebook has an entry "Visit to Pound May 29, 1947," with

the notes which appear (in part) on page 113 of Seelye, beginning "Pound got." (Note re: Bennett, "cremated" should be "cultivated.")

(23) Sunday 8 February 1948. Twenty-third visit, after eight months away from Washington. The notes from this visit were written up with the heading "EP February 9, 1948" (Seelye pp. 92–93).

This is the occasion Olson was speaking of in a letter to Robert Creeley of 17 June 1953: "I came home, got drunk, and hammered off the note did break it" (unpublished letter, Stanford). There is no evidence that "Olson reacted by abruptly stalking out in disgust" from the 8 February 1948 visit (Clark p. 132). Clark is writing fiction: "His show of feeling, he realized once he'd gotten home, was a product of his growing 'resistance at any longer being a son.' He became determined to immediately cease relying on Pound for 'direction of work, decisions ... to prime the pump.'" These supposed realizations and resolutions by which Olson made up his mind "to force an ending" to the Pound visits have simply been lifted from his "Faust Buch" notebook, a passage dated a month afterwards, 8 March 1948. What Olson thought out in retrospect is used by Clark to give a spurious sense of premeditation to the break-up with Pound, the real cause of which was Pound's elitism, witness the letter Olson wrote, striking back as an immigrant against Pound's Mayflower pose:

> BUT you do have to deal with us Olsons, Leite-Rosenstock-Huessys; your damn ancestors let us in. (AND AS ABOVE I DON'T THINK THE BATHTUB WAS SO CLEAN WHEN THEY DID.)

The letter, which can be found in full in *Selected Letters* (pp. 75–77), is signed by Olson as a "truculent ummugrunt." Clark's account suffers greatly from his not having had access to the letter itself.

Pound replied by return mail, with a customary postcard (at Storrs, postmarked 12 February 1948), saying that Olson should sit down with Confucius and not bother him with secondhand, mass-produced "bricabrak." "Goddamn him," Olson wrote to Creeley in retrospect (letter at Stanford, 17 June 1953) that "he cld let such a note have such an easy answer." Olson went to St. Elizabeths on one further occasion, but got more of the same—this time innuendo about William Carlos Williams's mixed blood (Seelye p. 101). For Olson, this was the end.

(24) Tuesday 24 February 1948. Twenty-fourth visit, the last. A description is included in the essay "GrandPa, GoodBye" (Seelye pp. 97–105), which, when he sent it to Peter Russell 17 November 1949, Olson referred to as

"the last notes I wrote, I think the day I last saw him" (unpublished letter, Buffalo).

When the Bollingen Award to Pound was announced on 24 February 1949, Olson wrote to Dorothy Pound that he was delighted. A postcard from Pound of 24 March 1949 suggested Olson had better come and say so in person. But this Olson did not do. He sent a note dated 2 June 1949 (Lilly Library, Indiana):

> look, it's no dice i don't get there
>
> the reasons are respectful   if goddamn stiff
> gramp
>
> shit, there it is
>
> when what's to be done is
> done I'll come   i'll look you in the eye
>
> > > love
> > > > olson.

It was not until the two were brought together fifteen years later at the Spoleto Festival of July 1965 that Olson felt able to fulfill that promise.

11
The Olson–Boldereff "Riot"

Clark, speaking of the growing "importance" of Olson's "mystery correspondent," Frances Boldereff, says that Olson "took the surprising step of
applying for a teaching job at the school where she worked, Penn State"
(p. 148). This statement is in error. Clark cites the article by Leverett T.
Smith and myself in *Credences* 2 (Summer 1982), "The Charles Olson
Papers at Raleigh, N.C.," in which we summarized a letter from
Pennsylvania State College of 30 March 1949, as "seeking testimonial in
regard to Olson's application for teaching post" (p. 79). We would not have
put it that way if we had known about Frances Boldereff. We should, in any
case, from the misspelling of Olson's name in the letter have been
suspicious that Philip A. Shelley, Head of the German Department at
Pennsylvania State College, the writer of the inquiry, did not have any
letter from Olson in front of him. This is the text of the letter (now in the
Raleigh files):

> Gentlemen: Word has reached me that Mr. Charles Olsen, a young
> poet and writer, has recently delivered a lecture or lectures at Black
> Mountain College. Would you be so good as to inform me confi-
> dentially concerning Mr. Olsen's accomplishments as a lecturer?
> He is under consideration to deliver a lecture at The Pennsylvania
> State College, and it is for this reason that I am anxious to know
> something specific about his effectiveness as a speaker as well as
> anything in general about his subjects and any other pertinent
> observations which you might care to make.

There can be little doubt now that word reached Mr. Shelley via Frances
Boldereff, actively promoting the interesting poet she had exchanged
letters with for over a year, but not yet met.

The reply came from David H. Corkran, Registrar of Black Mountain
College, dated 4 April 1949 (carbon copy in the files at Raleigh):

> Dear Sir: In response to your inquiry, we have found Mr. Charles Olson a popular and effective speaker. He is at his best in talking about Herman Melville. He is animated, imaginative and bold, having the capacity to stir up considerable discussion.

On 8 May 1949 Boldereff wrote to Olson in Washington, D.C.: "we got a terrific report on you from Black Mountain—I knew before it came but I was glad to have the people here have proof—now I have to go away and if you get invited next year, because I have so deeply believed in you please accept if you can to show them you are just as up there as I say." The significant thing is that she signs this letter "Frances now Ward"; and the reason she was going away was that she had just married a Duke Ward, who was taking her to Albuquerque. She was offering Olson the use of her "reconverted barbershop" house in Woodward (with "a friend if you so cared") not because she would be there, but because she wouldn't. These facts, plus the lack of any evidence that Olson encouraged this project, make it impossible to accept Clark's implied interpretation that their relationship had at that time already reached a stage where they were contemplating cohabitation of some sort.

We are indebted to Clark for details of the first meeting of Olson and Boldereff in the New York Public Library and subsequent meetings, information which is not in letters and which Clark obtained in interviews with Frances Boldereff Phipps in January 1987. Having listened to Frances myself over a period of four days in August 1983, I can understand how Clark came up with some of his conclusions. In her later years Boldereff had come to have rather a jaded view of Olson. And, for instance, Clark may be accurately recording her sarcasm when he reports, via her, Olson's parting words after a night in a hotel near the railroad station in Knoxville, Tennessee: "In the morning, when they parted, he kissed her goodbye with a magnanimous 'You deserved this, baby'" (p. 165). This vignette is damaging as it stands. If we had Frances's letters immediately following the meeting we would, I am convinced, hear something quite other than sarcasm. Unfortunately her letters for this period are missing. Olson's letter written immediately after Knoxville does exist (*CO/FB* #217, 15 May 1950). He said: "the honoring of you lies deeper than where you pose it, in the absolute recognition of you and of your force in my life." Clark could have quoted this as some rebuttal of the sarcasm, but he didn't.

I can also hear Frances Boldereff Phipps behind the thesis governing Clark's general approach to the affair: that Olson failed the challenge she represented. The accusation is cowardice: Olson might express a wish to "throw responsibility over" and start completely anew, but "never at moments when there was real opportunity to act" (Clark p. 136). Frances Boldereff is Opportunity and Olson is a Cripple in the face of it: this is the plot of Clark's novelette.

In keeping with his general thesis, Clark describes Boldereff in her early letters as holding back little (p. 137); Olson, however, "entered correspondence with her, at first in a tentative and exploratory fashion, answering her letters with rather guarded postcards and notes, his curiosity still hedged with caution" (p. 137). I see no fault in this. As it is, to make Olson seem stodgy, Clark has to exaggerate Frances's "openness." On reading Olson's poem "In Praise of the Fool," Clark says, "she had already seen his 'spirit coming through so naked and uncovered' that any future attempts at concealment between them would be beside the point" (p. 137). The fact is that when she used the words "naked and uncovered" she had not yet looked up Olson's poem, and in the context of her letter (#3, 4 January 1948) those words were not directly about Olson but about artists in general. She ends the letter, only her second one to him, referring to *Call Me Ishmael*: "you kept yourself out and yet are so in your book. I cannot pretend I do not know you. And I am so damned grateful you've no idea." Clark, with no little distortion, paraphrases this as her suggesting that "she and Olson should henceforth dispense with social preliminaries" (p. 137). Olson is "unnerved," Clark says, and so begins to "draw out the exchange with professional-sounding queries, soliciting her opinions, for example, on the type design of *Y & X*" (p. 137). I do not believe Olson was unnerved, and I do not at this stage—we are talking only about his second letter (#5, 11 May 1948)—see any "professional-sounding queries" in the plural. As for the typeface of *y & x*, why should he not be interested in her expert opinion as a designer? In any case, he didn't get a sample of *y & x* to her until the following November; so, whatever Clark meant by bringing this up, Olson did not actually solicit her opinion at this time.

Then Clark says (implying further disparagement of Olson) that Boldereff "put his discretion to the test by inviting him to visit her in Woodward, the Pennsylvania hill-country hamlet where she lived" (p. 137). This is not exactly true. What she did was send a sample of her design work around 20 June 1948 (#6), proposing an inscription to go with it: "For Olson—with whom I should love to get drunk." As Frances herself said in a later letter (#8, 26 June 1948), this was "not an invitation—it was a recognition." Woodward was not mentioned, and she ends the letter: "When will it be possible to see any of the other things you have been working on?" She is not expecting Olson to turn up with manuscripts; she is wondering when anything new is to be published. It is to this query that Olson is replying in his 23 June 1948 postcard (#7) when he says: "Fact is, the fishing is still good. I have finished one dance-play and am off into another." These words are not a rebuff to an invitation, they just slide past it. Frances takes off her hat to him in her next letter for just this finesse, and herself strikes a casual tone: "When you get time write me a letter—no matter how many months it is and tell me about America" (#8, 26 June 1948). Boldereff too exercises some caution.

Clark's yearning for melodrama is displayed again when he ends his discussion of the first exchange of letters between Olson and Boldereff by saying: "He had not yet let on a word to her about Connie" (p. 137). Why in heaven's name should he have done so? This is only Olson's third "tentative" postcard we are talking about.

A corollary to the thesis that Frances Boldereff was fast and straight while Olson was slow and crooked in their relationship is the contention that he lifted many of her phrases and ideas for his own use. Safe to say that Olson's flurry of work on "The Kingfishers" owed its inception "in some degree to the confidence-building exchange with Frances Boldereff" (Clark p. 146). In some degree, of course. But how much? Clark seems to think the poem grew out of a discussion Frances had stimulated: "Commenting on the spiritual poverty of the postwar society around them, he had written to her of his hopes for a new America, hailing the emergence of 'a green republic now renewed.' She replied that in the current explosion of materialism she saw no evidence of such renewal, and challenged him to provide some" (p. 146). No such discussion took place. Clark is relying entirely on three rather enigmatic lines of verse Olson appended as a postscript to his postcard of 23 June 1948 (#7):

> A crown in a forest of the city make
> attention turned as heads which hear demand
> the green republic now renewed.

And Boldereff's response (#8, 26 June 1948): "I am wondering how can you say 'the green republic now renewed'—oh! Olson please say if you mean that—I am sure the whole shell has to be sloughed off and of men alive I know maybe of four." End of "discussion"—for Olson says nothing at all about it in subsequent letters.

"The Kingfishers" was written quite outside of the frame of his correspondence with Boldereff. My belief is that the springs of the poem are elsewhere and of long duration. If Olson said it was the answer "to a question you asked me one year and five months ago," as he did in sending Boldereff "The Kingfishers" in a letter of 26 October 1949 (#49), it was because the poem had turned out to be an answer, even though it had not been written as such. (See Ralph Maud *What Does Not Change: The Significance of Charles Olson's "The Kingfishers"* [Madison: Fairleigh Dickinson University Press, 1998] p. 100)

There is no doubt that Frances Boldereff became the person Olson turned to "to share the excitements of his studies of the past" (Clark p. 147). She was the first to receive notice of his discovery of Maximus of Tyre, though this first encounter was only the borrowing of a quotation for a *billet-doux*. The quotation he wrote out in Greek for her (#21, 29 March 1949) was not transcribed "laboriously" (Clark p. 148) from Maximus's *Dissertations* at the Library of Congress, but from a copy of the Loeb Classical Library *Lyra Graeca,* ed. J.M. Edmonds (1922), that he had acquired. Neither is there any doubt that the short poem "Dura" (*Collected Poems* p. 85) came from Frances drawing Olson's attention (#28, 10 May 1949) to Franz Cumont's volume on the Dura-Europos frescoes, though there is no evidence that he could or did track down the book. Olson merely extrapolated Frances's own description.

It is not my purpose to detract from Boldereff's contribution but to attempt to be more accurate about certain circumstances than Clark's methodology allows him to be. For instance, the Sumerian material Boldereff sent to Olson was not a "file" (Clark p. 148) but a single offprint of an article by S.N. Kramer, "The Epic of Gilgames and its Sumerian Sources," which she had obtained visiting Kramer himself. First of all, to claim his priority, Olson sent Frances a poem beginning "I am Gilgamesh" that he had written eight years before (#31, 23 May 1949). Then, within a couple of days (#32, 25 March 1949), he sent "La Chute," directly derived from the article. The other two parts did not come so easily, so that Clark's word "quickly" (p. 148) does not really apply to "La Chute (II)" of July 1949 and "La Chute III" of October 1949.

As to the poem "The Advantage" (*Collected Poems* p. 105), it likely was triggered by one of Frances's "letter images" (Clark p. 159), but the controlling image of the poem, the springing up of violets, was something that Olson had been harboring a great while. In any case, Frances (despite Clark's statement to the contrary, p. 159) did receive a copy of the poem (#94, 11 January 1950); Olson wasn't hiding it.

Boldereff first mentioned Strzygowski's *Origin of Christian Church Art* in a letter of 26 January 1950 (#106). She recommended the book again in letter #138 (23 February 1950) and #151 (4 March 1950). When Olson dropped the name Strzygowski into his letter of 7 March 1950 (#152) he had not, I am sure, looked him up yet; he is just parroting her. Boldereff has another paragraph on the subject in letter #162 (14 March 1950). Only then does Olson get himself to the Library of Congress: "And this time you are my lead: it is Strzygowski i go to, for fountain" (#171, 23 March 1950). And finally in letter #191 (10 April 1950) we have evidence that Olson has really tried to read the book. A precise investigation of the events would not allow anyone to say (as Clark does, p. 159) that, upon Boldereff's telling him about Strzygowski, "Olson obediently trekked to the Library of Congress." "Obediently." What is Clark implying?

Olson, according to Clark, is doubly remiss, first in begging Frances for help, and then refusing moral support when she needs it. The first supposed solecism has to do with Olson's rental accommodation in Washington and the need to secure himself by purchasing it or having it purchased for him by sponsors, the latter being "the ideal solution," as Clark puts it (p. 149), which Olson "meaningfully" suggested to Boldereff. Looking at the letter (#31, 23 May 1949), I cannot see it as anything more than a neutral statement of fact, and Boldereff did not respond to it at all at that time. It was not until 17 October 1949 (#46) that Olson brought up the house question as a crisis and Frances responded with practical questions (#47) only to have Olson in his next letter (#49) dismiss it as not a crisis after all. It was not until much later—Clark has telescoped the time—that Frances approached wealthy friends about it and got a refusal (#136, 20 February 1950). At that particular moment Olson, it seems, was so engrossed in preparing for two three-hour discussion sessions on Melville that he did not even mention it—or perhaps there was a missing letter. In any case, there is no evidence for Clark's summation: "His hopes briefly rose, and when the dream deal did not materialize, he was brought back to earth with a jolt" (p. 149). This might be true of any one of us in that situation, but there is no evidence for it in Olson's case.

Olson caused Frances many disappointments—so many that if Clark wanted to fault him on that score he would have no need to exaggerate. Unfortunately, he does not seem able to resist overstating. For instance: "She abruptly quit her job, and declared she was about to arrive on his doorstep. She needed to come to an understanding with Connie, she said. Charles shot down the idea by return mail" (p. 160). The pertinent passage from Boldereff's letter of 2 February 1950 (#111) leaves some doubt as to whether she quit her job at State College or was let go: "The mundane details are that I no longer have a job." That's all she says. It does not sound as though she quit, certainly not to leave for Washington. She has picked up some work at a local printer: "I am working on several jobs at Nittany which I have just begun so I will be there same schedule perhaps for a month, two months, I don't know exactly." And then to stop any precipitous act of charity: "As regards money darling for the immediate present I can take care of myself—so please do not mention it to me or try to help me." There is no declaring she will arrive on his doorstep to settle things with Connie. It is only when, a few days later (#120, 9 February 1950), Frances decides that she will stay in Woodward as a freelance designer without going in to work at all that the utter frustration begins. The next day, 10 February (#122), she lets out a cry: "Everything is breaking up inside me—I pray you if you can not come to allow me to come for a few hours." This is a request, not, as Clark put it, a declaration; and Connie is not mentioned in all this. Moreover, by the end of the day Frances had calmed down and herself says: "I trust you absolutely and I am able to wait as long as you need me to" (#123, 10 February 1950). Olson does not get these Friday letters until Monday. Meanwhile he has just typed and mailed off to Frances the finished first draft of "Projective Verse." It is a poet producing at full steam who receives Frances's plea and writes on the Monday (#129, 13 February 1950): "o my lady   look: i cannot permit you to come here ... because i cannot dissemble and because i cannot, where the crisis is as intense here as there with you, add one straw more." He is doing "the very maximum in all directions" and continues: "i equally know (and this makes me full of the terror of life) that what is being done is right, god help us all, ... and shall seek to stay right right through every thing   And only because and only thus can any of us inherit what is in this ahead." While Olson is penning this, Frances in her Monday letter is saying: "My agony has passed for the moment" (#130, 13 February 1950). Clark compounds his mischief by further distortions: "She succumbed to his persuasions, backed off her demands, stayed put in her backwoods hamlet, kept on writing to him—there were sometimes two and three letters from her in a single post—and took on free-lance design work to support herself and her daughter" (p. 160). All of this because of Olson's rebuff. Nonsense. This is selling short an always independently-minded Boldereff. She stayed in Woodward as long as she wanted to and then left for work in New York City. Meanwhile, she had already, before the rebuff letter, embarked on a "big freelance job" (#125, 11 February 1950), one that resulted in a most beautifully designed book, *Walt Whitman of the New York Aurora* eds. Joseph Jay Rubin and Charles H. Brown (State College, Pennsylvania: Bald Eagle Press, 1950).

Olson's Roman Catholicism is a big subject. Frances Phipps used it scornfully against him in later years, and Olson's letter to her of 27 February 1950 (#143) may have been the start of the trouble. Frances's reaction, a combination of envy and dogma, was heavy: "I got violently sick and wept for one whole day when I thought my baby was turning catholic on me" (#148, 3 March 1950). It is Olson's reaction to her emotion that is of issue. Clark sees him as knuckling under with a turn-about avowal of aversion "to the 'filthy faith' of his childhood" (p. 161), but "filthy faith" is a phrase Olson had used in June 1948, long before, in a review of Graham Greene's *Heart of the Matter* he had drafted but not published and now sent to Boldereff to fill in his background. Thus, it is not the retraction Clark presents it as. Nor did Olson produce "a pair of long breezy letter-poems" to support his *mea culpa* or as "conciliatory garlands" (p. 161). The first, "A Po-sy, A Po-sy" was done before Olson received Boldereff's challenge on the Catholic question (#145, 28 February 1950). The second, "The Morning News," was a week later (#152, 7 March 1950) when the Catholic controversy had flashed itself out, leaving perhaps one phrase in the poem ("truly hermetique / Nothing catholique" lines 4–5) but nothing else detectable on the subject.

We will not get anything like a complete picture of this Connie-Charles-Frances love triangle until Olson's letters to Connie are published. The deeper sources of Olson's motivation will become more evident then. Meanwhile, I would like to clear up a few of Clark's misreadings of the situation. First, there is the poster. Frances sent it unsealed in mail that Connie saw and it caused consternation. It did not, as Clark claims, contain a note from Frances "urgently exhorting him 'to put off, to voyage' along with her into the unknown" (p. 165). The phrase "to put off, to voyage" is in an Olson letter of 15 May 1950 (#217) and he is referring in his own words to something Frances said in a letter of 4 May 1950 (#214): "I feel in my deepest self that you should now live alone." Clark says the poster message ended "with an image of their souls as twin rafts on the open sea" (p. 165). The twin rafts image also comes out of a later Boldereff letter (undated—I place it at 13 July 1950) where she refers to "that to me exciting and beautiful image of our rafts on the open sea." Since *Charles Olson & Frances Boldereff: A Modern Correspondence* was published I have discovered the poster inserted in Storrs Notebook #137. It is an announcement Boldereff designed for a Mozart concert by Sheema Buehne on 30 April 1950. On the back is the following note, given in full (it should take its place at *CO/FB* p. 321):

> Olson darling—
>
> I have been waiting for the real poster—darkbrown ink in white antique, but it does not come and I can't wait any more—If you don't absolutely adore it—the rhythm in it soothes hell out of me— I look and I look and there is some very right rhythm for me—and I ask you dear Olson if you do not like it—I will not be hurt at all— just to return—because I would not like it to be looked at if its beauty did not speak—it looks so undersigned Charles—so effort- less and Christ to me it is just like a beautiful fish hook in my loins.
>
> Yesterday I saw
>
> 1. a beautiful dead unwounded goshawk—stole a feather for you
> 2. A bright yellow and black striped snake—almost stepped on it and I stayed still and had the pleasure to see it go up to a dead snake, stroke all over with its dear tongue and seeing no more help was avail— quickly slid away—I <u>loved</u> it and that tongue licked my womb passage and healed me.
> 3. a big healthy groundhog or something else—big and furry and very nice <u>close</u> to me.
>
> I love you so much I am full of music
> I am washed clean like a new born child
> I am all pristine clearness and wholeness
> and loveness
> Frances

So one can see that, although it did not contain the proposals for flight that Clark thought it did, the protestations of devotion would be enough to create the "crisis" Olson refers to in his letter of 25 April 1950: "Your poster was the straw" (*CO/FB* #205).

What can we say of the love poems written at this time. "In Cold Hell, in Thicket" is the great poem of the triangle, and by its very nature belongs to both women. The others we have the job of assigning to one or the other. The ones sent to Frances, such as "The She-Bear," "Lady Mimosa," and "The Cause, the Cause," do not present a problem. I take it that the poems not sent to Frances were written for Connie, but in making that assumption I have to dispute Clark's contrary conclusion.

As regards "For Sappho, Back," Clark says that it is not surprising that Frances took the poem to be a "very accurate portrait" of herself (p. 171). There is, however, no evidence that she saw it until it was published. And I wonder if she read to the end, where we find the lines: "the hidden constance of which all the rest / is awkward variation"—an open compliment to Connie, I should think. And there is a previous line: "in the delight of her eye she / creates constants." "Help Me, Venus, You Who Led Me On" does not have anything of Frances in it. I am at a loss to see how the passage Clark quotes from Boldereff on page 171 has any bearing at all on the poem. The title is from Hippomenes's prayer for success in the footrace to win Atalanta's hand, by which Olson signals that he is going back to the first poem he wrote to Connie, "Atalanta" (*Collected Poems* p. 5). Clark has to admit that "Help Me, Venus" has "an oblique reference to his first Rockport encounter with Connie" (p. 171). But it's not oblique at all. The poem is all and entirely Connie's. Frances does not appear as "a beguiling Blakean 'silver girl'" nor was it in any form a "private message" to Frances as "Muse" (p. 171). It was never sent to her.

"Of Mathilde" (*Collected Poems* p. 194) is more of a problem, for it incorporates much from Olson's letter to Frances of 21 July 1950 (#258), is indeed a poetic rendering of his tribute to Frances there in the wake of his visit to her in New York. Clark believes it was addressed to Frances, while at the same time asserting that Connie was persuaded it "had been written expressly to her" (p. 174). "Of Mathilde" was never sent to Frances. Mathilde was Connie's middle name. I believe the poem was written for Connie using the same imagery as Olson used in his letter to Frances. Into such a thicket did love of two women take him.

Olson and Connie in Washington, D.C.
Kate Olson Archive.

12
Call Me Ishmael and the Melvilleans

Olson and Connie came up from Florida to their 217 Randolph Place house in Washington only to learn in the morning paper (13 April 1945) that Roosevelt was dead. "I started Ishmael that afternoon, the afternoon I kissed off my political future" (Olson in conversation with Ann Charters, *Olson/Melville* p. 9). The book was written "at a clip," partly on holiday at Enniscorthy, and "finished before the 1st A-bomb." Olson wrote to Merton Sealts on 28 July 1946, "I got back to the Melville book this spring and finished it yesterday" (Sealts p. 97). One of the new aspects of *Moby-Dick* that Olson wanted to get into the book (he was largely ignoring the pile of typed pages from the 1939–40 Guggenheim year) was the economic aspect of the whale-oil industry. In this connection Clark rightly mentions the notes about the expert, Remington Kellogg, found in Olson's "Key West II" notebook, but he should have added that it was not Kellogg that was used in *Call Me Ishmael*. The chapter "What Lies Under" almost exclusively relies on Karl Brandt's *Whale Oil: An Economic Analysis* (Stanford University Food Research Institute 1940), a fact revealed in Robert Bertholf's 1970 article "On Olson, His Melville" in *Io* 22 (p. 34).

Another new aspect was Olson's wish to get at the main themes by telling stories. Storrs has a document, "The Terrible Whaleman, Samuel B. Comstock" (Prose #197), which Olson typed out to send to editors. He told Charters how in 1945 he stumbled on this story of mutiny on the *Globe*: "I knew the Globe had been sailed back by the two cabin boys to the port of Valpariso. I was alone in the house, so I grabbed a cab to the National Archives and asked for the Consular Papers of Valpariso for 1819. Yes, out they came. I read the total first testimonies, the eye-witness of the crew as they were taken down" (Charters p. 10). Olson considered that this mutiny was "the psychic button for Melville that pushed the book." So Olson presents it in *Call Me Ishmael* as "Fact #2" (pp. 77–78). Clark has a good insight in saying that "this documentary insert became historical grounding for his 'Moses' chapter, with its sickle-wielding brother horde of castrators and father-murderers" (p. 105). But when Clark takes up the "First Fact," the Essex narrative, it is another matter.

During the first week of August 1945 Olson decided there was one extra thing that the "finished" *Call Me Ishmael* needed. He had to find a way to bring in the story of how a whale stove in the whaleship *Essex*. Olson knew about Owen Chase's *Narrative of the Most Extraordinary and Distressing Shipwreck of the Whale-Ship Essex, of Nantucket; Which Was Attacked and Finally Destroyed by a Large Spermaceti-Whale, in the Pacific Ocean* (1821). Melville's own copy had come up at auction, and in his M.A. thesis Olson had quoted from the auction catalogue some of Melville's marginalia. He was moved to pay a visit to Nantucket, Owen Chase's home, and had a fruitful week there. He examined a copy of Chase at the house of local historian Will Gardner, who on 19 August 1945 inscribed to him a copy of his own book, *Three Bricks and Three Brothers*. Olson actually wrote the pages of the "First Fact" based on the *Essex* story on the ferry back from Nantucket. Imagine his excitement, then, when in the Widener Library at Harvard a few days later he heard from Melville scholar Howard Vincent that Melville's copy of Chase's *Narrative* had just been up for auction again. Clark tells it this way:

> At a recent Parke-Bernet auction, Vincent told Olson, a wealthy oil-company executive and book collector named Percival Brown had acquired a copy of Owen Chase's *Narrative of the Shipwreck of the Whaleship Essex*. The copy contained annotations in Herman Melville's hand. Olson implored Vincent to help him get a look at the book, and his fellow Melvillean duly complied, setting up a meeting at Brown's New Jersey home, in the course of which Olson was allowed to transcribe the treasured annotations. (pp. 105–106)

This version makes it seem as though Olson had had no previous knowledge of Chase's *Narrative*, whereas he had, as we have just seen, been on the look-out for it for thirteen years and had just been on its trail in Nantucket.

Moreover, Vincent did not set up a meeting. In a letter of 16 September 1945 to Olson (now at Storrs), soon after their discussion, Vincent wrote: "I am writing to Perc Brown today asking him to hurry up on those photostats, and maybe that will get results. As soon as I get them I will copy them and then send them on to you for examination, unless by that time you have inspected the original." Olson in New York talked to his own contact in the book world, the renowned Arthur Swan, who encouraged him to write Perc (not Percival) Brown. Olson did so and, on invitation, went to see Brown in Upper Montclair, New Jersey, on 30 November 1945.

I lay out these facts because it has been generally held among Melvilleans that Olson unfairly "scooped" Vincent. Clark does not go quite that far, but others have, even the definitive Northwestern-Newberry *Moby-Dick* in its "Historical Notes" p. 653. I think the passage quoted above and the whole generous tone of Vincent's letter of 16 September 1945 shows that Vincent was not claiming any prior rights on the Owen Chase marginalia, though he did later on express shock at the speed with which Olson moved. Vincent thought it was "the next afternoon" (letter to Harrison Hayford 3 May 1972). As we have seen, it took over two months for Olson to reach Perc Brown.

It is a forlorn business to delineate the history of a quarrel, but these disjunctures are exactly where ethical values are exhibited in sharpest definition. Unfortunately, in this case, there must be missing pieces of the picture. We have as a starting point Vincent's very ebullient letter to Olson of 16 September 1945:

> Your book sounds like a more difficult and much more germinal sort of thing than what I am doing, and I approve it ... Your having spent twelve years of unremitting thought on Moby-Dick promises well, and I'm itching with curiosity to see your book.

This sounds like someone who would be the first to review Olson's book when it came out; but Vincent passed on it. Why? There must have been some reason if we could only put our finger on it. Olson's name was not included among those who had given "unselfish help and advice" in the Acknowledgments of Vincent's *The Trying-Out of Moby-Dick* (Houghton Mifflin 1949). And Vincent seems reluctant to mention Olson in the book. On page thirty-six he writes: "Professor F.O. Matthiessen, *American Renaissance* (New York and London 1941), pp. 412–17, 423–31, 431–35 and 449–51, is the first to study intelligently the effect of Shakespeare upon Melville's mind and art." After that stiletto word "intelligently" it doesn't do much good to add that Matthiessen based "his study on an article by Charles Olson, whose book *Call Me Ishmael* (New York 1947) stresses the Shakespearean side of Melville's genius." Vincent's one other remark on Olson in the book is equally vague: on page 374 he quotes the "Ego non baptizo" passage, and adds in a footnote: "In his study of Melville Charles J. Olson *Call Me Ishmael* (New York 1947) has made this scene an important part of his analysis of *Moby-Dick*." It's as though Vincent felt he had to mention *Call Me Ishmael*, but didn't feel like saying much.

Perhaps it was, after all, that Vincent felt "scooped." Or perhaps it was a more subtle personal offense that he felt. There is some hint of such in the reminiscence Vincent wrote Hayford in May 1972. "Later, in the Fall," he writes of what must be 1946, "he [Olson] called me from downtown Chicago and we met at the Harvey Restaurant in the Dearborn Station where we had a very agreeable lunch, where he told me more about CALL ME ISHMAEL, its thrusts and all that, and that it was in page proof and would be out soon. Nothing about Chase notes being printed." Vincent is intimating a lack of candor on Olson's part. He concludes: "That was the last time that I saw him. Or heard from him—directly, that is." I think this lunch in Chicago is probably quite crucial. But how can one know what really went on between the two men to cause mutual disappointment? Olson at this second meeting got an impression too. One cannot always bring oneself to be candid with someone—despite the ethical demand—when one has suddenly developed a mistrust of his essential sensibility. I make this conjecture on the basis of the later thumb-nail sketch in verse in which Olson must be encapsulating his sense of that Chicago luncheon:

> let him tell you, that no matter how difficult it is
> to work in an apartment in a bedroom in a very big city
> because the kids are bothersome and have to be locked out, and the wife
> is only too good, yet, he did republish enough of this other man
> to now have a different professional title, a better salary
> and though he wishes he were at Harvard or a Whale,
> he is, isn't he, if he is quite accurate, much more liked
> by his president?

This satirical portrait of Vincent is part of Olson's infamous "Letter to Melville 1951," subtitled: "written to be read AWAY FROM the Melville Society's 'One Hundredth Birthday Party' for MOBY-DICK at Williams College, Labor Day Week-end, Sept. 2–4, 1951." Addressed to Eleanor Melville Metcalf, the long poem was printed quickly at Black Mountain College and reached its recipient at the event, causing much consternation. Other speakers besides Vincent were pilloried in this polemical poem. In each case Olson had something serious to say; but why would he burn his boats in this way with the whole of the Melville scholarly community? It was bound to produce retaliation. I see the treatment of Olson in the Northwestern-Newberry edition as part of the second half-life of the reaction. An immediate response can be found in the Introduction to the

Hendricks House edition of *Moby-Dick* (1952), which Howard Vincent edited with Luther S. Mansfield. The "germinal" *Call Me Ishmael* of Vincent's letter of September 1945 has become here mere "poetic rhapsody about Space, Tragedy, and Myth" (p. xxix). Olson's verse pamphleteering, it seems, has badly knocked askew Vincent's critical acumen.

Furthermore, Vincent had done one major thing which Olson considered deserving of a serious rebuke. He had edited for Hendricks House the *Collected Poems of Herman Melville* (1947). Olson thought he had done a botched job of it, and said so out loud in the "Letter for Melville 1951":

> his edition of this here celebrated man's verse
> whom we thought we came here to talk about
> has so many carelessnesses in it that, as of this date,
> it is quite necessary to do it over.

Olson's righteous indignation over Vincent's work was uppermost in his mind as he wrote "Letter for Melville 1951."

Clark's treatment of "Letter for Melville 1951" is strange. I am sure that he relishes Olson's twentieth-century *Dunciad* as much as anybody, but he chooses not to share any of the delicious details. He also failed to correct Robert Bertholf's guesses about the identity of the three persons Olson satirizes. In his article "Charles Olson and the Melville Society" in *Extracts* 10 (January 1972) pages 3–4, Bertholf was obviously right about Howard Vincent; however, the "very bright man" at the end of the poem is not Perry Miller but Newton Arvin. Olson puns on his name, calling him "neuter," and several times quotes Arvin's book *Herman Melville*. (Arvin was listed as one of the speakers on the preliminary program that Olson received, but was not actually present: thus the confusion.) The other "main speaker," who will "talk about democracy," is not F.O. Matthiessen (as Luther S. Mansfield suggested to Bertholf it was) but Perry Miller.

Thus, the poem involves defamation of notable figures, just the stuff that one would expect to be grist to Clark's mill; but he turns away from it with a sniff: "'Letter for Melville' was actually less a message to the literary hero of his youth than an act of posturing performed for the benefit of his present legion of disciples" (p. 207). It has nowhere been suggested that "Letter for Melville 1951" is "a message to the literary hero of his youth." How does Clark imagine Olson thought the message would reach Melville? It is "for" Melville: to be a proper celebration of *Moby-Dick*'s centenary, as the Williams College conference could, in Olson's view, never be. Clark suspects a shallower motive: it is "an act of posturing performed for the benefit of his present legion of disciples."

But Clark is quite wrong about this. In the summer of 1951 there was no such "legion of disciples." Olson had not taught at Black Mountain College for two years and came to North Carolina in mid-July 1951 direct from six months in isolation in Yucatan. Larry Hatt, who printed "Letter for Melville 1951," was a newcomer to the college that semester, as was the press assistant Edward Dorn. It was before Olson knew his later protégé. It is true that some BMC students (slightly less impoverished, on average, than the faculty) clubbed together to get the "Letter for Melville 1951" printed. Clark tries to make this seem somehow distasteful, as though Olson was taking advantage of their gullibility; yet this jaundiced view has no factual substance. Clark knows no more than any of us about this, as the sole source is Olson's letter to Cid Corman of 12 August 1951:

> i had the wild idea, to take the LETTER TO BE READ AWAY FROM the Centenary Celebration of Melville's Moby-Dick at Williams College Labor Day Weekend (it was written in a moment of flame, two weeks ago), and fire it as a bit of verse pamphleteering (something I don't know has been much done since the Elizabethans) and by god if the kids last night didn't raise the 20 bucks to have it set by electrotype in Caslon, so that we can sell it at that damned stupid celebration, and also sell it as an olson poem! So, today, I imagine Hatt and Vanderbeek, and others are over in Asheville arranging the biz, and here am I confronted with the necessity to rewrite it! (*CO/CC* I.187)

It is strange that Clark can read this account of a lively educational enterprise and interpret it as "posturing" performed for a "legion of disciples."

He dismisses the poem with a phrase of his own, "inflammatory anti-academicism," and the word "megalomaniac" borrowed from Paul Metcalf (p. 207). I wonder what the context really was in which Metcalf used that word. He had not corresponded with Olson since May 1950, when he had crossed swords with him on another matter, as described in Metcalf's *Where Do You Put the Horse?* (The Dalkey Archive Press, 1986 p. 28). It is probably in this context that the word "megalomaniac" was used. He and his wife hadn't liked Olson's inscription to them on a copy of *y & x*: "For Paul & Nancy, early recognizers, now that the others are catching up." Apparently, they thought it arrogant. But within two or three years relations had improved, and there were several pleasant social engagements, including the visit of Olson to their Edisto Beach retreat, described by

Metcalf at some length (pp. 22–23, 29). Olson supplied a statement for Metcalf's Guggenheim application and also for the book-jacket blurb of *Genoa* (1958).

I give Paul Metcalf the last word on this matter, from *Where Do You Put the Horse?*, where he is describing the Open House of 14 September 1975 at Arrowhead, Melville's old home in the Berkshires, celebrating the 125 years from the time of Melville's purchase of it:

> At age fifty-seven, I was one of the younger people there. We watched the overdressed and elderly, the quiet rich of the Berkshires, doggedly hefting their frames out of their Chryslers to lend their presence and perhaps their pocketbooks to yet another historic moment; we toured the house, read the posters each announcing a proposed restoration, with price attached; we chatted with the long-skirted, lapel-labeled hostesses (in order to read a name, you had to stare at a breast) and found everything from total ignorance to serious scholarship in knowledge of what they were talking about; we listened to the speeches over the public-address system, under the rented jonquil tent; witnessed the presentation of the latest inflated artist's edition of *Moby-Dick*; we gabbled under the great white pines on the becalmed green lawn, and admired the flower beds, tailored by the Berkshire Garden Club; we drank the pale yellow punchless punch, and nibbled the little petits fours; etc., etc. … and then I came home and reread "Letter for Melville 1951," Charles Olson's bitter, personal diatribe against the Melville Society, against all official organization of the celebration of Melville's work. (p. 32)

Metcalf is here confirming that, for him at least, Olson's "Letter for Melville 1951" is not a medley of insults that have lost their point, but something to return to for cleanness after compromising himself.

13
The Mainstream Runs Out

In January 1946 Olson got a nice present. *Harper's Bazaar* gave him his first published poem, "A Lion Upon the Floor." It had been a while coming. That poem had been written a year earlier, and probably sent out a few times to periodicals, though it does not appear on any of the lists such as in the Storrs notebook #55 ("Washington Fall, 1945 I"):

> list of poems & prose rejected "up to now"
> For Adam (Atlantic)   Said Adam (Atlantic)
> Report from Field (Virginia Quarterly, Harpers)
> Enniscorthy (Virginia Quarterly, Harpers)
>   Prose Thoughts on Yeats, Pound, Joyce (New Republic)
>
>   Then new submissions
>   3 to Devlin   Translation
>   Report from the Field
>   Proposition
> new Pound to Levin   Nov 6
> Pacific Lament to Kouenhoven at Harpers
> Winter to Nation   Dec 8
> Valentine to Harper's Bazaar sent Dec 9

Perhaps he made personal contact with Mary Louise Aswell at *Harper's Bazaar* and "The Lion Upon the Floor" was submitted and printed right away.

"For K" appeared in the following issue of *Harper's Bazaar*. "Pacific Lament" went over to *Atlantic Monthly*, where it appeared in the March 1946 issue. The April 1946 issue of *Harper's Magazine* contained "Lower Field–Enniscorthy." This first flush of success is quite remarkable, and we should pause and relish it, as Olson must have done. Then we can follow it further: "In Praise of the Fool" *Harper's Bazaar* December 1947; "Only the Red Fox, Only the Crow" *Atlantic Monthly* March 1949; "In the Hills South of Capernum, Port" *Harper's Bazaar* April 1949. And there the mainstream publications end.

He had tested the limits somewhat earlier; and by this time he had no illusions. He had had an informal commission to do something in prose for *Harper's Bazaar* (letter to Monroe Engel 23 April 1947). The result was "Origo," which arose from his enthusiasm for Frobenius and Fox's *African Genesis* (1937), a book Pound had put him on to. Olson had written to Douglas Fox on 19 April 1947:

> Finished the first draft of a piece last night which gives me a chance I have long waited for, to make what I take to be a novel use of two of your tales, the Kabyl First Man, Woman and 50 Chillun and Gassire. I shall enclose on a separate page the opening article and the way I acknowledge you, in order that you may have a sense of the intent and present form of the piece. The Kabyl, due to the design, is condensed and somewhat rewritten, and Gassire I break up some at the beginning but from the partridge on use pretty much as you have so finely translated it. (*Selected Letters* p. 66)

Olson also incorporates Frank Cushing's retelling of the Hopi origin myth as found in Paul Radin's *Story of the American Indian* (1937). One can see why this piece would be a shock for *Harper's Bazaar* and why, after its rejection by them, Olson might feel his bluff had been called. He never tried to publish it again. The Storrs typescript, Prose #18, remains unpublished and Clark does not mention it.

Unsuitable as it may have been for the mainstream, it shows that Olson was already a mythologist who wanted mythic narrative to communicate everything that needed to be communicated. I see it as presaging the "Causal Mythology" lecture at the Berkeley Poetry Conference of 1965, where, from the height of his maturity, Olson could speak to a receptive audience in such a way that four poems could practically by themselves carry the meaning of a "lecture." With "Origo" there is a naivety in Olson's supposing that he has earned the right to speak primordially. He was moving very quickly in the right direction, but he had not got there yet. There is a touching note of Connie's (extant at Storrs) of 8 April 1947 in the midst of Olson's effort to rise to spiritual disciplines. Connie is writing to him in New York City: "How far are you toward moving into your new world?" she writes. "You seem very tragic and very beautiful to me today." Connie, I feel, had an instinct for what was happening and how it would at that stage fail.

But what *was* Olson trying to accomplish with Origo-Imago-Dreme? In a letter to Robert Creeley of 25 October 1950 he is musing about how important sleep and dreams are to complete our experience of "WHAT

GOES ON." He reminisces about the time he tried to prove "the 12 hrs [of sleep and dream] as equal of the other 12":

> Blocked out this, once couple
> of yrs ago, when Harper's Bazaar offered me 250 bucks, for a piece!
> Course I fucked it up. With the very idea: was this, three parts, moving
> differently, one narrative only, one images only, one facts, nothing but
> these three differing movements. Didn't come off. BUT this was the
> titles, and they'll give you the clue:
> ORIGO   IMAGO   DREME
> all one, ya
> … I keep going back to base premise picked up,
> somewhere:
> life is preoccupation with itself
> … I take it, that's just what we do have, what we damn well
> are, all the time, 24 hrs, and that the 12, are only the chance to see it
> more. (*CO/RC* 3.135–37)

In other words, sleep is where we have dreams that are basic mythic material, and no less a reality. Olson cites for Creeley a much cherished passage from the ethnologist Malinowski, which, significantly, he found in Jung and Kerenyi's *Essays on a Science of Mythology* (p. 7). Malinowski's subject is the Trobriand Islanders, "but," says Olson, "it doesn't matter (it works, anywhere, including, now, you and me, this instant):

> Sez he:
> The myth in a primitive society, i.e. in its
> original living form, is not a mere tale told
> but a reality lived. It is not in the nature of
> an invention such as we read in our novels today,
> (((look at that lad, going after
> the enemies!)))
> but living reality, believed to have occurred
> in primordial times and to be influencing ever
> afterwards the world and the destinies of men …

> Myths never, in any sense, he continued, explain: they always set up
> some precedent as an ideal and as a guarantee of the continuance of that
> ideal ((what abt that phrasing)). (*CO/RC* 3.135–36)

In presenting "Origo," Olson severely kept away from etiology, when any one of us, including the editors of *Harper's Bazaar*, would be in a mindset to ask, "What does this myth explain?" Olson hoped that we and they would not be asking for an explanation but would try to allow the stories to sink in as preoccupation with life in a way that cannot be examined by ordinary means. Olson's failure with "Origo" reflects the fact that he has not been that long on the path of the mythopoetic and that his successes up to this point have been in the expository world of debate and political strategy. We should recognize what a drastically "new world" (to use Connie's phrase) Olson is proposing for himself and realize he is likely to make some false steps initially. The Gassire story itself, the almost unendurable series of losses, must have been telling him something about rejection and how one perhaps has to forfeit the easy victories. He would not totally know what this myth of blood on the lute meant until eight years of poverty in a $28 per month flat in Gloucester began to produce the sounds of *Maximus IV, V, VI.*

Another dead end that Olson had to face at this time was the university literary journal. The saga of the *Western Review* is not touched upon at all by Clark, but it is a first class example of the way Olson's moral nature worked. Ray West was included among the circle of Poundians, so Olson sent something to his magazine, *Western Review.* Unexpectedly, West accepted the poem "There Was a Youth Whose Name Was Thomas Granger" for the spring 1947 issue. This confirmed, for Olson, Ray West's open-mindedness; he suggested in a letter of 7 June 1947 that it might be possible for him to break his journey in Lawrence, Kansas, on the trip to the West Coast that he was undertaking. It turned out not to be possible, which they both expressed regret for. West accepted "Siena" for the winter 1949 issue, and the "David Young, David Old" essay for the fall 1949 issue. Then something began to go wrong after West moved to Iowa. In a letter to Olson of 4 January 1950 he said he liked "The Praises," but on 28 January he returned it because of "opposition" in the editorial board. Olson's response is included in *Selected Letters* (pp. 103–105): "What happened today I predicted would happen, if you were not strong, the moment I learned last summer that the magazine was going to Iowa." Olson knows which of the committee members did him in. But he tries Ray West again, with the poem "At Yorktown," just to be sure. He also responded to a query on Pound from West with a letter of 20 April 1950, enclosing "GrandPa, GoodBye." Then he waited.

On 6 October 1950 Olson received "GrandPa, GoodBye" in the mail with a printed rejection slip (though it had not been submitted for publication) and there was no sign of "At Yorktown" at all. Olson sat down and typed a forceful letter (at Utah State Library), which ends as follows:

Honest, Ray West. I can't be sore enough, enough to wham you, simply because I cannot forget what you, as over there, in the West, did; and how, once you went Middle (o my prophetic arse-hole) you are (as far as I can see, and you, seem to have no will to disprove) are deceased.

It's

LOSS, that's all, loss, however much fools may (for false purposes) delude you. For if you treat me this way, you are treating others, who are, I'm willing to put it on the line, the betters of your contributors & yr fellow editors.

West did not reply to this letter. At least there is nothing in the Storrs archive.

The finger-man in Iowa was Paul Engle, long time director of the Creative Writing Program there and an operator in the world of readings and grants (see *CO/FB* p. 252 for more on this). On the trip west Olson and Connie had stopped in Iowa because Engle was a friend of Helena Kuo, the owner of the car they were sharing costs on. Olson wrote to Pound soon after, possibly 10 July 1947 (letter at Indiana): "Got into trouble in Stone City, Iowa, thanks to you … P for pisspot Engle (friend of Kuo) has version of visit to you at Rapallo which I did not find amusing." To West in a letter of 1 February 1950 Olson wrote: "I know why he [Engle] put the finger on me, because he once had occasion so to speak of a finer poet than either of us, that, if I were a man, he had to take my scorn for him, and my contempt for his verse, which he did" (*Selected Letters* p. 104). The veto of "The Praises," added Olson, "is in the nature of a pay-off." A totally believable story. If only it were not so believable.

14
Cagli, Crosby, and the
Making of *y & x*

Corrado Cagli brought several gifts into Olson's life. This section must begin with an attempt to duplicate the moment when Olson walked into Cagli's exhibition, *From Cherbourg to Leipzig: Documents and Memories*, and saw his Buchenwald drawings for the first time. This was April 1946. There had been photographs in the newspapers, but now Olson is seeing the enormity of the Nazi camps through Cagli's sensibility. His beloved friend, whom he had met and enjoyed the company of in May 1940, had been in the U.S. Army, and with the first liberating troops to enter Buchenwald. Being an artist he had made sketches, which were now on the gallery walls in front of Olson.

Corrado Cagli, *Buchenwald 3*, 1945.

I like what Clark has to say about "La Préface," the poem that came out of Olson's experience standing there: "In 'La Préface,' the death-ground of Buchenwald became the birth-ground of a new archaic, a 'new Altamira cave' whose walls were windows open on a future of indeterminate possibility" (p. 113). There have not been many poets of the English language who have been able or willing to be deadly serious about the death camps. Olson is speaking to himself as much as anybody when he says in the poem: "You, do not you speak who know not." But Cagli has made him know, and the words come out totally determined by that confrontation.

> "I will die about April 1st ..." going off
> "I weigh, I think, 80 lbs ..." scratch
> "My name is NO RACE" address
> Buchenwald   new Altamira cave
> With a nail they drew the object of the hunt.

At their first meeting when Cagli knew very little English they talked with hands and objects like primitive men after the Tower of Babel.

> Put war away with time, come into space.
> It was May, precise date, 1940. I had air my lungs could breathe.
> He talked, via stones   a stick   sea rock   a hand of earth.
> It is now, precise, repeat. I talk of Bigmans organs
> he, look, the lines! are polytopes.

It is the same, now they have met again. Olson has ideas for a Bigmans series of poems, while Cagli is talking about Roberto Bonola's *La Geometria non-Euclidea* and drawings in the fourth dimension.

> Birth in the house is the One of Sticks, cunnus in the crotch.
> Draw it thus: (   ) 1910 (
> It is not obscure. We are the new born, and there are no flowers.

It is Cagli who inducted Olson into the mystery of the Tarot, hence the "One of Sticks," which is the card for creation, source, birth. Since both men were born in 1910, the date works for both; the open parenthesis is their rebirth. They are enduring now the preface to all life that comes after war and its horrors.

The title was not entirely a metaphor; the poem was written as a foreword to Cagli's exhibition brochure when the show moved to Chicago. It may even have been Cagli's title. In his letter to Olson of 26 April 1946 he thanks him "for la préface." He could have been sent an untitled draft and by welcoming it in that way have supplied the title. Olson's first thought

Olson and Cagli at 217 Randolph Place NE, 1946.
Kate Olson Archive.

would hardly have been to have a French title. His dear friend from France, Jean Riboud, had not yet, by four months, made his appearance in New York City—at least according to his biographer Ken Auletta, in *The New Yorker* (6 June 1983 p. 60). It is difficult not to think that Olson had already met Riboud, who had been in the French Resistance and an inmate of Buchenwald for two years: "when he emerged, he had tuberculosis and weighed ninety-six pounds" (Auletta p. 46). Later Olson will write "The Resistance" as a sort of prose equivalent of "La Préface" and dedicate it to Riboud. "Olson and his wife, Constance, became special friends of Riboud's," says Auletta (p. 60). "Every two or three months, Riboud took the train to Washington to spend a week-end with them. The three would stay up talking until dawn, sleep until mid-afternoon, talk until dawn." Olson was his best man when Riboud married Krishna Roy on 1 October 1949. "La Préface"—if the date given for Riboud's arrival in the U.S.A. is correct—represents an amazing predictive synchronicity: the real subject of the poem was about to appear on the scene.

Jean Riboud visiting Charles and Connie in Washington, D.C.
Kate Olson Archive.

There is a photograph of Olson and Cagli on the grass of the courtyard at 217 Randolph Place, Washington, probably during a visit of June 1946, when a manuscript was created between them called "Cagli and I on Love" (Storrs Prose #183). This seems to be notes on their conversation, Cagli for the most part, or possibly totally, with Olson as amanuensis. It is not something that needs to be quoted. Take my word for it, Cagli is highly heterosexual, quite macho with the opposite sex. Strange therefore that Clark should say of the Cagli/Olson relationship that it was "never openly sexual" (p. 113). Why would he think of such a thing?

Clark has gone again to Olson's notebooks, to the "Faust Buch" (Storrs #41), where Olson, in a note dated 8 March 1948, refers to his "relations with Finch, Melville, Dahlberg, Cagli, and even Pound sexual at base" (*Minutes* #26 p. 17). Olson continues: "The thing I do not understand is that, though this pattern looks mighty homosexual to me, the sexual root in me is male enough." Olson is denying any homoerotic feelings. In any case, the fact that Melville appears in the list should give pause in interpreting the word "homosexual" there as an expression of sexual preference. Olson is simply admitting to himself that he has been more interested in men than women as a measure of where he has got to: "the way I have leaned on each of the men mentioned for direction of work, decisions, gone to them to prime the pump. In each case, however, the love has been covert, and the work posed as my own." This is more of Olson's self-reflection that can easily be cited as weakness, as Clark seems always to want to do: "a pattern of excessive dependence, a conveying of powerful affect beyond the bounds of mere casual camaraderie ... an almost rapacious imitative stirring on his part" (p. 113). I do not think that the musings of the Faust Buch, Clark's sole source for this, justify such a summary. Olson is looking at past flaws; the notebook entry is written on the day he decides not to go to a Cagli opening to which he has been invited. It is actually more an independence day. "I would rather be less that I dream myself to be and be myself than any longer strive to be something each of these men could admire." And again, advice to himself: "Be stubborn, when you are clear, or sure, in yr own courses ... You have been frightened of everything and everybody that you respect. Because you are not sure of yourself. Fear is either shame or intimidation. Why should you live with either? They're not worth the candle of yr own life" (*Minutes* #26 pp. 17–19). There is a stirring quality to this call upon his own courage.

We have, however, jumped ahead a couple of years. We still have to note how much was achieved through Olson's respect for Cagli. This includes a first book of poems, *y & x* (the lower case is Olson's intention and practice). On 29 July 1946 Olson was proposing to James Laughlin of New Directions a pamphlet, "IN MEMORY OF: A Poem by Charles Olson. A Drawing by Corrado Cagli" (in Storrs Miscellaneous files). The poem is not extant—it was perhaps on Melville—and Laughlin turned down the idea; but the notion of collaboration stuck with them. On 8 August 1946 Cagli invited Olson up to Barnegat City on the New Jersey coast, "the same old ocean which sponsored the beginning of our friendship at Gloucester" (Storrs letter). A logo-title for *y & x* was done there, and taken by Cagli to Caresse Crosby of Black Sun Press, whom Olson had also got to know through Pound. Crosby's reaction to the idea was "wonderful," Cagli reported; they would all three get together on 26 September 1946. Apparently Crosby gave something in advance for the book, for Olson wrote her on 14 November 1946 that he was rather desperate for the rest of the advance. She replied that she had "no funds just now for y & x," but enclosed a check for the Olson poem she was including in her annual *Portfolio*.

This poem was "Upon a Moebus strip," one of the five poems chosen for y & x. Of all the Tarot poems Olson had been working on, the one he retained for the volume was "The Green Man," based on The Fool. The other poems chosen were "La Préface," "The K" and "Trinacria," the last being the surviving poem which fulfilled the original intention of correspondence between poem and drawing. In a letter of 9 December 1946, Cagli wrote (letter at Storrs):

> It seems to me that there is something very mysterious going on there if, in the field of dimensions, drawings turn out to be poems and poems flow back making change to the source of the drawings. I always liked your poetry but now I love it more because any time you show me another poem another door is opened … I feel very strong about us now, like if we had found together a muse of gold.

After fits and starts y & x was published late 1948 in an edition of 520 copies with a palindrome format, extending, when unfolded, to be one sheet printed on both sides, a most beautiful book. Cagli wrote: "I like it tremendously." There is no place where we find Olson gushing over the book, but we can be sure he did so in person to Caresse, who had been the furnace of this alchemy of poet and painter. Olson loved her for it, and for everything she stood for.

I would like to give a sense of Caresse Crosby, not by listing her wildly generous acts over many years as found in her autobiography, *The Passionate Years*, but just by showing her as someone Olson could talk to about everything—for instance, in the letter where Olson announces his principle of awkwardness as opposed to the suave, as he saw the distinction in the Sienese painters opposed to the Florentine, and as he saw in himself and Caresse opposed to "the enemy."

> Am now making "Notes on the New Dimension": idea, why we critters take Duccio, Sasetta, Giovanni di Paolo, etc., even up as far as Piero and Ucello, as more interesting than the big and suave boys. The coins I'm handling, the counters, are: awkwardness (as permanent cloth of spirit), the oblique as a via to confront direct, –as guerillas, maquis—the enemy. The enemy being: quantity, materialism, the suave: Chiang Kai Check …

This letter (published in full in *Selected Letters* pp. 84–87) and others like it deposited in the library at Southern Illinois University show a genuine rapport between Olson and Crosby. It was not the artificial relationship that Clark's calumny tries to make it out to be: "Though Olson considered Crosby 'empty' as a person, he was greatly pleased to have such a prestigious publisher for his first verse collection" (p. 115). Considering the volume got barely a review in the press, one might feel that Clark is going too far with the word "prestigious." Olson knew of the historical high spots of the press, including D.H. Lawrence's *Sun*, but he also knew that he had left mainstream success behind. Our main quarrel, of course, is with the word "empty," which Clark picks up from a later context and by which he slanderously tries to make out Olson to be a hypocrite. The word appears in a letter to Connie during that enormous review of their total life together during their separation in the fall of 1952. Olson has been writing long letters to her practically every day for three weeks and starts this letter of 8 November 1952 as follows (unpublished letter at Storrs):

> Another thing which bowls me over abt this period is my austerity ... I never was more severe ... I have to watch myself a little that I don't screech when I venture out of this cell ... I feel merely cold (severe)—& hot inside ...

In this personal crisis he is identifying in himself a new person, one not as social as he has been, now "more bent on having things straight." An upheaval in his psyche caused by the separation makes him blame himself for being hitherto indulgent about himself—and, equally, about others. Olson is on a new path of non-indulgence:

> Nor do I know that it would work—haven't had occasion to judge it except in the narrow band of my isolation and the wide band of such really empty people and "friends" here—Caresse, Rufus, Peter and Joan, Pietro, the Madsens, Richmans, and the like.

So there it is, the word "empty": not applied to Crosby in particular but the whole "demi-monde of art and politics." Olson is spending his days and nights with Carl Jung as his sole companion. Anyone else might seen "empty" in comparison with the author of *Symbols of Transformation* and *Man in Search of a Soul*. Olson is in a severe mood, a heightened state of resolve, where mundane things are scorned. Clark misappropriates the word "empty," making it seem like Olson's final judgment on an individual. It was a passing phase. If Clark had been one of the company at Caresse Crosby's Roccasimbalda Castle in the Abrussi the day after the Spoleto Conference, 3 July 1965, the same place that Pound had visited a few days earlier to read to Caresse the poems of Harry Crosby in the garden, the place, as Olson wrote to Vincent Ferrini, which had "365 rooms, literally, and flying the flag of the Citizens of the World above it like the only Renaissance I have seen in Italy," if Clark had then asked Olson the question, I believe he would have replied that his dear hostess had a fullness of life, incomparably so, as, except once, he had always said.

15
"Red, White, and Black"

Olson's large ambitions had, by 1947, resulted "only in the relatively brief and condensed book-length essay on Melville" (Clark p. 119). I suppose that's one way of looking at *Call Me Ishmael*! But, fair enough, Olson had indeed been for years hankering after a long work on the whole American experience. This is amply demonstrated in the compilations from manuscript that constituted George Butterick's *OLSON #5*. Olson's interest is even earlier than is indicated there. A substantial error on Butterick's part in the dating of "An Outline of the Shape and the Characters of a Projected Poem called WEST" (pp. 14–18) led Clark astray when he said that it was in the winter of 1946–47 that Olson began work at the Library of Congress on "a long poem centered on Indians, Spaniards and gold and bringing in as principals Ulysses, Columbus, Faust, Montezuma, Cabeza de Vaca, Cavelier de La Salle and Paul Bunyan" (Clark p. 120). It can be conclusively proven that this "Outline" that Clark is referring to was made as far back as April 1941. The preoccupation with Yeats's "gyres" and "Giraldus" of *A Vision* would be soon after Olson's first reading of the book, not later. More conclusive is the dating by Olson of his first reading of William Prescott's *History of the Conquest of Mexico* on the flyleaf: "Spring 1941— towards the 'West.'" Butterick did not have knowledge of this inscription when he dated the "Outline" as "ca 1946." We can now see that it is the "Outline" that Olson meant in the "Key West II" notebook of 1945 when he referred to "notes on the poem to be called 'West' you wrote 4 yrs ago" (*OLSON #5* p. 11). Another clue is that the outline does not, in spite of Clark's listing him, include any mention of Cabeza de Vaca, who was not in Prescott and became a discovery of Olson's much later (see the June 1946 notebook extract in *OLSON #5* p. 12).

Olson's main impetus for getting back to the big book on the West was that the publishers of *Call Me Ishmael*, Reynal & Hitchcock, had a very bright young editor named Monroe Engel, to whom Olson wrote about it in mid-August 1946. Other concerns intervened, and it was only when Olson met Engel in New York during a Christmas trip that he was moved, on returning to Washington, to draft a "Project for a book, untitled, which let's call OPERATION RED, WHITE & BLACK." He sent it off to Engel, who replied on 14 January 1947 that he "liked the outline tremendously" (letter at Storrs). A contract for the new book was prepared, but Engel then announced that he was leaving for Viking as of 15 March 1947 and wondered if Olson wanted to change publishers too. Olson apparently could not do a switch that quickly, so he stayed with Reynal & Hitchcock, and accepted a check.

Then Olson decided that, instead of writing about the "West," he would live it, by going out to California. This interruption is part of the story, so we will follow Olson and Connie on their trip. It actually began in Gloucester with a telegram inviting Olson to participate in the Northwest Writers Conference in Seattle. How did they get across the continent? This becomes an interesting question because there is conflicting information. Relying on Jane Atherton, Clark says:

> the couple were dropped off by Mel Atherton at the Boston bus depot ... Then, while waiting to board the bus, he [Olson] struck up a conversation with a pair of college students who were about to head west by car; soon he'd cashed in his and Connie's bus tickets, having talked his way into a free ride for them both to Chicago. There he managed to pull off the same trick, this time hitching a ride all the way to Portland, Oregon, with a Chinese-American woman in return for his assistance behind the wheel. (pp. 123–24)

None of this is true. I don't know how Jane Atherton could be wrong about dropping them off at Boston bus station, but it must have been some other occasion. We have a letter of 30 June 1947 to Merton Sealts which says they are leaving Gloucester by train, that day: "we are catching the 12:37 train, and have a 2:00 connection for New York ... I must be in N.Y. tonight to keep appointment for possible ride out." The next news is a postcard to the Engels from Deadwood, South Dakota, postmarked 8 July 1947. A week later they have arrived in Puyallup, Washington, and Olson writes to Ezra Pound about the trip: "had 24 hrs to take up offer of ride from NY to Yellowstone, (an ad placed by Woman Writer, Helena Kuo the name, Chinois,) a share-cost, share-drive deal. Yellowstone, for two, $16.86. Then we hitched to Missoula, and, weary of horrid autos and a dull, protracted continent, we caught a train to here." That would seem to settle it. Clark apparently did not have access to Olson's letters to Pound at Indiana Library.

Olson's performance at the University of Washington has always been considered "erratic" (Clark p. 124) or worse. Olson certainly felt he had failed himself, and his opinion had seemed to be confirmed in the word that went out from Prof. Heilman of the Department of English, University of Washington, to the effect that Olson wasn't a good bet as a visiting poet (unpublished letter to Ed Dorn 14 January 1957 at Storrs). Hence Olson's exuberance when, ten years later, a member of that earlier audience was present at his reading at the Poetry Center of San Francisco State University on 21 February 1957 and said she did not agree (the tape kept running after the reading and recorded the following conversation):

> Mr. Olson, I met you in Seattle …
>
> That was a disaster.
>
> A disaster?
>
> But I was stage fridden.
>
> Oh, I didn't notice that.
>
> You didn't see that? Hell, I couldn't find the words.
>
> You were marvelous.
>
> They gave a report that I was ungentlemanly. I couldn't get an engagement on this trip because of what was said about me.
>
> It was wonderful, and then we went on that salmon expedition.
>
> [Olson turns to someone, probably Betty Olson] Listen to this, in terms of that Seattle.
>
> Eleven years ago I saw him at the Seattle …
>
> [Olson applauds with his hands] You see? The people, sir. To hell with the executives!

It undoubtedly would have helped Olson to have known that for at least some people in that audience at the University of Washington his performance had been of such value as he proceeded down the coast from there to arrive in San Francisco on about 5 September 1947.

"In San Francisco, poet and critic Kenneth Rexroth, with whom Charles had recently struck up epistolary contact, met them at the Greyhound station. Rexroth put them up at his apartment, and 'did the turns' of introducing Olson to local verse luminaries like Muriel Rukeyser, William Everson and Mary Fabilli. On Rexroth's advice, he also sought out Robert Duncan" (Clark p. 125). I don't know where Clark got the business about

Rexroth's meeting them at the Greyhound Station and taking over. He footnotes a letter (found in *CO/RC* 6.59) which mentions that Rexroth "himself did me the turns on the West Coast 3 yrs ago handsomely." That's all it says. It does not appear that Clark interviewed Rexroth; there is no correspondence at Storrs from Rexroth before a Christmas card, December 1948. In his letter to Ezra Pound 24 August 1947 (Indiana) Olson simply announces: "Go today to San Francisco, & shall look up the Cali4nians, starting with Robert Duncan."

Clark totally neglects to mention the most significant person (in terms of future contact) whom Olson met in Hollywood. Robert Payne was a mild-mannered Englishman, who wanted to be a poet but found himself writing biography, travel books and novels, and was in Hollywood trying to break into script-writing. The two became quick friends, partly because Payne was also a night person who thought it natural to work or talk till dawn. It was apparently Muriel Rukeyser who brought them together, for Payne reported back to her: "Did I tell you how much I liked Olson?" (letter of 22 November 1947 in Berg Collection, NYPL), adding some details:

> We went one evening down Hollywood Boulevard and he bought, in the light of red neon lamps, a newspaper from a dwarf, and recoiled in terror and love: and spoke urgently of Stravinsky while I spoke of Chaplin, till the two became one, and we saw Petroushka at last with his flat feet and bamboo cane. I wish he could have stayed to do Moby Dick.

Because of his personal connection with Jay Leyda, Melville scholar and film historian, Olson had been drawn into the discussion of a film adaptation of Melville's classic. With some poetic license, Rukeyser had seen Olson's *Call Me Ishmael* as a potential "shooting script." "I have no impression Hollywood agrees," Olson wrote to her on 1 October 1947:

> But John Huston has asked me to do a critique of his script of a Moby-Dick movie, if he and Blankery, his producer, can get Jack Warner to agree to it on his return next week. Jack Warner, it appears, is haunted by another whale—a $365,000 job made for "The Sea Beast" which sounded in 50 fathom the day they launched it, and did not come up. Result: he has not yet agreed to allow Huston to do a Moby-Dick. (*Selected Letters* pp. 71–72)

It is in this same letter that Olson mentions Payne and adds, "Glad to know him, by the way."

The two men had merely brushed against each other, as it were, before Olson, who did not have to take Hollywood very seriously, had returned to his writing desk in Washington, D.C., with Jack Warner's expletive, "That — whale!" as the punch-line in his account of his adventures. At least, it pleased Ezra Pound, who said: "Well, seven months, one story, not bad" (Seelye pp. 98, 134). Clark rather spoils the story by missing out the cost of the mechanical whale and that it was for a prior movie, and also by misquoting the punch-line (p. 128).

Another significant meeting in Hollywood was with Stravinsky, in his home, where Olson's height was penciled on a closet door along with those of previous visitors such as Auden (as told by Robert Craft in *Stravinsky: Chronicle of a Friendship*). Soon after arriving back in Washington Olson was able to attend a concert conducted by Stravinsky and afterwards wrote "An Homage" (*Collected Poems* p. 75). Clark says that this was written "following a brief conversation with Stravinsky after a Constitution Hall concert" (p. 134); but, since there had been the previous meeting in California, the poem is not based on such a flimsy occasion. Readers might test for themselves the appropriateness of Clark's judgment on the poem: "His tortuous attempt at achieving post-symbolist synesthetic effects ... remains as conclusive proof of an observation made by his composer friend Frank Moore that 'music was mysterious to him'" (p. 134). Those of us who knew the brilliant Frank Moore will recognize the tone, but Clark might have tempered it with an acknowledgement of Olson's modesty in this regard. He refers later to Olson's hearing David Tudor perform Pierre Boulez's "Second Piano Sonata" at Black Mountain College, whereupon "both Tudor and Boulez were instantly enshrined in the writing teacher's canon of approval" (p. 209), intensifying the derision by saying that "Boulez was solemnly proclaimed 'the first composer since Bach.'" The phrase quoted is from a letter to Creeley at the time. The full passage is needed to give us a sense of Olson's modesties and enthusiasms. He is trying to get at the concept of "THE SINGLE INTELLIGENCE" and feels that he has just been given Boulez as an instance of it (*CO/RC* 7.111):

> ... a huge man I came upon yesterday whom you MUST give yrself the chance to hear, now that you are in France—where he is
> I, at the moment, go this far, as to say, he is the 1st composer since Bach—for me (granting, of course, my peculiar ignorance, or arrogance, about music as an art!

PIERRE BOULEZ—only two things of his exist here (the 2nd Sonata, which I heard yesterday impeccably played (piano) by David Tudor; and a recording in NY)

　　but for god's sake, go get him, when you are in Paris—he is 25, and I shall try to find out his address for you—Christ, does he come *straight* from himself, compose as a man, with none of the shit of "music," or experiment

The most significant event during Olson and Connie's 1947–48 visit to the West Coast had nothing to do with the literary scene, (the real rapport with Robert Duncan came much later), but was Olson's getting to know the West by walking the ground. Carl Sauer, professor of Geography at Berkeley, had done that ahead of Olson and with a technical knowledge that Olson admired. Sauer was a real brain and a stern taskmaster. Olson was propelled by him into serious research at Bancroft Library, Berkeley, and at the State Archives in Sacramento, on the Donner Party and the Gold Rush. He couldn't help himself; he dived into primary documents, some of them previously untouched by scholars and, to cut a long story short, participated in an ongoing project organized by George Hammond for the Book Club of California by editing, with an introduction, #2 of the "Letters of the Gold Discovery" (dated February 1948, but actually appearing in June 1948), titled *The Sutter-Marshall Lease*. Clark with some edge calls it a "lost" (in quotes) document and "a two-page pamphlet" (p. 127), but Olson judged that this work was well worth staying on for into the new year 1948, even beyond his grub-stake. He had, in the end, to send an SOS to Monroe Engel for funds (letter 27 December 1947 at Harvard). He felt he had a right to do so because he really was back on to "Red, White & Black" in earnest:

> for 4 months I have been living from pillar to post up and down this coast doing research for the book & discovering such material that I have been led on, first day by day, then week by week, until I invested everything, our fare home, and then some … You know my method. This phase is the hardest, slowest, and, especially on the road, most expensive. Now things are very serious, have been all this week. Connie must return to Washington and I must go down to Berkeley to the Bancroft to relate new material there to what is here.

He is, in this extremity, asking Viking for $250, "accepting the fact I have already signed a contract for the book as earnest of my responsibility to them." Engel came through, and Olson could turn with some equanimity

to the crucial practical task of applying for another Guggenheim Fellowship. Storrs has a carbon of Olson's preliminary letter to Henry Moe of 10
January 1948; he got a project description to them by 26 January 1948, the
one printed in *OLSON* #5 (Storrs Prose #209). It is an impressive plan of
work, the kind of challenge that Olson could rise to superbly when he was
cornered. So, before he left California he had made a good step toward his
goal.

Clark doesn't agree. He calls the trip "an interesting adventure," but
believes that "by the end of it his planned long work on the West was no
closer to reality than it had been when he started out" (p. 129). How can
Clark say that, knowing that the Guggenheim application that Olson
slaved at for two weeks resulted, on 1 April 1948, in a grant of $2500 for
twelve months to do *West*?

16
"The Fiery Hunt"
and Other Dance Plays

While waiting during the early months of 1948 for news from the Guggenheim Foundation, Olson got diverted into writing dance plays. Clark is wrong, however, to allege that Olson, when he got it, spent his fellowship money in an unauthorized way. "He gratefully accepted the money," says Clark (p. 135), "regarding it as compensation for his long labors but at present little inclined to revive the West book project." What actually happened was that Olson accepted the fellowship but did not draw on it at that time. He even borrowed money from Henry Murray, writing in a thank-you letter of 20 July 1948: "I had to forego the Guggenheim granted to do the narrative book on the West, and you struck me at ebb." Explaining about his dance plays to Josef Albers in a letter of 30 September 1948 (at Raleigh) Olson said: "because of this work ... I am unable to take up a Guggenheim granted last spring for another purpose." If for nothing else, Clark should have made a correction on this matter in the second printing of his book. Olson's scrupulousness here was remarkable, whereas Clark has him perpetrating a sort of fraud.

It was after Erick Hawkins of the Martha Graham Dance Company came to Washington and did "Theatre Dance Pieces" at the Symposium on Contemporary Arts in March 1948 that Olson's theatre ideas were given focus. There were discussions, and Hawkins gave Olson some notes toward a dance play to be called "The Fiery Hunt" about *Moby-Dick*. He had been working on it for two years. It was not an "old scheme" of Olson's, as Clark surmises (p. 136), but of Hawkins's. Olson, however, responded with alacrity. The typescripts are all in the archive at Storrs. One of the sheets in the file is headed, "What are the elements in Hawkins' plan?" Olson took some and left others. What he chiefly added was the striking image out of *Moby-Dick* itself of the whiteness associated with death, as in part IV of the finished play (*The Fiery Hunt* pp. 23–24):

What ISHMAEL does not so early understand is the peculiar atmosphere of the deck. For everything, himself, Ahab, the ship's elements, show sharp and unnatural. Suddenly the world around is the color of the whaleboat and the quarterdeck, the color of bleached bones. And there is a presence—falling in. He gives voice to it while Ahab holds where he is:

> What whiteness is this that the night has left,
> what added fear to what this man has brought?
>
> Such light is holy in another place,
> of priests and brides, New England house
> and sand, of altar cloth and bed,
> imagined space and dreamed-of god,
> of woman, book, bones, fields at night,
> a fence, or gold-caparisoned horse.
> But on this sea, in this blank morning of our year,
> with this wild leader in his wild pursuit,
> this color without color locks us in
> a palsy, new-found fear.
> This white that stares me in the face
> looks at me like a dusted enemy more fierce
> than Ahab or than death:

Instead of recognizing such passages as flawless verse set within imaginative stage directions, Clark talks about Olson "handicapped by a lack of dramatic conception": "His Ahab bellowed "Mountains are egos! Towers are egos!" while his Ishmael crooned of 'angels with hands in jars of sperm'" (p. 134). "Bellowed," "crooned," what kind of critical language is that? In my opinion, the stichomythia is neat, and eminently playable:

AHAB:	ISHMAEL:
I, I alone	Am nothing, leader
Ahab, Ahab	straw, straw
I'll use you all!	Destroy us, rather
The Whale! the Whale!	You! you!

"The Epilogue" is masterly exposition in well-measured verse, the punched rhymes appropriate for a staged dance play:

> A man's fate
>   how he abate
>   the negatives in his given:
> parents, place, income, hate
>   neighbors, rulers, friends

these pluralities
        a man's fatalities
                with which, from child, he's riven.

His self the other
        within a frame
                that curious mixture called
his name: Ishmael   Ahab   Stephen   John

his only instrument
        to serve a purpose
                earn him fame.

He starts
    pushed by a ball
             itself pushed by another
endlessly back
      in billiard series
             to that long cue
from which life's play began
            this man:
cell, god, fish, bird
      breach birth mother

The push no accident
            nor he (though all else be)
If power is in him
        was in nature's feeble first long step
to make himself
        identity.
He earns his fate
      to that degree
            he push against all limits, bound
palpable, unknown
      thrust up against him:
devils, wars, failures, notions, sounds.

He the hazard
      and the faith
  desperation what he need
            those limits to exceed:
    drive without truth
        rather to destroy
his own squeezed sham
      the unbelief.

> There is no other way
>   no outside answer
> no god on whom to fix a blame
>   no truth.
>   For good and evil sown together
> make man himself his only weather.
>
> To think to pitch on whale's white hump
>   the evil and the wrong
> and thus dispose of fate—
>   here Ahab erred
>   and in that error failed
> his hate!
>
> (*The Fiery Hunt* pp. 32–33)

This is what Clark deigns to call an "abortive foray into dance theater … not only a failure on its own terms, but a further waste of time and energy that might better have been invested in his West book" (p. 134). What books, methinks, Charles Olson could have done if he had only used his time and energy profitably!

Olson had faith in "The Fiery Hunt" (though he didn't like the title much) and in July 1948 shipped off the last reworkings to Hawkins. He didn't hear back. Clark says that "the play was adjudged unsuitable for staging by Hawkins" (p. 134). I don't know where he got that from; but if true, then we must say that Hawkins was wrong. I don't know of any productions of "The Fiery Hunt," but I await such with confidence.

By 20 July 1948 Olson was on to a new dance play, "my own, this time, in which I have had only two predecessors, and they Chaucer and Shakespeare." "Troilus: A Mask" cannot be judged in the same way as "The Fiery Hunt." The poetry is fine, but it remained unfinished. As Olson said in his letter to Albers of 30 September 1948, these verse-plays needed an environment like Black Mountain College in order to flower interactively with an audience. The summer session of 1949 gave Olson his chance. We know a number of "Exercises in Theatre" were directed by Olson on 28–29 August 1949, but we do not have any of the scripts. When Olson and Connie finally took up full time residence at Black Mountain in the summer of 1951, they were surrounded by talent. Olson immediately did a Nijinsky play for Tim LaFarge; the text of "The Born Dancer" is included in the *Fiery Hunt* volume. It was for Nick Cernovich that Olson embarked upon his greatest triumph in this genre, "Apollonius of Tyana." Clark summaries what he sees as the main themes of this work (p. 206), but he draws back from saying that it is a masterpiece, which it certainly is. It is a secular pilgrim's progress, where this important, though rather neglected, historical figure, the philosopher Apollonius, attached to Tyana (as Olson was to Gloucester), makes moves in a spiritual biography. To a large extent the author puts ideas into Apollonius's mouth that he himself is grappling with. The result is both historical and contemporary, an interflowing of wisdoms. Again, I do not know of any productions, but the play seems to me eminently performable.

It certainly takes a prominent place in Olson's development. In a letter to Frances Boldereff of 14 July 1950, Olson referred to "my new friend, Apollonius of Tyana." He had been reading G.R.S. Mead's *Apollonius of Tyana* (1901), which became his sole source for the dance play a year later. He was impressed with Apollonius as bearing out the point Jane Harrison had made in *Themis* about the primacy of the old fertility gods and their local shrines. As he put it in the letter:

> he spent his life, the whole first century, trying to remind every people, as he traveled carefully the whole Mediterranean world, get back to yr local hero-god, take yr power up here, don't buy the Olympians, Greek or Roman, stick to your own ground, and your old cults, only purify, purify, purify! (*CO/FB* p. 419)

This would certainly interest a poet who a couple of months before had written the first *Maximus* poem, "I, Maximus of Gloucester, to You," addressing the city itself, his own local, reminding it of old pieties and pricking its conscience, as Maximus in the second century A.D. had done for his town of origin, Tyre (see Butterick's *Guide* p. xxvii).

Olson makes the five "moves" of Apollonius an image of his own preoccupations. Practically nothing in "MOVE one" comes from the Mead source. It draws rather on the same materialistic thinking as Olson's essay "The Resistance." Apollonius/Olson is seeking The Way: "to heal, is also how you eat and how you find out how—somehow—to maintain your resistances" (*Selected Writings* p. 139).

The second "move" is from Antioch to Baghdad, where he did what was most difficult for a man "who talked to live" (p. 140): he took a vow of silence. "He listened instead." (This is more the source than it is Olson!)

The third "move" is as a preacher into the midst of the bustling world:

> He knows, as he moves through Alexandria, Athens, Rome, Cadiz, that his job, at least, is to find out how to inform all people how best they can stick to the instant, which is both temporal and intense,

which is both shape and law ... The problem is, how to extricate what he wants from the mess he is surrounded by, how to manage to locate what he himself feels: that life as spirit is in the thing, in the instant, in this man. And then to fix it, in such a way that no one can see him act or hear him talk without, from that illumination, knowing how rich their own life is.

This is as much 1950 as 50 A.D. "He is now 40 years old," writes Olson, "and at last aware of the dimension of his job" (p. 147). Apollonius's age is not known; this was Olson's age at the time.

Preparing for "move four," Apollonius comes to understand that "what he has not done, with all his concentration, is to commit himself" (p. 149). The move is to India in a "dance of recognition": "that quick way any of us seize the thing which is right for us," while at the same time obeying the dictum that "no man should impose his mode of life on others" (p. 151).

Emperor Domitian put Apollonius on trial. When friends counseled fleeing, his fifth "move" was not to go, but to stay, with a resolve that so struck Olson that he passed it on in a letter to Creeley (*CO/RC* 2.89) and to Robert Duncan in a letter of 21 December 1953. Apollonius stood his ground and said, "There is always the moment that suits wisdom best to give death battle" (p. 155). Apollonius is acquitted by the court and so is able, in the dance play (the actual circumstances of his death are not known), to return to the figure of Tyana, his city, and the two dancers become one silhouette, thus ending as enjoyable a thing as anything Olson ever wrote.

It is too bad that Clark cannot find any words of praise for it. He talks about it as "an image of the questing self" (p. 206), but he doesn't get the quester past the talking stage, quoting, to end his paragraph: "in fact, he was one of those who talked to live." Rather, Clark seems eager to get on to a letter that Olson wrote around the same time, and begins his next paragraph with a slide from "Apollonius of Tyana" to the said letter:

> In the volubleness of Apollonius there was not only autobiographical but psychological resonance. Questions of orality were now coming into increasing prominence in Olson's writing, particularly clouding his communiqués on cultural matters. What else but a testament of oral compulsion is the "sheep's heart" letter, a mid-July epistle to Creeley which last-minute misgivings kept Olson from ever sending? (p. 206)

We have to take up this matter. Clark is implying that the letter in question is an "oral compulsion" and that, on reading it over, Olson felt too ashamed to send it, even to broad-minded Creeley. What caused the mis-givings? Well, nothing. There were no misgivings. Olson did not "with-hold" the letter.

It is hard to think back to a time when, if you forgot to put a carbon in your typewriter, you couldn't mail a letter without losing it as something you yourself could refer to. On the Tuesday following the Sunday letter, Olson wrote to Creeley (17 July 1951): "what i unloosed there i have been running on, and can't let it go, like a stake or fetish I dare not let out of my hand! But I will." (*CO/RC* 6.149). On 22 July 1951 he refers again to the eight-page letter which: "i still can't get back to to get off to you" (*CO/RC* 6.177). If one had real second thoughts about sending a letter, one would not keep on about it.

Then things intervened: "Apollonius of Tyana," the rewriting of "Human Universe" for *Origin*, the birth of daughter Kate, chapters of a book on Shakespeare, and so on, until the subject of the eight-page letter came up again on 19 February 1952. Olson wants to type out a copy of it, but again it doesn't get done because, when Olson sits down at the type-writer, he instead writes the substance of it into a more formal essay titled "Culture," which he sends instead: "BY GOD, look what has happened … the JULY LETTER SAT—and now gets off its ARSE, if not yet directly to you!" (*CO/RC* 9.145). There are no misgivings here, only a rush of things that prevents him copying out the letter.

The "misgivings" are what Tom Clark imagines Olson might have had because of the subject matter of the letter. And certainly one might have misgivings if the letter was as Clark summarizes it:

> It had been precipitated by a confusing emotional scene brought upon him—importunately, he felt—by his friend Ben Shahn. The artist, plainly in a distraught state, had approached him with the distressing news of Bernarda's just-diagnosed breast cancer. Shahn thought his wife was dying and wanted to share his grief. Fond as he was of the man, Olson found himself repelled. The intensity of the emotional demand was more than he could deal with, and its imposition all too reminiscent of the pressures he'd once had exerted upon him by Edward Dahlberg. (p. 206)

I would say that the situation was not at all reminiscent of Dahlberg. Olson doesn't say it is. He describes it this way in the eight-page letter itself:

> You see, Ben came to me the night before, Friday, asked me to step outside in the dark, and by the time I caught up with him, he moved out so fast down the steps and to the grass, he was what a

> man hates to be but caught, gone, done in—crying, so crying he
> couldn't speak so that I could understand the words, they were so
> blubbered, god help us. What it was was, that, that day, he and
> Bernarda had seen a doctor and found out she has a cancer on the
> breast and is to be operated on tomorrow. (CO/RC 6.137–38)

Olson says nothing about being "repelled." Quite the opposite: "It was a
time, yesterday, to hold the Shahns' hands, both of em, poor things, with
this goddamned business staring them in the face."

The repulsion, if you can call it that, was felt the following day after
Nick Cernovich had done a solo dance on St. Francis that Olson found
very touching, "God damn tears, almost out" (CO/RC 6.137). Olson is
taking Cernovich aside, "chiefly to tell him to throw the St. Francis title the
hell and gone," when Shahn comes up and says, "I violently disagree." The
repulsion was to the way Shahn's sensibility intermitted between Olson
and his desired effect on Cernovich. Olson had set himself the difficult
task of proposing the dance be reset in a new frame, and Shahn's voice
urges holding to passions more easily invoked. Olson is torn by this diver-
gence for two hours, with the wives along and the unspoken breast cancer.
Yes, when we identify the precise ground—not the night before when the
thing came sobbing out, but the daytime corrida of discussion—then we
can say with Clark that, for that time only, Olson was repelled. But he is
able to report, as of the following day, that "at lunch just now Ben joined
us, after the food, as straight as ever … It's all become a crazy business.
And is already we three: Ben as close to me, more close, than ever" (CO/RC
6.141).

There is, however, something more to this Sunday letter: the subject of
Shahn's Jewishness. Clark warps it by suggesting that it is a central cause
for Olson's repulsion:

> Later in the letter Shahn and Dahlberg emerged as co-bearers of an
> ancient tribal burden of unconscious guilt, seeded in all Jews as
> part of their original monotheistic legacy, and "Arabian desert
> wrongness" inherited from a "God that herding people picked up."
> (p. 206)

These are not Olson's conclusions; but he bears some responsibility for
Clark's being able to hint at prejudice. He actually talks about what it is to
be Jewish. In describing how Shahn came over after Cernovich's dance to
register his disagreement, Olson stresses that it was before Shahn had
heard more than a sentence: it was "in that goddamned restless eating

nervous unhappy way that great Jews have always dogged my tail" (*CO/RC* 6.139). And he can't leave it there, because, once said, once Jewishness has been raised, so much more must be said to avoid its being taken wrongly.

> i know the will: it is to grab the attention. And not in any sly way, or even competitive way. From the same fatal natural greed to get on with life, they think as though it could be eaten in that instant— this, is the center of, that sensuality, which is them, is what has blessed and damned them in one act—for they are chosen, were (were, from the beginning, which none of the filthy anti-semites can say without thus doing exactly what they insidiously know they want to do, start a pogrom (*CO/RC* 6.139)

In spite of trying to clear the air by distinguishing himself from the "filthy anti-semites," Olson has done a no-no: as a non-Jew he is claiming to talk about Jewishness. Is that even allowed, or is the subject an absolute taboo? Well, if it is, Olson presses ahead to try to get at some truth, ignoring the taboo:

> … from the beginning chosen to be the corrupters by the very burden of the heart, the heavy heart they carry, which is not human heart, but is an enlarged sheep heart, a heart of sacrificed animals (it was Abraham who had such, why, he lived so long, why, the god of his creation, mark you, the Jewish God, wanted to know if Abe's heart was exactly that heavy, was not human (it is a lie, that story, that test is a human test—it is the test of an animal god of an animal tending people who, that early, had so lived in that sort of a connection to blood (the slaughtering of same, perhaps) ((for so long, and for such a long time out of cities, out of the cities to the east they had watched, from 5000 BC, come into being from a people they were different from; for such a huge time, in those Arabian and Semitic places, apparently, left out, outside the city, herdsmen, and because never city, never, possessed of human time & nerves, always, animal time and nerves, until, now, as I have known them (it is their animal hearts that did, for so many many years give me the width of heart I, then with only a human heart, and such is not good enough until all the other organs are sufficiently advanced, is not an actual heart, does not know its own suffering (any Jew knows that 1st, and ultimately lives longest exactly here, like a bullock, or like Abraham did, 900 years, or whatever, thus, does not know, how, the heart is, when it has to become animal, has to arrive at such a state instead of departing from same)—I have only known my heart for one month.

If Olson is talking about Jewish differences here, as he is, and centering the difference metaphorically in the size of the heart, he is also saying that this Jewish heart has somehow been what his own heart has moved toward and within the last month attained. This personal remark is not explained, but it means that he is not alien at all to Jewishness. He goes on to acknowledge that his Jewish friends and acquaintances must have felt his kinship from the start. He is here referring of course to Edward Dahlberg and Dorothy Norman, with perhaps Harry Levin of Harvard, too:

> they knew (and said) long before anyone else, this man, this olson, is capable! And shall I not love them or no, shall i not remember them, until I die, because, that generosity was given me? (*CO/RC* 6.140)

This personal resolution has the appearance of settling the problem. But no. Olson is honor bound to reach an objective truth about this "chosen" people. He turns to the conventional counters, Einstein, Marx and Freud, as the highest representations of Jewry:

> This is something I can't go around. And so long as such stays true, they are, the chosen, they do have the absolute right to think, as they do, that, the goyim are not quite good enough! I say, to all the rest of us, prove em wrong. Leave em alive. Prove em wrong. Otherwise, shut up—and shut up yr jackknives. (*CO/RC* 6.144–45)

Remember that this is an eight-page letter, and goes on and on. Olson recalls Dahlberg's notion that "the Jews have superior liver and bowels, that these are the seat of life ... that the seat of anti-Semitism is in the weak liver and bowels of all goyim" (*CO/RC* 6.145). Mere myth, but Olson wants to assert that "reality is implicitly mythological":

> The Jews, I take it, have been the heart of civilization as it has been alive in the West for the 1st 4700 years. I would bet, if one examined the texts carefully (Leviticus, in particular, as the most honest of all the books, tho, the Talmud, should, be equally revealing) that the earlier imagery was thick with liver, bowels, and stomach process. But in any case, it is, this business of, the seat of life as inside man, and the blood system of feeder and flusher of organs, which settled humanism very early. And that what I have so often been talking about as such—humanism—has, ultimately, to be taken back to this point of historical time—this point which is no time at all, when you have to sit on a bench here a few yards away from me and watch a man, a dear dear man, at that terrible moment, cry, cry out his whole heart, because, his wife, is presented

with this thing. Oi, Weh, is so very accurate. There is no consolation we can offer any other. There it is. And how thoroughly, in
such a moment, it all is true. Why not, at that moment, are they not
the chosen? Why not? I do not know that they are not.

We are forced to quote Olson at length to demonstrate how wrong Clark
is to stigmatize this long letter to Creeley as something Olson would have
misgivings about. There is no skeleton in the closet here. "Judaism, and
still the living Jew, are the truest and root founders of humanism" (*CO/RC*
6.143). Isn't that a good thing to have said? I think Clark is nervous that
Olson is willing to raise the Jewish question at all (something that Carl
Jung got into so much trouble for in 1936). Indeed, it is a bit brave; but
then, it's only what Apollonius of Tyana would, in his own way, have done,
with the same conclusion as Olson (*CO/RC* 6.145): "I can do only one
thing. Be as *I* am."

17
Black Mountain—I

Josef Albers may have been rigid in some ways (his paintings seem to indicate this) but as Rector of Black Mountain College he was flexible enough to offer Olson something that he was delighted to accept. Olson was not ready for a full-time appointment but Albers said he could come to the college for a few days every month. Poverty-stricken as he was in October 1948, Olson jumped at it. During his December visit a crisis at the college came to a head and a grateful Olson was very willing to back Albers. In fact, he spoke for Albers, literally, when Albers lost his voice during the days an outside group of potential trustees were checking out Black Mountain College at Albers's invitation. Clark tells it this way:

> Olson stepped into the breach to chair a climactic meeting. Addressing the panel of visiting dignitaries from New York City, Andover and MIT, he outlined his own plan for saving the college from imminent bankruptcy and closure. It was an imaginative scheme drawn from Pearl Buck's *All Men Are Brothers*: the nation's most valuable "mandarins"—artists, scientists and thinkers— would take off on "a broken pilgrimage to nowhere," touring the country to acquaint potential students and sponsors with Black Mountain, and at length wind up back to North Carolina, thereby rescuing from extinction not only the college but all useful culture and knowledge. The impracticality of the proposal was lost for the moment in his obvious enthusiasm. (p. 144)

So far so good. But Clark then lurches into what was an entirely different occasion:

> With seasonal cup of mulled Tokay punch held high, eyes wide and brows lifted in challenging inquiry, he asked "what was wrong with" fourteen seekers of truth wanting nothing more than to be "left alone on a mountain?" His plan was politely ignored, and the college shortly saved by other means, but this performance was an

auspice of things to come: it marked Olson's debut in a role later to become familiar, the crazy head monk of the monastery. (p. 145)

Clark has confused the story as told by the sources, in the first instance Martin Duberman in his *Black Mountain*:

> Six outsiders accepted an invitation to meet at the college on December 12–13, 1948 to discuss their possible future connection as trustees: Mrs. Graham Blaine of New York City, Professor John E. Burchard of MIT, Beaumont Newhall, Bartlett H. Hayes, Jr., of Andover, Massachusetts, Dr. Samuel Cooley, the local Black Mountain physician, and Alex Reed, who had been a weaving student at the college in the mid-forties ... When the December meeting convened, the prospective trustees spent most of the first day asking a series of questions: "What has been responsible for the turnover in the student body?" "What would our legal responsibilities be under the incorporation laws of North Carolina?" "Can assurances be given that internal troubles will not continue to appear at Black Mountain?" During the second day of conferences, they offered some tentative suggestions: Tuition should be raised to $1,800; instead of fee reductions for students, a loan fund should be set up, and in any case, maximum assistance should probably be limited to $900; to meet the current deficit, money should be borrowed on the property; the strongest fields should be art, music and writing, "with visiting faculty supplying supportive offerings in other fields;" a campaign for "quick, dramatic publicity" should be inaugurated; the alumni should be organized; and a concrete program and budget should be drawn up for the year. Beyond those questions and suggestions, the six felt unable to go. Before committing themselves to become trustees, they wanted to check further on what their legal status and responsibilities would be, and then to have another meeting the following month. (hardback p. 310, paperback p. 324)

Duberman certainly seems to know what went on during those December evaluation days. Whereas Clark presents his readers with a meeting that Olson dominated with his wild ideas, tipsy on Tokay punch, Duberman has no record of such a thing. Why? Because it never happened. Clark has misread the chief source, the sole source for Olson's part in things, an interview Olson gave to Andrew S. Leinoff, transcribed by George Butterick in *OLSON* #8, particularly pages 77–78:

> Like I said, what's wrong with fourteen people being left alone on a mountain? What's wrong with that. As a matter of fact, that's one

of the reasons why I have such a passion about Black Mountain, is that I felt even then—and that was the first year I was there and that was when the place was in the statutory condition she'd basically been in since her founding—this would be the spring of 1949 ... I had that funny feeling: What's wrong? It would be a marvelous example of what is the situation in this nation that four-teen such people, and they were rather a considerable bunch ... They were a faculty but they were a, like, again, a society of, a funny little group of human beings. A society, like they say. So I said to them once at a faculty [meeting]—and it was marvelous to say it—and I was getting pretty drunk, really, drinking that lousy but marvelous, best of, sort of punched cheap wine—not muscatel or port but—tokay. Which is a son of a gun. I mean it left me so that I walked right down the hill without touching the ground at all.

"So I said to them once at a faculty [meeting] ..." Since Olson has already discussed the visiting trustees meeting, the word "once" will refer not to that but to some other time. Please, Clark, don't let's suppose that Olson was so out of control that, when Albers asked him to speak for him in a very serious crisis meeting, he got drunk in front of messrs Burchard, Blaine, Newhall, Hayes, Cooley and Reed. No, there were faculty meetings quite often and, as I read it, it is at one of these earlier or later meetings that Olson made this point, the more strongly that punch was flowing. Clark's interpretation would only be offered by someone who was looking to portray Olson as an embarrassment to everybody.

Olson always behaved well when the occasion called for it. One reason why I am certain nothing untoward happened at the December meetings is that just afterwards—and as a direct consequence of the new resolve to try to reach more people with a publicity campaign—Albers asked Olson to write out his impressions of the college for such use. This request would not have been made if Olson had gone beyond the pale. This "short promotional statement" is mentioned by Clark, but he does not say where it can be found. Since it has remained unpublished except as an appendix to Leverett T. Smith and Ralph Maud, "The Charles Olson Papers at Raleigh, N.C." in *Credences* 2:1 (Summer 1982) pp. 89–90, I present it below:

> Black Mountain College as seen by a writer-visitor, 1948
>
> To say why Black Mountain College is as attractive and powerful as it is, is as difficult (and sweet a task) as to characterize a human personality one loves or by whom one is profoundly moved. For

Black Mountain is more like a human individual than it is like anything else.

It is not the least like any other college. It is not named as they,
after dead Presidents, benefactors, States. It is named for a live
mountain, and the hills of that range shadow its lake and meadow,
lend their contours (which the ice admirably left them when it
withdrew) to the college as it distributes itself at each end of that
sidehill road which ought right now to be a more important image
of American education than Mark Hopkins' log.

Black Mountain's secret is a combination as ineluctable as that of
the human organism—bones, and the breathing apparatus of flesh,
the pores. It is easy to see the freedom of Black Mountain—no
degrees offered, no examinations in course, no separation of men
and women, nor faculty from students, no bells. The hidden part,
the structure by which it stands, has stood, will stand, by which it
and its parts move, is discipline, and the promotion of it. This is a
matter of the exactitude of its faculty, of the intent of the students
it draws, of the base of its curriculum, the arts. He or she who does
not discipline himself or herself in this North Carolina air, who
does not learn from his or her freedom the principle of work (which
is the principle of intensification) dies off to the place as dead cells
or bad bones.

Because Black Mountain is small and all is to be seen and heard,
even the murmurs as well as the steady hum we call life, it is
possible, from class to class, meal to meal, exhibit concert film
lecture dance, from milking to tractor, scraping the road to clear-
ing away the burned laboratory, it is possible (there are examples
present) to understand that man does not thrive by knowledge
alone but by the ingestion and use (by himself) of each particular
that falls, or he makes to fall, in his way. That usage, and its
usufruct, is not possible by any other road than labor, labor of all
the senses and the organs, the labor of the individual itself.

Because Black Mountain is that road it leads to itself and takes on
the character of the individual I here praise, American education
goes from its door.

This is a beautifully balanced piece of belles lettres, dispelling the
notion of Black Mountain as an "experimental" college and showing how
freedom itself suggests its complementary condition, discipline. It is this
piece that was an auspice of things to come; it marked Olson's debut in a
role later to become familiar, the observant, loyal, caring, helpful leader,
trying to make the most of available resources. No crazy head monk, he.

18
Flea-Bitten

The question is: why should Olson have got mixed up with such a paranoid character as Edward Dahlberg in the first place? Olson landed on Dahlberg's doorstep while Dahlberg was vacationing on Cape Ann in the summer of 1936. On Olson's part there was an understandable wish to impress a known writer; on Dahlberg's part an understandable wish to gain a protégé. How could this quite normal conjunction of needs stoke such hellish fires and freeze such infernal rivers of feeling on and off for twenty years?

It was not a total waste of time, at least not initially. Dahlberg launched Olson into *Twice A Year* and the New York art scene, gave him an alternative to the Harvard academic model and ingrained in him a prose style which took enormous personal strength for Olson to raise himself out of. These are things that had to come from somewhere if Olson was to become the Olson we know; and Dahlberg was it.

I do not intend to follow the long road of "in love, in sorrow," to use the phrase from a letter that Paul Christensen made the title of his book, *In Love, In Sorrow: The Complete Correspondence of Charles Olson and Edward Dahlberg.* The one thing that still intrigues is the *Flea of Sodom* question: did Olson have a right to refuse to review Dahlberg's book? Clark tells the story in a nutshell:

> Dahlberg, unpublished for almost a decade and hungry for that promised review, began pestering him relentlessly about it. Regarding this desperate appeal as psychological blackmail—the extortionate demand of an abandoned father—Olson resisted stubbornly. (p. 183)

Was Olson at fault in this refusal? In a letter of 17 April 1950, anticipating the publication, Olson had made some remarks about reviews, mentioning his friend Harvey Breit of the *New York Times Book Review*

(p. 119). This was close to a promise, and in a letter of 25 June 1950, still before publication, there is a definite promise:

> I shall drop a note to Harvey soon (better to be cool, with that fellow, he is so scared of, us HAMMERERS!)—and though I am scared to death about the doing of the review, (it is not my form whatsoever, nor my way of putting my sense of you forward: you are too close to me for those public places: too close, for critique— for critique as I imagine critique, that is) but, for you, I'll do, do, do, do (p. 131)

As it turned out, that was four "do's" too many.

When the London edition of the book came from Dahlberg with a flourish of an inscription dated 31 July 1950, Olson wrote by return mail: "I have suffered too much, Edward, to speak easily of the sage & parable you have put forth here" (p. 135). This was an early warning; and next day, more:

> I'll be honest, and hope I do not have to raise myself up soon and do a critique of you, my dear wise friend. For it is an overwhelming experience to have this book in my hand. You see, you are most close to me, I am here present, and, beyond all else, your images are some of the very same images I have taken up for myself. (p. 140)

To which Dahlberg replied that he did earnestly wish for a critique from Olson, reiterating it two days later:

> I am hoping out of the attention that might come from this book to get some sort of college post, so you see, Charles, I do need that kind of help from you. If I tell you there is not a single person to whom I could appeal, save yourself, to do this (outside of Herbert Read in London), you might believe this to be wily hyperbole. But it is the whole truth. (p. 150)

To which Olson responds in a letter of 29 August 1950:

> You have me very troubled. If I were asked to do the Times review, I'd do it, for the reasons you advanced, that, such a review might serve your other necessities. Follow you here, absolutely. But it would be a usurpation of my forces and my senses of you to do a "review", a form I abhor. And that, plus my distaste for "using" Breit who left me myself so exposed in the same place, leaves me still with a huge reluctance to write him again. I would so much rather leave this thing to his doing, on the base of that earlier letter, if he so chooses. And meanwhile go ahead working on what is my

own plan, to do a considerable critique, without reference to the magazine where it might appear, and then, when it is done, send it out ((this is the organic way in which I have worked now so long, that any other conventional method—or arbitrary one—especially where it is such a major thing as your work, and my first real grappling with it, for critique—would be scattering, to me)) ... For I should want to say nothing of Edward Dahlberg which did not stand in the same mortice as the thing I might say of Herman Melville. For Edward Dahlberg is more than my friend: he is of my own substance, a personage of my own fable, and I heave him out with the gravest torment, as if it were parts of my own flesh (pp. 151–52)

Olson adds at the end of the letter: "And do not be troubled. We shall do what has to be done. And it shall be done, if not in the big spread stupid place, in a small place where it can be properly done" (pp. 153–54). Dahlberg in his next letter seems to concur in this (pp. 155–56). But soon the New Directions edition is out and Dahlberg no longer concurs. They quarrel on the telephone, and Olson writes two very frank letters on 21 and 28 September 1950. The next letter we have from Dahlberg is calm, as though nothing untoward had happened. But he still wants the review. The lines are drawn.

A full treatment of this end-game would require an analysis of Dahlberg's psyche and a reading of *The Flea of Sodom*, both of which I beg not to be forced to do. There is a letter from Olson of 11 November 1950 in which he tries, for Dahlberg's eyes, to demonstrate some of his thinking about *The Flea*, but that doesn't count. From Dahlberg's point of view, only a public splash would meet the demand. For Olson, *The Flea* is only a part of the problem: the real job is the whole Dahlberg Pantokrator— and who would want to take that on?

The last skirmish of this *ne pas de deux* begins with a Dahlberg letter of 16 November 1955: "Let me ask you, and can you reply truthfully, and without evasion, why did you refuse to defend THE FLEA OF SODOM? ... What bread, little as it is, was stolen from me by those assassin book-Cains, the communists, and with your help! You can't deny it, because your acts prove it. You were always furtive with me" (pp. 219–20). Olson's reply of 18 November 1955 is finally not furtive, and the truth comes out. Olson considers Dahlberg widely wrong, "so importantly wrong" that if he had to say anything in print about him he'd have to say "why and how" he is wrong, and he doesn't want to. Olson at last says the words: "I don't want to" (p. 224). He is still a little furtive. He only calls Dahlberg "wrong." He spares him the whole truth. He doesn't reveal how utterly demonic he now believes Dahlberg to be.

Where, then, did right reside in this issue? One of the things we are thankful to Tom Clark for is that he interviewed Olson's old friend Ephraim Doner. Doner fairly settles the matter. "Edward," Clark quotes Doner as saying, "demanded a price. He was like the God of the Hebrews— 'Remember what I did for you'" (p. 61). Olson was truly burdened by the early push he had been given; the final gift from Dahlberg was that he forced him, if he were to survive as his own man, to create his own powerful gods. Would it have killed him to publish a little review somewhere? In the midst of such a re-forging, apparently it would have.

19
"The Kingfishers"
and the Archaic Postmodern

In my book, *What Does Not Change: The Significance of Charles Olson's "The Kingfishers,"* I did not dwell on previous interpretations of the poem, mentioning only George Butterick's scholarship in order to amplify it and Guy Davenport's conjectures in order to deny they are the best of all possible explications, which—despite Davenport's modesty—they had been touted as. Thus, Clark's two-page analysis of "The Kingfishers" is not therein criticized, and so I offer the following rectification of that omission.

Clark's criticism ends with some kind of homage to the poem, but his first approach is to belittle Olson's achievement by suggesting that it was Frances Boldereff who really got him to do it and that he could not have finished it without "the confidence-building exchange" of letters with her (p. 146). I have dealt with this put-down in covering Clark's misrendering of the whole Boldereff affair. Suffice it here to say that Olson had conceived of doing such a poem long before he had any communication with Boldereff, that it was not discussed at all in their letters, and was finished and sent off to publishers before they met.

Clark begins his discussion of "The Kingfishers" by saying: "Its first embryonic movements came in February, with another of his epic-scale conceptions, a plan for a long poem to be called 'Proteus.' Only two fragments of this were actually committed to paper" (p. 146). It seems clear from this that Clark never saw George Butterick's long-awaited revelations about the poem in his article "Charles Olson's 'The Kingfishers' and the Poetics of Change" *American Poetry* 6:2 (Winter 1989) pp. 28–69. Butterick reproduced the ten typescript pages of "Proteus" and referred to other drafts, a number of which comprise appendices A–F of *What Does Not Change* ("Proteus" is Appendix G). "Proteus," then, was not only planned but executed. "The Praises" and "The Kingfishers," are not "fragments" of an unfinished epic; it's just that Olson, in the end, preferred to slice it up into two poems.

Clark: "One grew into 'The Praises,' an ambitious propositional poem in its own right, affecting an aggressive Poundian vernacular tone ..." (p. 146). Let us stop right there. Pound is just too easy a stick to beat Olson with. I'll let Olson himself answer this one. In writing to Creeley on 4 October 1951 he said: "THE KINGFISHERS, which, time & again I have heard, 'Pound,' feels so completely mine that, by it as gauge, I must take it all such people are idiots, total & depraved." And again: "This whole question is intricate. It burns my ass, that, so often, these idiots cry, 'Pound,' everytime they think they have a critique of my own work. yet, fuck em. I'll not be driven off a value because of such ... But what burns me is, that, the superficial resemblances are used to beat me with. Fuck em." (*CO/RC* 7.244).

Clark: "The Praises" reflects "wide reading (principally in the history of geometry and Plutarch's *Lives*)" (p. 146). It is not Plutarch's *Lives* that is the source but Plutarch's *Morals*, or *Theosophical Essays,* as we find it in the title of the edition Olson actually used, a translation by C.W. King (1908). The vague phrase "history of geometry" hides the fact that Clark does not know that fifty-two lines of the 133-line poem are taken from one source, Matila Ghyka's *The Geometry of Art and Life* (1946).

Clark: "Equally slow to come together but ultimately far more success-ful was the second poem developed from the abandoned 'Proteus.' Here Olson's drive toward large statement was contained and given figurative resonance by the vivid central image of the kingfisher, allusive symbol of the spiritual renewal" (p. 146). Clark is chronologically challenged. "The Kingfishers" came before "The Praises." But more important, he got symbolic the meaning of the kingfisher wrong. With its "dripping fetid" nest it is a symbol of decadence.

Clark: "The image had its source in a seemingly trivial incident. At a party in the studio of a Washington artist friend, Olson overheard a drunken art curator mumbling semi-coherently about 'the blue of the king-fisher feathers.' The episode lodged in his imagination to resurface—in typically cryptic and mysterious fashion—at the heart of his fable of cultural revolution" (p. 146). This incident was not at the heart of the poem but a starting anecdote. It does, nevertheless, lead into a substantial theme, and I don't think Olson was trying to be cryptic or mysterious: the trade in kingfisher feathers provided the wealth that created Angkor Vat and the ending of the export to China meant economic disaster: "When the attentions change / the jungle leaps in."

Clark must have heard through the grapevine about the Washington artist and the drunken art curator—or perhaps he had, after all, read Butterick's article where these facts were first made public. But if he had, how could he not tell us that the name of the mumbling guest was really Gernand (not Fernand)? This would have solved a perplexity that has attended this passage from the start. I further doubt that he knew the article, for he does not know that Mao's words in French in the poem were not read aloud "from a French periodical" by Jean Riboud but were quoted by him in a letter. This letter (at Storrs) is undated; Butterick thinks it is "probably from November–December 1948." However, it was more likely to be nearer the time of Mao's speech, which was December 1947.

Clark: "Mao's revolution was but one manifestation of a recurrent transformative energy Olson evoked by beginning his poem with an echoing paradox from Heraclitus: 'What does not change / is the will to change'" (p. 147). Clark in mentioning Heraclitus is following Davenport, but one might have thought he had more sense than to fall for Davenport's convoluted footnote, the premise of which is that Olson was an expert in Greek. Besides, Butterick's article (p. 55) refers to a page of prose in the archive at Storrs, which reveals exactly how this famous first line of the poem came into being. It came at the end of a discussion about the laws of human nature and history, "the permanence of human effort shifting as it does its direction" (p. 55).

> Why it shifts is not so easy to say. Is it for as elementary and animal a reason as the simplest need of the nerves—for change? I should imagine this is a more accurate way to put it than we generally do when we talk of goals. They change. What does not change is the will to change

There is no period. When we turn over the page, we read the typed words:

> What does not change / is the will to change

and two attempts at the opening stanzas of the poem. I concur with Butterick's conclusion in his *American Poetry* article: "We have, then, evidence as close to the actual moment of creation as we are ever likely to get" (p. 55). There is not the slightest evidence that Olson went outside the thrust of his own argument to reach that famous line.

Clark: "Olson imbedded his oblique, discontinuous narrative with further archaic elements, details of Aztec and Greek rites taken from Prescott and Plutarch and arranged alongside tags from Eliot and Pound like tesserae in a complex mosaic" (p. 147). I do not think "The King-fishers" is a pattern of elements but a coherent argument using imaged ideas. Clark can only see Olson "employing the major modernist juxta-positional mode"; we will not understand Olson's advance on Pound and Williams until we see that he is neither an imagist nor one satisfied to have "no ideas but in things." His basic mode is moral statement aided by analo-gies and some Eisensteinian montage. Even Clark, who has pinned the drab label "mosaic" on the poem, realizes in the end that something different is happening: it is "a first-person statement in which the poet at last rose above his modernist influences to position himself, like some ancient city founder planting his oar, at the jumping-off point for all his work to come" (p. 147).

One cannot argue with that! The poem is meant to put the lid on old modernism. There are no Eliot "tags." Indeed, Clark missed the opportu-nity to drive home how much this is an anti-"Wasteland." At one stage in its composition Olson wrote to Robert Payne (letter of around March 1949—see *Minutes* #14/15):

> I had locked myself in for three weeks in an attempt to do a 1st long poem. Yesterday I put it together and looked it over, compared it to THE WASTELAND, and decided, as a practicer of the gentle craft, I better do more work at the last.

One of the worksheets at Storrs contains the following schemata:

Anti-Wasteland

I   objective record & vista of the city

II   the morning
     the birds

III (the desert become the city

IV   (the city gone jungle
                I–III recur)

V   the going on—change again
                the Long March

"The Kingfishers" did not follow this scheme exactly, but the intention is clear. Olson's city will not be an "objective correlative" (Eliot) but an "objective record," within economic history.

Our Lady of Good Voyage Church, Gloucester.
Photo: Charles Olson Society.

Clark does not touch on this rivalry with Eliot and appears not to know of the telling postcard that Olson wrote to Pound from Gloucester on 14 June 1947, a picture of the Blessed Virgin on top of the Portuguese church, with the message: "Here is my Lady that Possum stole." (This postcard is quoted by Helen Gardner in *The Sources of Four Quartets*. Pound sent it to Eliot and she saw it in the Eliot papers.) Olson is thinking of part IV of "The Dry Salvages" and the apostrophe to the "Lady, whose shrine stands on the promontory." Olson later wrote to Creeley about Eliot's preemption of "my madonna, buono viaggi, Gloucester, and how he misuses it" (*CO/RC* 1.28). Olson was right. Eliot had not been in Gloucester since he was a youth and did not in fact remember a Lady of Good Voyage but thought that "there ought to be a shrine of the B.V.M. at the harbour mouth of a fishing port" (quoted by Gardner p. 34). Olson knew the particulars, knew that, for instance, this statue seen by all the fishing boats leaving the harbor held in her arms the model of an old masted vessel:

> (o my lady of good voyage
> in whose arm, whose left arm rests
>
> no boy but a carefully carved wood, a painted face, a schooner!

This is from the first *Maximus* poem of 1950, but Olson already with "The Kingfishers" knew he had to deal with particularities. Hence, the birds of the opening lines; hence Gernand of the party and his remark about kingfisher feathers; hence Mao Tse Tung's words presented to the poet by his friend Jean Riboud; hence the encyclopedia facts about the kingfisher's nest; hence the quotations from Prescott and the *E* on the stone from Plutarch—these are found objects that make the argument. For in "The Kingfishers" Olson is still a declamatory orator. What he is trying to persuade us of is that we must move from the world of T.S. Eliot and its alienation.

Another connection that Clark misses is to Ben Shahn, in his role of artist of the working people of America. On 9 January 1950, Olson sent a typescript of "The Kingfishers" to him saying, "This, if anything, belongs to the Shahns" (letter in the Archives of American Art). In saying this, Olson must be implying that the poem is looking toward a people's future. Ben Shahn would certainly take the first line in that spirit of solidarity: "What does not change / is the will to change." If Olson was happy to have Shahn think so, then it must be so.

We must not, however, be so reductive as to say "The Kingfishers" represents only that kind of political vision. Clark is right to find a further vision implied in the last line of the poem ("I hunt among stones"). He says it is "the search for renewable value in a rediscovered archaic" (p. 147). Yes, the archaic is the whole key to the postmodern future. But I think Clark perhaps uses the word too casually. Is he aware of how much weight Olson places on that aspect of the postmodern? When Clark mentions "postmodern" later he doesn't give the impression he understands the connection to the archaic. He doesn't seem to be anything but jocular about it, calling "postmodern" a "new and useful piece of jargon" (p. 208). He doesn't even want to mention that Olson was the first literary figure to use the term (preceded only by the historian Arnold Toynbee).

"The Kingfishers" resists the modern, but has not yet arrived at the postmodern. One evidence of this is the opening line of part III of the poem:

> I am no Greek, hath not the advantage.

I have to admit that it was here I went off the track in the volume *What Does Not Change*. I wanted to push the poem into the postmodern. The "Human Universe" essay showed an Olson at war with "the whole Greek system" (*Selected Writing* p. 55). He was interested in the pre-Greeks as the way into the future. But I was out by a couple of years; the gap between "The Kingfishers" and "Human Universe" is very significant. "Greek" in the above line is associated with the image of the *E* on the Delphic stone, the very beginnings of Western civilization. We don't have the advantage of that primacy. So the poem gives this fairly conventional nod to Greek origins, and represents an Olson who has not yet progressed to write "Human Universe" in order to "get on to some alternative to the whole Greek system."

In his book *The Origins of Postmodernity* (1998) Perry Anderson mentions "The Kingfishers" in a way that makes the above distinction clearer. Anderson grants Olson primacy in the use of the term "post-modern," but has, however, only a limited view of Olson's achievement. He does not seem to have been aware of the account given by George Butterick in "Charles Olson and the Postmodern Advance" *Iowa Review* (Fall 1980) pp. 4–27. If he had been, he could not have thought of Olson's postmodern as merely political "in the classical tradition of the avant-gardes of prewar Europe" (p. 12); he could not have turned readily from Olson to Fredric Jameson: "The Kingfishers," he says, "could virtually be read as a brevet for Jameson's achievement" (p. 75). This might, in a sense, be true, for we have acknowledged "The Kingfishers" is at core an old-fashioned political poem. It is vintage 1948–49, when, if the *archaic* postmodern was perhaps a twinkle in Olson's eye, he did not yet have the means to express it. By 1951 when he began using the word "postmodern" Olson had made new discoveries which had so much to do with the earliest history of mankind that in order to get it straight one has to add the adjective, the *archaic* post-modern. Butterick in his 1980 essay was quite aware of this, as anybody would be who had access to the full record of the years 1950–53 up to the Institute of the New Sciences of Man at Black Mountain College. Butterick pointed out Olson's "interest in the origins of man himself, in an effort to bring him beyond the modern" (p. 12). The archaic is the indispensable other on the pathway forward from the present. "The formula seems inescapable," says Butterick; "the deeper man returns to his archaic, primordial, pre-rationalist condition, the further beyond modernism he advances" (p. 12). Perry Anderson while ready to admit that Olson was first in line in his use of "postmodern," has not pressed himself to discover what is quite blatantly the truth: that Olson is not the first in the particular line that Anderson puts him in front of.

It is as yet difficult to gauge what Olson's ultimate place might be in the history of ideas. His primacy with the word "postmodern" has not done his reputation much good to date. The term has just run away from him like the gingerbread man. How can anyone at the moment associate "postmodern" with Olson when the word has been perverted far from his original meaning, indeed inverted into the opposite of what Olson meant by it? Postmodern is now generally understood to be modernism pushed to an extreme of alienation which allows no hauteur of identity on which to hang a coherent tale. For Olson, the postmodern was a reversing of the modern, not an intensification. The modern psyche did not feel that it belonged: this can be agreed upon. But postmodernism as now usually understood assumes that there is nowhere it could belong, whereas Olson's assumption, in his first formulation of it, was that "any POST-MODERN is born with the ancient confidence that he *does* belong" (letter of 20 August 1951, *CO/RC* 7.115). If Olson could have stopped right there, if he could have trademarked his term "postmodern" and sued anybody who used it any other way ... but the gingerbread man ran. I cannot be bothered to follow where he ran to, but if I could be the wily fox and snap him up so that we could start all over again with Olson's original "postmodern," then I would consider myself in the service of a saner future.

While the word "postmodern" went off in critical theory to mean something else, what Olson meant by the word uncannily thrived in real life. Olson meant to predict a path into the future, and lo! within a decade it happened as predicted: there was dancing in the streets! It is fashionable in some quarters to scoff at the 1960s and those who hold it dear. I was there, and I cherish the memories of an era in advance of its time. I know its dark side, but I also know that it was essentially good and was one stretch of a long path that will not, I hope, die.

Let's be more specific. The ethnopoetic endeavors of Jerome Rothenberg and Dennis Tedlock, accumulating through the '60s (the first issue of

Alcheringa was Fall 1970), demonstrated that the ethnic "other," the tribal, was not out of reach. Proper attention to text and a confluence of feeling and knowledge could bring us closer to those spirits who are more a product of ritual and earth-need than well-brought-up educated persons. *Alcheringa* acknowledged (in #15) its descent from Olson by including previously unpublished poems pertaining to the earliest mythologies such as Sumerian and Hittite, and his "The Art of the Language of Mayan Glyphs." These were part of the attempt, as the editors put it at the back of the issue, to show that "the source and mainstream of poetry" resides in the "tribal, archaic, subterranean, folkloric, oral, etc.," adding that "the same line to source continues into our own century in the conscious reliving of origins by profoundly contemporary innovators like Olson." It was the vitality of these tribal affections that enabled Olson to stand on the platform at the Berkeley Poetry Conference of July 1965 claiming that the poets were the real power in the land and that he, not LBJ, was President. Thus, within a generation, the prophecy of 1951 had been fulfilled. Olson said there, referring to that moment in the Wheeler Hall of the University of California, "This is what Creeley and I would call 'home.'"

Or to take another strand of the "archaic postmodern," the archaic part of ourselves (i.e., the dream content and its connection to collective archetypes), Olson is revealed as a Jungian. He wrote to Jung in December 1952 in "total admiration (more than for any living man)," inviting him to Black Mountain College for the Institute of the New Sciences of Man (*Selected Letters* p. 181). Again, Olson of the '50s was prophetic in regard to the advances in depth psychology, all the good work that has been done by attention to the soul. I am thinking particularly of James Hillman, a quoter of Olson if not a cohort.

Another strand is the mathematics of "the infinitely small." Olson early on had a sense of the importance of minute changes and feedback; he attended to Norbert Wiener's *Cybernetics* (1948) while it was still in galley proofs. He took the term "proprioceptive" from Wiener, and in his 1959 essay "Proprioception," eschewing anything of the mystical side of quantum theory, he sought to have us focus on "the DEPTH implicit in physical being—built-in space–time specifics, and moving (by movement of 'its own')." Without that deep knowledge of the body's order, he asserted, neither the unconscious nor the self "have a home" (*Collected Prose* p. 182).

"Complex systems can exhibit powerful self-organization." The author of these words is the biologist Stuart A. Kauffman of the Santa Fe Institute in the preface to his book, *The Origins of Order* (Oxford 1993), in which with full mathematical evidence he advances the laws of the human universe, the "adaptive processes that mold systems with their own inherent order." When Kauffman came to present his thinking in a more popular form for Oxford University Press in 1995 he titled the book *At Home in the Universe*, without knowing how much that would have pleased Charles Olson.

Olson never actually used the term "archaic postmodern," presumably because to him there was no other kind of postmodern, no other way into the postmodern but the archaic. His radical view of our position in history suggests that, rather than play the hand we have been dealt by various dealers since Plato, we can fold, and play a different game by attending to what D.H. Lawrence in *Fantasia of the Unconscious* called "ancient knowledge." This would be Tarot, say, as opposed to contract bridge. We have been taught how we are supposed to be able to win, but in the great scheme of things (it has been noticed) we are not winning. The supposedly civilized world needs to stop all the destructive "victories" and find the basis for a different way, which goes back to what "Know Thyself" meant at Delphi long before Socrates, and even before Homer, whom Olson liked to call "that *late* European poet."

One crucial moment of revelation for Olson can be pinned down to the morning in March 1949 when an offprint of S.N. Kramer's "The Epic of Gilgamesh and its Sumerian Sources," from the *Journal of the American Oriental Society* 64 (1944), came through the mail from Frances Boldereff. Clark considers Boldereff a prime initiator, the Inanna of Olson's awakening, but the curious thing is that, again, we are drawn back to 1941. We have noted previously that before anything else, before reading the Kramer offprint even, Olson set to rummaging through his papers for an old poem of that date, titled "Tomorrow," and beginning "I am Gilgamesh": a rather disingenuous way of claiming priority. He wanted it known that he had made some kind of leap forward years before.

We don't know the exact source of Olson's Ur-Gilgamesh poem. William Ellery Leonard had done a version for Viking in 1934; the poem actually doesn't require there to have been a source more than a summary of the Sumerian myth. Here, then, is the first act of the archaic postmodern, eight years before the concept itself began to be formulated:

> I am Gilgamesh
> an Ur world is in me
> to inhabit.

We do not need to guess what Olson saw in *Gilgamesh* when he says it plainly in his early essay "The Gate and the Center" (1951): "As I read it, it is an incredibly accurate myth of what happens to the best of men when they lose touch with the primordial and phallic energies and methodologies which, said this predecessor people of ours [the Sumerians], make it possible for man, that participant thing, to take up, straight, nature's, live nature's force" (*Collected Prose* p. 173). The essay notes a few general precepts of government which come down via the king lists, and makes a broad claim: "The whole question and continuing struggle to remain civilized Sumer documented in and out" (p. 173). Olson feels that there is something objectively different about the pre-Socratic ages, and in 1963 found Eric Havelock's *Preface to Plato* a confirmation of his scourge of Plato's destructive "logic and classification" (as he put it in the "Human Universe" essay of 1951). Olson is saying that, since Western civilization has gone awry, we had better work with what we have from before the degradation. The Sumerian and Mayan are the "backdoors of our own culture": "And if I am right that the Americans are the last first people, then just such a place of beginning as the Sumerian and the Mayan, tipping between ancient and present man, is a live place" (*OLSON* #10 p. 60).

Some years later Olson called this link between then and now an "uroboros." This is in a letter to Donald Allen of 15 May 1960, where he is moved to summarize *Gilgamesh* as follows:

> a ruler of the City who has gotten out of his own hands and so reeks he goes to his Mother and lays his axe (ceremonial I assume) in front of her and she tells him a thing or two—a lot of events then follow including the bringing in to him from the woods a buddy who has been transformed from a Nature Boy to a man of principle (like unformed clay stone wood bone shell—for a gorget): this man dies this effects G   G goes off to find ... (*CO/DA* pp. 79–80)

And then Olson interrupts himself to say: "We were the last 'first' people, we have the advantage ... The American–Sumerian hoop is a true uroboros."

A passage in Kenneth McRobbie's memoir in *Minutes* #6 seems to bring this subject to a focus. He recalled an occasion on which Olson "showed a defensiveness, masked by indirectness, concerning the word 'socialism,' retreating into generalities about 'the polis' and Sumerian collectivism" (p. 13). McRobbie may have meant this as a reproach, but it made me go back to the place where Olson is not defensive, where he says once and for all (and doesn't keep repeating himself thereafter) what he sees as the value in Sumer:

> … from 3378 BC (date man's 1st city, name and face of creator also known) in unbroken series first at Uruk, then from the seaport Lagash out into colonies in the Indus Valley and, circa 2500, the Nile, until date 1200 BC or thereabouts, civilization had ONE CENTER, Sumer, in all directions, that this one people held such exact and superior force that all peoples around them were sustained by it, nourished, increased, advanced, that a city was a coherence which, for the first time since the ice, gave man the chance to join knowledge to culture and, with this weapon, shape dignities of economics and value sufficient to make daily life itself a dignity and a sufficiency.

This is from Olson's "The Gate and the Center" (*Collected Prose* p. 170). And with this sense of social morality in mind and Sargon's injunction that "the guardianship of the earth is the ruler's especial province," Olson looks to the future:

> I have this dream, that just as we cannot now see & say the size of these early HUMAN KINGS, we cannot, by the very lost token of their science, see what size man can be once more capable of, once the turn of the flow of his energies that I speak of as the WILL TO COHERE is admitted, and its energy taken up. (p. 172)

With McRobbie's prodding, we can see that the "archaic postmodern" is possibly a way of saying whatever it is that will provide the foundation for a world without greed. The fresh start that the "archaic postmodern" proposes is a regaining of "that fantastic condition of the human race when everything mattered" (*Muthologos* II.166).

When Tom Clark quoted the line "What does not change / is the will to change" he said (p. 147) that it "was to become a rallying cry for a generation of poets soon to follow up on Olson's bold cultural challenge." It would have been gratifying to have had the full evidence for that assertion. I hope it is, and will continue to be, true.

20
The First *Maximus* Poem

It might be thought perfectly obvious that "I, Maximus of Gloucester, to You," the first of the *Maximus* poems, began in Olson's letter to Frances Boldereff of 17 May 1950. Isn't its inception there right before our eyes? In the second paragraph (see *CO/FB* p. 335: and the facsimile of the letter below) Olson declares himself scared that he might never write another poem after "The Morning News":

> It is the craziest sort of feeling, this, of not being able to match the done! (I suppose this plane is the sex of writing art, the underpart, the nervousness because love is not born. One loves only form, and form only comes into existence when the thing is born. And the thing may lie around the bend of the next second. Yet, one does not know, until it is there, under hand.

Clark (p. 166) supposes—and it is a very reasonable deduction from internal evidence—that Olson was, at this point in the letter, moved to stop and turn his last few sentences into verse, gliding right there and then into:

> the thing may lie
> around the bend of the nest
> second

—where, Clark conjectures, Olson hit the *s* key instead of *x*, accidentally turning "next" into "nest," and then, Clark's hypothesis goes, deciding to retain the typo: "From the 'nest' mischance issued a key image: 'the bird! the bird!'" which then immediately got him to the seagulls of Gloucester:

> o Anthony
> of Padua sweep low and bless the roofs,
> the gentle steep ones on whose ridge
> gulls sit …

And so on for the rest of that page of the letter and another full page after that. This theory proposes that Olson composed the poem impromptu on the typewriter without pause.

But nothing in the Boldereff correspondence nor in this letter in particular would make it natural or compelling for Olson to turn to Gloucester as a subject. The better presumption is that the Gloucester lines were already written. Olson had had a request from Vincent Ferrini in Gloucester on 3 May 1950 for a contribution to his proposed magazine to be called *Voyager*. George Butterick was of the opinion that the poem was written "as a letter to Vincent Ferrini" (*Guide* p. xxx). Olson himself confirmed it in a letter of 2 July 1950 to Ferrini (*Origin* #1 p. 61) when he said that Ferrini had "invoked" the poem from him. In the title "I, Maximus of Gloucester, to You" the "you" are Ferrini and like-situated New Englanders (the swordfisherman, for one, is directly addressed in the poem). Butterick believed that an already existing poem to Ferrini was being quoted to Frances Boldereff (*Guide* p. xxxi). This puts a different perspective on the composition question.

The matter would be easily settled if there existed in the Storrs file a holograph first draft to Ferrini that was obviously prior to the letter to Boldereff; but there isn't. In spite of that lack of evidence I choose to think that Olson would have already put together some lines about Gloucester after Ferrini's request of 3 May and that they were on his desk as he wrote to Frances on 17 May. However, they would not, I surmise, have contained any talk of love. The thrust of the Gloucester ur-poem would be political. The letter to Boldereff is, then, an act of fusing together the assertion about love which had come up in the letter and the feeling for polis which Ferrini's request had invoked.

In other words, the Lady of Good Voyage was already there in a Gloucester poem for Ferrini's magazine *Voyager* and was not a representation of his muse, Frances Boldereff. I do not think that the reference was "coded for translation" onto the level of the poet's current amatory interest (Clark p. 167). Anyway, the love in the poem is not love of woman or "any romantic thing" (as Olson put it in the last few lines of the poem) but love of form, especially the form of a city. At the same time, Olson might never have been able to use the word "love" if he had not had Frances to say it to in just the way he does say it: "the nervousness because love [i.e. that which gives form to the poem] is not [yet] born."

wednesday may 17 1950

darling:
            my mind is aswarm (it is the coming back, to work, after the
affirmation of you, and the flooding of speech of two weeks, especially,
so far as speech goes, the change in my sounding of, verse: what would
have specially pleased you, was a lecture i gave on blake at black mountain, with that extraordinar-y passage at the end of his Lavater notes, as
depart, and the mental traveller, as text. Perhaps i could not have won
you with the Pound at Alabama, the passage which includes the lines,
"the ant's a centaur in his dragon world". But I do believe the Lear
passage on procreation, despite yr accurate objections to S. and woman,
would have caught yr attention. You see, that production at bmc last
summer turned out to be a teacher of me. I tried to join music & instrument to speech. And the upshot was, no. What I have gone on to do, is
to make verse, and its projection, self-contained. When you have a copy
of the summer issue of PNY, and have the chance to read the PRO verse in
print, - well, i have the feeling that is only scratching the skin of
it

       THE MORNING NEWS, strangely enuf, seems to project most - Creeley
will publish it in his 1st no. (do not know the name of his MAG), and will
review y&& x. And - of course - I am scared i shall never write another!
It is the craziest sort of feeling, this, of not being able to match the
done! (I suppose this plane is the sex of writing art, the underpart, the
nervousness because love is not born. One loves only form, and form only
comes into existence when the thing is born. And the thing may lie around
the bend of the next second. Yet, one does not know, until it is there,
under hand.

         the thing may lie
         around the bend of the nest
         second, time slain, the bird! the bird
         there, strong, thrust, flight! o kylix!

                                        o Anthony
         of Padua sweep low and bless the roofs,
         the gentle steep ones on whose ridge
         gulls sit, and depart,
                         the flake racks,
                                        o my city

         love is form, and cannot be without
         important substance, a weight
         say, 50 carats, each one of us
         our own goldsmith s cale: feather to feather added,
         and what is mineral, what is the curling hair, the string
         you carry in yr nervous beak, these
         make bulk, in the end, these
         are sum, my lady of
                         good voyage, in yr left arm
         no boy, but carefully scrolled wood, the delicate
         mast, a bow-sprit for
                         forwarding

         the underpart is, though stemmed, uncertain, is
         as sex is, as money is, facts
         to be dealt with, to be - the demand is - played
         by ear

Letter from Charles Olson to Frances Boldereff, May 17, 1950.
Box 184, Charles Olson Research Collection, Archives and Special Collections
at the Thomas J. Dodd Research Center, University of Connecticut Libraries.

                                which
by ear, but, that ‖e matters, thet which insists, will last

                                        o that, people of my city,
where shall you find how, where, when all is bill boards, when all
even silence is painted, not even a gull can be heard, when
sound itself is neoned in, when, on the hill, over the water,
she, who used to sing, when the harbor glowed black, gold,
when bells came like little boats over the oil slicks, and a man
slumped attentionless on the narrow bench against the pink shingles

                                        o sea city

one loves only form,
and form only comes
into existence when
the thing is born,

                        born of yourself, born
                        of hay and cotton struts
                        of the streets and weeds
                        xixxxxxxxx   in,
                        you've carried, o bird

                                                of a bone of a fish
                                                of a straw of will
                                                of ‖color, of a bell
                                                of yourself, torn

        love is not easy but how shall you know, New England, now
        that pejorocracy is here, now
        that streetcars, o Oregon, twitter
        in mid-afternoon, offend
        a black-gold loin? how shall you xxxxx strike, swordsman,
        the blue-red back, when, last·night, your aim
        was mu-sick, mu-sick, mu-sick,
        and not the cribbage game?

                        &Gloucester-man, weave
                        yr nerves and fingers ‖new,
                        American, braid,
                        with others, such
                        extricable surface
                        as faun and oral,
                        satyr, lesbos vase

                        kill, kill, kill, kill, kill
                        those
                        who advertise
                        you out

in, in, the bow-sprit, bird, the beak
in, the bend is, in, goes in, the form
that which you make, which holds, which is
the law of
object, what you are, what you must be, what throws up
the mast, the tender
mast!   the nest
                under the hand

I'm sure, frances, that, despite troubles, these webs which
spin, get spun across the space, the wild and at time intolerable space,
are flowers of life, are facts to bow to, gentle maitresse. Anyhow, I
give you the deepest sort of recognition, speak out from hidden islands
in the blood which, like jewels and miracles, you invoke. And I, as
hard-boiled instrument, as metal hot from boiling water, tell you, he
recognizes what is lance, obeys
the dance,
            mio chorego,

                        eros, eros eros!

                                        a kylix, sharles
                                        Olson

It opens, frances, thus :

                    I, MAXIMUS

                    Off-shore, by hidden islands in the blood,
                    like jewels and miracles, I, Maximus,
                    a metal hot from boiling water, tell you,
                    what is a lance, who obeys
                    the figures of
                    this dance

                    1

                    The thing.....

((and closes))

                    mast!

                    The nest,
                    I say,
                    under the hand,
                    as I see it over the waters,
                    from this place where I am,
                    where I hear, can still hear,
                    from where I carry you a feather,
                    as tho, sharp, I picked up a nerve,
                    in the afternoon delivered you
                    a jewel, it flashing more than a wing,
                    than any romantic thing, than memory, than place,
                    than anything other than that which you carry,
                    then that which is - call it a nest, call it
                    the next second -
                              / than that which you   / can do

The parting paragraph of the letter to Boldereff is:

> I give you the deepest sort of recognition, speak out from hidden islands in the blood which, like jewels and miracles, you invoke. And I, as hard-boiled instrument, as metal hot from boiling water, tell you, he recognizes what is lance, obeys the dance ... (*CO/FB* p. 338)

This became the opening cadence of the finished poem:

> Off-shore, by hidden islands in the blood,
> like jewels and miracles, I, Maximus,
> a metal hot from boiling water, tell you,
> what is a lance, who obeys
> the figure of
> the dance ...

That is, the end of the letter produced the verse which Olson then re-typed as a postscript to the letter: "It opens, frances, thus:"—which strongly suggests that at this point there is indeed a finished poem, the "it." And this "it" must have its existence on some sheet he is copying from, presumably the typescript at Storrs (Appendix B in *Minutes* #29), a fair copy of "I, MAXIMUS" dated "olson may 17 L" (the same date as the letter to Boldereff).

My speculation is that, grasping the moment, Olson turned immediately after signing the letter and typed out a revision of his Gloucester draft poem incorporating the way it had extended itself in the body of the letter. He has added a beginning based on what he has just said to Frances in salutation, and, moreover, an ending, which he also types for her to give her the now completed poem, albeit in parts (*CO/FB* p. 338). In short, we do not have the draft prior to the letter, but we do have the "may 17 L" typescript prior to the postscripts of the letter.

The remainder of the documents in the Storrs file help to fill out the subsequent variorum history of "I, Maximus of Gloucester, to You" beyond the sparse details in the Clark biography. The poem sent to Ferrini (receipt acknowledged in a letter from him dated 20 May 1950) was not the "may 17 L" typescript but one that Olson quickly sat down and typed afresh, slightly revised and signed "charles olson stage fort avenue gloucester, MASS" (the only address he had ever had in Gloucester and where his mother still lived). The reason this typescript exists in the Olson archive is that Ferrini, misunderstanding Olson, returned it on 7 July 1950. What Olson was asking in his letter of 2 July 1950 was that Ferrini release it for publication elsewhere now that *Voyager* was not going ahead. He explained he didn't need the typescript because he had a carbon. This carbon, too, is in the Storrs file (Appendix C of *Minutes* #29). He had already been looking it over, thinking it would go in a chapbook he was preparing for Richard Emerson of the Golden Goose Press. All the marks on it, mainly spacing adjustments with a smattering of other changes including an expanded title, were presumably done on 29 June 1950 when he typed out a fair copy and sent a carbon to Frances Boldereff. The top copy was sent to Emerson. It was subsequently returned, so that he had it to send to Robert Creeley on 11 September 1950. Soon after, when Cid Corman is starting up *Origin*, Olson asks Creeley to send Corman the poem. Creeley sits down and re-copies the poem, submitting it for *Origin* (*CO/RC* 3.84). Butterick in *Guide* (p. xxx) is therefore in error when he says it was "the heavily revised carbon copy that was sent to Corman for the first issue of *Origin*." Butterick's reference to the date 22 March 1951 as the *terminus ad quem* for the revisions on the heavily marked carbon is because the letter to Cid Corman of that date refers to it (*Guide* p. 5). But the situation there was that Corman had forwarded a request from Jack Sweeney of the Poetry Room at Harvard for some such thing for an exhibition, so Olson responded with the revised carbon, sending it through Corman as a sample of old worksheets. As we have seen, the revised poem had reached Corman long before via Creeley, and it had been accepted for *Origin* by 12 October 1950 (*CO/RC* 3.92). That Robert Creeley was an intermediary may account for the dropping of the word "important" in the second line of part two in the *Origin* printing. Until one sees the actual typescript Creeley sent to Corman (it may be at Texas) it would be unwise to state categorically that Creeley acted as an editor here. If we are right that Creeley received the top copy matching the carbon that went to Boldereff on 29 June 1950, he should certainly have typed the word "important," for the word is there. (We can relieve Creeley of complicity in the other textual problem, the "how" instead of "now" in the fourth line of part five. Olson himself made the typo in the Boldereff carbon.)

When it came to supplying the first ten *Maximus* poems to Jonathan Williams for the collection of 1953, Olson first put in the *Origin* version slightly revised. We can see this in the Storrs file: a typescript attached to a proposed title page, THE MAXIMUS POEMS 1–10. But then Olson had second thoughts. Clark tells us there was "extensive revision done before the typescript was sent on to Williams" (p. 234). He gives no details, not mentioning that it was enormously changed, the first five lines omitted altogether and the sections drastically rearranged so that the poem now begins, "By ear, he sd." (Appendix D in *Minutes* #29). Olson talked about his reasons in a letter to Creeley of 24 April 1953 (at Stanford):

> after i had the final mss done (with carbon for you and myself), it almost pulled me overboard! that is, i was so damned pleased i had a big one, i forgot the oars! but Con pulled me back. And for this week I have been rewriting, to pull in, and at the same time allow more line to whoever's interested.

To get the final book done "like a bloody canvas" (the letter continues) Olson used just the one sheet of bond in the final typing—"I was not filing the damned nails as much as one damn well does if it's a single piece of paper." This explains why there is no carbon of the final version sent to Jonathan Williams on 30 April 1953, now among the Williams papers at Buffalo. I have not studied this second typescript of *The Maximus Poems 1–10*, but judging by the printed result Olson made sure the word "important" was restored, and also banished the "how." This wrong-headed "how"—nothing more than a typo for "now"—is one of the few quarrels one can have with Butterick's text for the California *Maximus Poems* and should certainly be changed in some future edition. (I do not know, nor can I imagine, what the procedural mechanics might be for effecting such a change.)

How it came about that Olson reverted to the *Origin* ("Off-shore") version for the collected *Maximus Poems* (Totem/Corinth) of 1960 has not to my knowledge been divulged. He put the "By ear" version into Don Allen's anthology, *New American Poetry 1945–1960,* published by Grove Press in May 1960, but for *The Maximus Poems* only a few months later in November 1960 he had made the switch. The one intervening event that might have made a difference was the publication of Ed Dorn's *What I See in the Maximus Poems* (Migrant Press) around May 1960. Dorn spoke exactly to this point—he was, of course, reading *The Maximus Poems 1–10* version:

> And the low quarter exists for me in the first line of all: "By ear, he sd/" To me it is simply a false preamble to a work which I feel vastly, and subsequently doesn't comprise the remaining substance of the poem.

At a time when Olson had had (except from Robert Duncan) very little feedback, Dorn's comment here might had a greater impact than would normally be expected. The result, anyway, is there, in Olson's restoration of the first version of the poem in all later editions. I cannot but agree with the decision. The first version was, as we have seen, hardly an organic growth, more of a grafted plant; but the "By ear" version was pruned in a most severe way during a nervous push to get out the *1–10* volume.

Butterick in his *Guide* took the "By ear" version to be the original and the "Off-shore" version to be revised from it (p. 5). This error was due to an uncritical reading of Jonathan Williams's note at the end of the Totem/Corinth edition (1960) where he refers to the edition's "revised first *Letter*." By this, however, Williams was only stating that a *different* version from the *1–10* volume had been substituted by the author; Williams assumed it was a *later* revision, not remembering that the *Origin* version was the prior one. That this must be so I pointed out in an article, "Charles Olson: Posthumous Editions and Studies (Part 2)" *West Coast Review* (January 1981) p. 39. In *Editing THE MAXIMUS POEMS* (Storrs: University of Connecticut Library, 1983) Butterick rectified the error (p. 5).

21
"Symposium on Writing"

Under the above title Richard Wirtz Emerson published in his magazine *Golden Goose* (Ser. 3 No. 2 [Autumn 1951] pp. 89–96) what appears to be a round-table discussion involving William Carlos Williams, Kenneth Patchen, Leslie Woolf Hedley, Henry Rago and Charles Olson, with Emerson asking the questions they answer. A headnote explains:

> Early in 1950, the Editors started assembling notes by poets on several aspects of their craft. In August while making some record-ings of Dr Williams' poetry for broadcast on the weekly poetry program "Voices" (prepared and presented by R W Emerson for Station KCSU in Columbus), the questions on which the original symposium was based were used while recording a special discussion program with Dr Williams. Hence, the questions for the present symposium are partial transcription of that program (broadcast 7th October 1950).

Anyone casually reading this would assume that what follows it in the *Golden Goose* is some kind of edited discussion. It certainly has the customary format of one, the speakers' names followed by what they say, Emerson putting to them five questions on how they write. It is something of a surprise, therefore, to discover from the exchange of letters between Olson and Emerson (at Storrs) that there was never any such discussion, and that the answers were gathered from each poet separately and amalgamated in a simulation of a symposium broadcast.

As a matter of fact, this discovery is something of a relief, for Olson's answers had seemed extremely inappropriate as part of a discussion: very irreverent and, if voiced in such company, quite drunken, one might have felt. For instance, the first question as printed is: "What would you say about the mental and physical condition of the poet. What is his condition when he writes his best work. Is he relaxed or tense, tired or refreshed,

alone or …?" William Carlos Williams's answer is substantial and inform-
ative, ending with: "I think the psychic element must dominate, and your
body be secondary, but tense." Then Olson is represented as coming in
with an abrupt, "Who the hell cares?" Very rude indeed, except that in
reality he was not in the same room as Williams and had no knowledge of
Williams's answer to the question. He would never have been rude to his
revered predecessor. This "who the hell cares?" was his response to Emerson's question in a letter.

We might ask, then, why Olson wanted to be so abrupt with Emerson.
We get a hint in what we have already seen of Emerson—he is the kind of
person who could lump together these collected answers in order to fake
a discussion and put everybody in a false light. He had not of course done
this at the time the questions were asked, but he had done enough to
annoy Olson, whose prescience was working overtime. What Emerson had
actually done was behave like a fairly normal officious magazine editor.
Olson wrote in a letter to Robert Creeley of 29 June 1950 (at Stanford,
published in *Minutes* #59/60/61):

> (he is, rawthah, a horsesass, y'know, askin' me, for a photo,
> moind you, and be I a married man, and, may oi have yr signature,
> AND, wld you please answer, for another issue, along with 20 other
> wryters (right-arses), the foollwing questions:
> > I mental-emotional conditions most conducive verse?
> > II age most conducive?
> > III does verse, most, fr., mental a/o spiritual
> > > happiness a/o unhappiness
> > > discontent a/o frustration
> > > awyew wayew ayeweya?
> > IV is, 1st draft, the end of it—er do you reeeeee-pairrrrrrr?
> > > flats, perhaps   Or do you aaaaaa aaaBANDON
> > > yrrrrrrrrrrrr work?
> > V IS A POEM BORN, or DO YOU SHITE IT OUT?
> keeeee-
> RICESTTTTTTTTT
> > but (as you would, I'll take care of the latter.

Olson did take care of it on 7 July 1950, telling Frances Boldereff in a
letter of the same day (manuscript at Storrs):

> got off to emerson olson bib., and answers to his questions on, the
> craziest goddamn things you every saw, (you'll see my answers if he
> publishes 'em), and no photo, refused, no info on me, no: all that
> crap is calculated to distract attention from the JOB DONE.

In other words, in answering Emerson the way he did, Olson was trying to arrest the whole process of turning poets into well-behaved marketable personalities.

Below are presented the questions Emerson actually asked in a letter of 27 June 1950 (now at Storrs)—he rephrased some of them in the printing of the mishmash. "There is no real hurry," Emerson wrote in the letter, "except that the large number of people involved makes it difficult for me to know when I've got all angles covered—plus getting all contr's blended together in a uniform format—so while I dont like pushing anyone on such a thing, yr early reply wd be a big help (plus the fact it wd insure spontaneity)." Yes, Emerson was doing his little magazine editor thing, thinking he could cajole his poets into being both prompt and lively. If Olson's answers appear uncouth in manner, it is because he wants to rebuff Emerson's expectation that he can get everybody to cooperate. Olson was not about to perform like a trained seal.

> I. What is the mental and physical condition most conducive to writing a poem?
>
>> Who the hell cares? Sd Fred the Grrrrreat: every man must save himself as best he can.
>
> II. From your own experience, what wd you say about the age (years) most conducive to writing poetry?
>
>> Haven't the faintest idea. The question is an altogether different one: WHEN you have anything to SAY. Take a good squint at one, Arthur Rimbaud. And get on with it, bro., get on with it.
>
> III. Does poetry come from mental and/or spiritual happiness or unhappiness (discontent, frustration, etc)?
>
>> God help us. Just stay sane. But not like Goethe, o, no, NOT at such a price. Better be Holderlin (or Christopher Smart), if that's what you have to pay. Anyhow, avoid all such nonsense of da da de da. You will, anyway, if you're putting it out. And for the rest, anybody else? Let it go Hugo: "l'humanite, c'est l'infirmite."
>
> IV. Is a first draft final—or are there revisions and repairing, etc.— if so, how much?—the business of a poem not being finished but abandoned.
>
>> Nobody's g.d. business. Not *how*, or *who* made it, but WHAT IS IT, when it's staring you right in the puss.

V. By its nature, is the writing of a poem spontaneous or premeditated (a poem born or made—do you "sit down and write a poem")?

Letz uz put it zis way:
> "Iz it a poem   Or was it shited out"
> And behave accordingly, writer or reader.
> Thank you.

When *Golden Goose* Ser. 3 No. 2 finally came out in March 1952 Olson wrote to Creeley about "Symposium on Writing" and its "damn twisting of me":

> you will recall the nonsense two years ago: what goose does is cut up my answers (smert, to begin with—hate them, so goddamned smert) & destroy whatever point they had which was their close slangness working over against all his own pietism (*CO/RC* 9.174).

The danger is that literary history might take "Symposium on Writing" at its own face value. To be sure, Olson was being "smert" with Emerson, but the fake discussion format makes Olson appear downright rude far beyond any intention. Hopefully, the piece will never be reprinted. Clark did not mention it. Since it puts Olson in a bad light, Clark's restraint is surprising.

22
Black Mountain—II

When Olson got established at Black Mountain College back from the Yucatan in 1951, did he give himself free rein as an intellectual bully? This is the impression Clark seems to want to leave with us: Olson as "the forceful, opinionated Strong Man" (p. 209). Clark calls on the testimony of Ed Dorn, who "shrewdly" points out Olson's problem, as a teacher, with democracy: "He got his method from his predecessors, Pound, Eliot, and they were all such fascists" (quoted p. 209). On the contrary, Olson got his method by reading like mad and thinking things out for himself. His personality he got from his father, stubborn at times, but mainly good-humored. As for the classroom, have we forgotten the days when the teacher was assumed to know more, and know it better, and make no bones about it? "Opinionated," I grant; opinions about everything. For instance:

> … the performances of this extraordinary pianist, David Tudor, who arrived Friday (he is here as Litz' accompanist, but he knocked her evening right out of her hands by playing Schoenberg's Opus 23 as the 1st no of the evening so beautifully that nothing else mattered, even Litz's fine 1st dance, Part of a Suite for a Woman, and Harrison's own several pieces for piano (very clear and delicate stuff, what i wld think are probably the equivalents of Bill Merwin or Larry Richardson's verse—those most able Neo-Classicists—who are more able than the Intermitters, Lowell (who is a bore), Berryman (who has a head like brilliant embroidered drawers), Jarrell (whose brains are all he has—peculiar how, all of these, get more like Karl Shapiro every year … (*CO/RC* 7.20)

But wouldn't any of us have given anything to have been in the classroom the day after that Tudor-Litz performance to hear these same opinions? And compiling an "Index" of forbidden works is fun, great pedagogy, especially when "inscribed as law," as Clark claims they were on the basis of his interview with Robert Duncan (p. 209). Teachers have to be dogmatic to give students something to exert themselves over. It isn't as though this was a college where anyone was giving out F grades to ruin careers. No, it was just the great freewheeling Black Mountain that Olson's directorship produced in 1951–56. Clark, however, wants to see not the fun, but rather a certain meanness in it all:

> Dismissed to the Index ... were the experimental all-black and all-white canvases of student painter Robert Rauschenberg. Rauschenberg was not "destined for fame," nor to rank among the "truly great" (p. 209)

In his attempt to make Olson look foolish about Rauschenberg, Clark may have got a winner—or anyone might think so, until one consults his source, Mildred Harding's memoir "My Black Mountain," which has been excerpted in *Black Mountain College: Sprouted Seeds,* ed. Mervin Lane (1990):

> As Rauschenberg labored among his collages ... the Mountaineers—delighted with his revolutionary originality—debated. Would he be truly great? Was he destined for fame? "No," said Olson. "Yes," said John [Adams], and compared Bob with Mozart. (p. 298)

This sounds more like a free-for-all than an imposed Index.

As for the serious work of the college, we are given a glimpse of Olson being "kept on his toes" in faculty meetings:

> Adversaries included a pair of natural scientists, biologist Victor Sprague and anthropologist John Adams. Sprague on one notable occasion hit a nerve in expressing his distrust of Olson's autocratic teaching approach, stating flatly, "I'm not convinced you believe in the many." (Clark p. 212)

Sprague's comment was not about Olson's teaching approach; the context indicates a more general political meaning. Clark's sole source here is a letter to Creeley of 1 December 1951:

> ... an incident last night with new protozoologist here whom I like very much, a guy named Sprague, definitely their best addition academically, simply that he is a superb research man (in parasites which immobilize crawfish & shrimp) and the sort of sincere man who suffers, thereby, a proper naiveté ... Sprague was looping from corn whiskey by dinner time, and also had been dragged down, suddenly, from the rear by the death of a friend, a man named Carl Behre (Bare-ey), owner of the Pelican Coal & Ice Company of N.O., and brother—this seems to be where Sprague came to know him—

of Elmer Behre, zoologist, at LSU. Ok. Now Behre's widow had written Sprague offering her husband's library to BMC—a library of Marxist economics, plus a good deal on China & India. What Sprague wanted to know was, could he, in good conscience, accept the gift … "It all hinges on you. I've lost a lot of sleep over you. I'm not convinced you believe in the many …" (*CO/RC* 8.214–15)

Sprague is wondering if BMC and its current Rector are sympathetic enough to be worthy to receive his late friend's Marxist library. Sprague would not be basing his doubts on Olson's classroom behavior; he probably hadn't seen any of it.

As for the other "adversary," John Adams, Clark says he "would more than once insert deflating commonsense interpolations into Olson meeting-monologues":

> In a November meeting, for example, Olson was rather long-windedly calling for the immediate replacement of all prior educa-tional concepts by a completely revolutionized form of pedagogy adapted to the altered condition of post-modern man when Adams interjected dryly that he "doubted anybody here knows what Mr. Olson is talking about." (p. 212)

Clark's source here is the secretary's minutes of the BMC faculty meeting of 21 November 1951 (published in *OLSON* #2 pp. 16ff). These are, as is customary, a précis of people's remarks, and therefore there can be no way of knowing if Olson was longwinded.

Adams did not interject anything, dryly or otherwise. It was Max Dehn who spoke after Olson, then Lou Harrison after that, and Max Dehn again. It was only then that John Adams made his contribution:

> Mr. Adams said that he [Harrison] and Mr. Dehn were talking about what education ought to be and that Mr. Olson was talking about what education is, the idea of Nietzsche to have education grow out of and be involved with vital life experiences; that the final and best synthesis would be when both come together, the above and the abstracting and generalizing; that he doubts if anybody here knows what Mr. Olson is talking about.

Considering the support that Adams had given to Olson previously, I take his final remark (as taken down by the secretary) to be one of sadness that the Black Mountain faculty (or some of them; not, I think, himself) persist in resisting Olson's views.

There is a second exchange between a supposed wild Olson and a cautionary Adams, presented by Clark:

> And when in another meeting Olson hit a similar risky note, declar-
> ing it essential "to go blind in education as in other areas," Adams
> put in succinctly that such policies were bound to land the college
> in "chaos." (p. 212)

Olson in the meeting explained (as Clark doesn't) that by the words "going
blind" he meant merely that "you don't make a priori definitions of what
you intend to accomplish" (Duberman paperback p. 359). Rather than
Adams being "succinct" (as Clark has to have him, to be a contrast to
"long-winded" Olson), he is in the minutes of the meeting credited with
longer contributions than Olson. The whole passage, as presented by
Duberman from the faculty records, represents a serious discussion with
commonsense exhibited by both parties.

To continue with our look at Black Mountain in 1951, clearly for Olson the
most momentous occurrence was the birth of Kate Olson on 23 October.
Clark makes it seem a disappointment for Olson that the baby wasn't a boy:

> His most powerful wish was to see her produce a son. Confiding to
> Creeley his anxious hopes for a boy-child, he added that among
> the potential names he'd been pondering were Obadiah (after the
> Old Testament prophet, descendant of David, majordomo of the
> House of Ahab) and the simple patronymic "Son of Olson." Connie,
> in her turn, was made so acutely aware of his preference for a male
> offspring that upon emergence from anesthesia after giving birth
> to a healthy infant in the Asheville hospital on October 23, her first
> words were "A girl—how terrible." (p. 213)

Clark has certainly misread his source here (even the date, which is a letter
to Creeley of 31 July 1951 not 3 September 1951). Olson is quite expressly
open to a girl child; he is just worried about the name question:

> in fact, the lad or the lass inside has just taken another rise—is up
> again against her chest—what i figure, is, the rise for, the drop!

> damn nice business, this, of, to have Con having this wonder bean!
> but how to name it (Ann) is, a problem when, the name is
> O L S O N (nothing goes with such, it is itself a false patronymic,
> because, son of. So, I sd, if boy, why not, Son of Olson. And be done
> with it! The result was, Obadiah, says somebody! O O . And if girl
> (which, I cannot bring myself to cast my heart—it would be ridic-
> ulous for me to interfere!—let it come, and if it comes girl, well, by
> god, wouldn't that be very nice (or as nice, in any case, what
> matters to me is, how good is IT, male or female? (*CO/RC* 7.34)

There is no "anxious hope for a boy-child" here. Obadiah was not his idea for a name, and "Son of Olson" was hardly serious. As for Connie's "a girl—how terrible," this was when she was coming out of ether, as Olson describes to Creeley immediately after the birth:

> Have just left Con, coming out of, the ether, and figure you two are the ones I want to have the news first
> "a girl—how terrible," says Con (& surely, figuring, I wanted, a boy—just because, I suppose, it is still assumed a boy is more important?
> Actually, as I am suddenly relaxed, it seems very beautiful—I saw the child first (that is, before Con), brought straight from the delivery room, and it is a very pleasant thing (I notice most sort of big feet—my hunch is, it looks like her mother, the skin, and, the head. (*CO/RC* 8.84–85)

The way Clark puts it ("The patriarch's evident disappointment over the interruption of the Olson male line" p. 213) is again an obvious misreading. Moreover, to make his point, Clark has to ignore "The Ring of," a gem of a poem, which was sent to Creeley ten days before, but which Olson always associated with Kate, anticipating a Venus birth.

Olson with Kate, early 1952.
Kate Olson Archive.

23
Olson's Automobile Accident and Other Matters of November 1952

Anyone reading Olson's letters to Connie during November 1952 when they were apart, Olson in the Washington house and Connie at Black Mountain with Kate, might be in awe of the intensity and incisiveness of the self-examination proceeding therein. Never was a separation so energetically conducted and so thoroughly written out! The clarity is of heroic dimensions. Olson's use of psychology (mainly Jung and Fenichel), especially mythology and dream analysis, pushes beyond all previous methodology. And the search for the truth is totally honorable.

It is to be regretted, therefore, that Clark once again cannot see as exemplary what should be obviously so to anybody. He recasts this crucial November 1952 into something rather tawdry and pitiable. For instance: "Absorbed in his personal campaign to become 'President of his own Disunited States,' on election day, November 4, he slept through most of the Eisenhower/Stevenson presidential contest" (Clark p. 230). This picture of a slothful Olson has not a grain of truth in it. Olson spent 4 November from 10 A.M. to 4 P.M. writing a sixteen-page letter to Connie, during which task, as he told her on page fifteen of the letter, he had to go throw up in the bathroom because of the tensions of the path he was leading himself on. But he continued, and wrote a two-page postscript before going to the post office. On returning he wrote another two pages in response to a letter which had arrived from Connie. In this latter note he expresses himself "almost happy, to have said so much—found out so much—about myself   still shaky in the legs from the vomiting   will not eat (having supper with Peter & Joan,—taking them out to King's for the returns" (letter to Connie 4 November 1952). Clark has this as:

> At some point in the evening he went out to mail the letters to his wife, and on the way home stopped off to glance without much interest at the Eisenhower celebrations on a friend's television set. (p. 231)

This is fiction. And it should be borne in mind that Clark has no source other than the very letters that we are also examining. Clark's fictional adaptation continues:

> Back at Randolph Place, he returned his attention to the business of self-analysis, producing the one piece of published writing to come out of this most introspective of times: "The Present Is Prologue," a brief note on his growing consciousness of the influence in his own life of those "founders who [lay] buried" there, his parents. The short essay served a double use, in extending his self-investigation a further step and as his response to a biographical questionnaire from a forthcoming reference work on twentieth century authors. He dispatched a copy to Connie to follow up on his election-night letters. (p. 231)

None of this happened on election night, which we can be confident Olson spent as we would expect him to, talking with Rufus King and other friends into the early hours. The autobiographical piece (to which George Butterick gave the title "The Present Is Prologue") was actually written two days later (6 November 1952) when a request arrived in the mail from the fellow Worcester poet Stanley Kunitz, who was compiling a First Supplement to his *Twentieth Century Authors* for the H.W. Wilson Company. In an introspective frame of mind already, Olson was able to type out a page-and-half right away and send it off, enclosing the carbon in a letter to Connie the same day: "I hope you tolerate it—even like it! For it was fun to rush in on and do, without further fart-thee-well! The only trouble is, it stole the time to go more into the holes in my soles!" (letter 6 November 1952).

The uppity tone of these last remarks of Olson's is enough in itself to refute Clark's picture of total gloom. Phrases like "totally devastated" and "his disgust with himself" are Clark's deliberate mistaking of what was going on during this period of separation and reevaluation.

As a further example, we can take the unfortunate automobile accident of 17 November 1952. Clark describes it as follows:

> His disgust with himself, however, could only lead him deeper into destruction. Cruising the city streets in a distracted stupor, he ran over a young black girl who seemed to appear out of nowhere in front of his car. (p. 231)

This makes Olson sound culpable, driving in a psychologically impaired state. But this is more Clark fiction. The facts are otherwise. To begin with,

Olson did not run over the girl. Olson described the incident in a letter to Connie of 17 November 1952. (Again we might reiterate Clark has no other source than this very letter.)

> Had an ugly bizness coming home tonight from posting mail to you. A coloured girl, age 9, ran in front of me as I turned from Lincoln Rd into R st, and was knocked down when I braked. She was already going away when I got out. Refused to let me take her home—sd her mother would beat her! But two men I asked did follow her while I got the car out of the way—& was offered witness by a very decent guy who had missed her coming the other way.
>
> Anyhow, took her & her mother to Children's—same place, same room, & some of the same nurses. That woman doctor handled her—& did a find job, even X-rayed her leg for sure. And nothing, thank God—just shook up, & sore.
>
> But god, what a dirty feeling—one I have dreaded the thought of as long as I have driven a car.
>
> The cops came to the hospital, and I have to appear in court a week from Wednesday. All seems clear, & the only little fuss was eye-brows over a D.C. resident, with a Va. licence, & a N.C. car. Rufus is standing by.
>
> I already have a release on further liability from the parents (a nice couple with another daughter 5 living in a basement (2 rooms) off Quincy Place. I hope you don't mind—I heard the girl tell the cop she only had one doll. So I gave her the one Santini gave Kate—just to take the curse off the whole business for her.

Is this accurately summarized in Clark's account? I cannot think so. "The accident left him in a shaken state," Clark writes, "and he had to call on Rufus King, a radical lawyer friend of Caresse Crosby's who had helped him out in the past, to get him through a court hearing. Fortunately, the victim's injuries were not serious, and her parents agreed to sign a waiver releasing him from liability. Relieved, he pressed on the child a doll given him by friends as a Christmas present for Kate" (p. 231). Every sentence here is designed to take something away from Olson, distorting his sensitivity and warmth in the gift of the doll (Clark tries to exacerbate the implied offense by calling it a Christmas present), and his care to get the girl to the hospital even though there were no signs of any injuries. (Why does Clark use the word "injuries" when there weren't any?) Rufus King had become Olson's friend as much as Crosby's. It was with King that Olson had spent election night. And there was actually no court hearing as such to get through. Perhaps Clark had not read the passage in a later letter to Connie (23 November 1952):

> Due in court Wednesday on the accident. Don't expect any trouble. Rufus has a lawyer on the inside with his eye out. He tells me it isn't anything but a counter deal—no judge—the Corporation Counsel's Office. And I am protected by two witnesses who were very damn nice to come forward and tell how the girl shot out.

Clark doesn't give any sense of Olson's humane concern. If he had read how this passage continues he would surely have had to do so:

> I visited her and her family again. And she was skipping, & altogether back to normal. Really, it was all damned damned lucky—I braked so fast I can't believe it. It was coming from black to light faster than a light goes on. Funny thing about that sort of shock: how it drops you down into the very pavement of life. Stops all personal stuff in its tracks. Widens out. And makes one just look out from the place with the biggest sort of eyes. What a thin ice we skate on with machines. And what a destructible thing a human body is. The girl's legs & arms—her name was Geneva Lewis—were such thin stems. Her parents are poor now (they both work). But one can see them 9 yrs ago as even poorer—& the mother was telling me how the other daughter (age 5) weighs more than Geneva! Yet, all she got was bruises!

Olson adds, as any of us might, "I drive different!"

Yes, here is an "allegory of a poet's life," indeed—though Clark doesn't utilize it as such. In a sense, Olson had knocked Connie down. And no matter how quickly he had braked and no matter how lucky the escape, the relationship could never be the same again. He would drive differently from now on. Clark cannot see this parallel because he is too busy portraying the accident as self-absorbed carelessness. The truth is that both in the case of the accident and with Connie, Olson was, in a crisis, most alert and entirely caring.

We must look at the trial separation more closely, if only to dispute any accusation of duplicity. It was a couple being exceedingly honest with each other. There is a holograph note in the Connie Olson papers at Storrs which, I believe, was either given to Connie or was a record of what was said to her about a visit to Frances Boldereff in New York on the weekend of 11–12 October 1952. Connie didn't have to guess, as Clark proposes

(p. 229); Charles told her. Or maybe she guessed, and then he told her. Anyway, this is what the note says, undated but conjectured to be Monday 14 October 1952:

> shall he tell you, flat, that he spent the weekend with that dame— & that he intends to take Rufus up on a free ride to NY this weekend, to spend another with her
>
>   (& telling you just, that, if he doesn't tell you, he'll never get over the sense of block with you—that to slap you in the face is a cruelty a man seems to be born to do to his woman

This frankness, I deduce, is what caused Connie to take herself and Kate off from Washington to Black Mountain.

Connie's letters of this period are missing (having been returned to her at her request) but at least twenty-five of Olson's, some of them very long, are extant at Storrs (having been returned to him). They indicate deep challenges for Olson. He begins as "a proud fucking male" in what is probably the first of them (though the initial two pages, and consequently the date, are missing); he will "fight off any thought that I have failed you, that I have failed our marriage, that I do wrong by Kate & you":

> I know you are right, too, that work is the answer. Yet I have to be extremely careful. As you know, I have so often used it, like personality, to skip by—to put off—locking with life. So I am going in like a bull on eggs. And feel confident. But will be slow, very slow.

Olson, 27 October 1952, in reply to Connie's first letter to him, gets a first sense of light:

> When you sd yesterday you saw me as now engaged with my unconscious for the 1st time, it fitted. I'm sure you are right. All the light bursting in on me this fall looks like it … And repeat: can use every light you throw. And wld rather have it direct from you, who loves me, than from anyone, anything, least of all books, even Jung's.

Clark is right to pick out Olson's description to Cid Corman of what is going on: "It is one of those central, crucial engagements some men do, I suppose, walk up to (in the dark, &, I guess, in the middle of life) Anyhow, it is wholly exclusive, & excluding—allows nothing in but itself. And for the first time in my life I am finding out what it is to have a wife, and friends" (*CO/CC* 1.300). But Clark does not follow the rise and fall of the works and days of this separation and the make-over that it, to some degree, was. Clark merely calls it "the tracking-down of his 'UNC,' or unconscious, the final quarry in his self-investigative hunt" (p. 230). This collection of letters will one day be published and will do what extracts cannot do: show what it took for Olson to worry a new self out of temporary loneliness.

About two weeks of Olson's introspection had gone by when Connie produced a change of momentum in the letters, which Clark describes as follows:

> She proceeded to offer a history of her unspoken doubts and frustrations in the relationship, culminating in the crushing—for him—revelation that as a result of her failure to be made emotionally "complete" by him, she has sought fulfillment in a secret love affair with a Washington artist friend of theirs.
>
> A totally devastated Charles retroactively experienced the jealous husband's gamut of emotions, becoming first irrationally angry ("This is the end. ... this proves all women are betrayers"), then remorseful and self-pitying, finally abject and conciliatory. (p. 231)

There is such a mass of letters and variety of pushes that one can hardly blame Clark for being unable to summarize it all properly in a paragraph. Rather, one might blame him for even trying. The only thing that would get it straight would be to present Olson's letters in full. The letter of 9 November in response to Connie's revelation was fifteen pages, followed by a 9–10 November letter of four pages, a 10 November letter of eighteen pages, 11 November two pages, 12 November two pages, 13 November twenty-two pages, 14 November nine pages, 15 November fifteen pages (see *Selected Letters* #59), 16 November five pages, 17 November seven pages, 21 November four pages, 23 November fourteen pages, 24 November five pages, 26 November eight pages, 29 November eight pages, 1 December eighteen pages, 5 December thirty-two pages. And then Connie called him and he joined her in Black Mountain. The full edition of these letters will show a "gamut of emotions" all right; but saying, as Clark does above, that Olson ends "abject and conciliatory" is to force a false plot-line on the sequence. The main mood is determination. For example, on 11 November 1952, two days after the supposed bombshell from Connie, Olson wrote an "Announcement":

> I don't care if I never write another fucking poem
> > I am going to know
> who I am.

In the end, it was Connie who was worn down. Olson told Corman, when he got back to Connie and Black Mountain, that she had had "a breakdown from total exhaustion" (*CO/CC* 1.310). He said it was probably "because of weaning Kate." It was also, I should think, from having to take on all the weight of Olson's letters. Despite his best intentions, he had been unable not to be overwhelming.

Olson with Connie and Kate, December 1952.
Kate Olson Archive.

24
WCW

In Miscellaneous file #147 at Storrs there is the following note to Flossie Williams, wife of William Carlos Williams and, in March 1936, newly a widow:

My dear Mrs Williams

I have written and written to you about Bill, and kept not sending them fearing you'd think them effusive, or more than you might want to pay attention to, now. But they were attempts at expressing to you my own sense of him and I think I'll enclose them, for you to throw away if you wish, or if it should be any relief or pleasure to read more about him, then certainly these do go on.

Please share my sympathy with your sons as well.

Charles Olson.

The fact that this manuscript is at Storrs means that, after all, Olson did not send it, nor the two letters he had written, which are also extant there. The first of the two was printed in *Selected Letters* (#97); the second I transcribe below, for the record and as evidence for gaining a true measure of his relationship with WCW. For he is here making every effort to be without guile, and thus supplying primary material. Perhaps we can detect undercurrents. That the letters were never send may alert us.

28 Fort Square
March 6th 1963

My dear Mrs. Williams,

Your husband was a brother/father for me, a man I felt, without ever thinking about it. It was one of the reasons, I do believe, that I was never able to say anything "interesting" about him, at least in print—and wanted to so badly, because I loved him so: in fact did once write a 14 page letter (Yes I did, that *once* have plenty to say) to Louis Martz. You probably will recall his "Road to Paterson", and he called Bill Pelagian, but meant the British Bishop who was against original sin, and I thought Martz meant Pelasgus the Culture-Hero of the Peloponnesus, and I wound up like Walter Johnson to tell him why I thought Bill wasn't! But fortunately caught up that I had made a mistake, & never sent the letter.

It was like that time in your living room when both you and Bill called me on my remark about him in the Mayan Letters, that he didn't know from nothing about what a city is. And I'm sure you will never forgive me for saying that—or were at all persuaded by my talking about the electric light pole out your front window.

The point was, Bill, for me, was not an influence but a truth—a living figure like Kit Carson or somebody whom nobody will ever again be able to be in the world once he was without having to go around, peer at, dig down under, even to be mad and crazy and cut into the soil around him—even to strike with a shovel his roots, and he living right then and there. Do forgive me that, for I'm sure that must have been what I was doing and it was part of ignorance for sure but a struggle with him because I felt him so close—it was "family" (if you will hear that that other way—like he himself, I should imagine, and the things he did for me: the way (like) he writes about Sam Houston (?) (He makes Houston feel like a governing hero for himself.)

He did things for me, as you know, that no one else did—and I'm not sure they weren't of the same kind, that is, that he also felt some funny involvement which wasn't comfortable, or as usual in such "literary" matters—either that, or I was never a friend, in the sense he had so many, or a follower (and I mean that highly, like some much younger men as Creeley say and now so many more.

I always had "trouble" with Bill—and I think he with me, and I should like you to know it from my side anyway, because I did love him and hate it that he has had to die. I also am proud I said to you that day in the restaurant near your house, when you and I had a chance to talk, that I do think the Beauty Burden of Loveliness and more of those stories are the *greatest stories ever written* bar none, especially the Burden of Loveliness.

And his *rhymes*—only recently I saw for the first time (in Sorrentino's article on Duncan, Bill's extraordinary (like Euripides) four or five lines on America the golden—the Altgeld—the rhymed damned! (That's not right but that's not the point.)

I hope you yourself are all right and will take care of yourself. Please share my love and sympathy with your two sons (whom i have never met) and if at any time there should be any least thing you might have reason to call on me for I hope I can do it. Bill was a hero for me, in so many words I'm sure. That's what it is all about. He is a hero. And it is very hard to think of any man who was a hero as Bill was for a very long time—and, when a man is a hero, there never was or will be another exactly like him. It is different than the difference in other men. In a hero the difference is that he is a hero. I am thinking of his own provocation in writing the American Grain—or that piece which poured belief into my own younger veins, Against the Weather, in the second Twice-A-Year—with its emphasis (still not known to me) on St John of the Cross.

If anybody in the world today walked right out into what they used to call the Elysian field it was Bill, Monday—and I pray that you will feel nothing else but that that is so even though I know it is hardly possible that anything feels that way so easily or forever. But isn't it one of the things about him that some such picture as that fits him in particular even if everything he ever did was to cut such stuff right back to where it was and sat and say it his way as against the world?

Well, he was my hero, and I always did feel this Pelasgia–Houston thing about him.

> Love to you who loved him,
> and comfort and belief now that
> everything he did is done,
> Charles Olson

PS. "Excuse" me. I've re-read this letter—and it all sounds a little grand, but I know (like I say) that I have always "lived" more with Bill than I studied him or even read him, and I'd like to let it stand—simply for that one idea that he was a hero (there may not be anything particularly original about it, it occurs to me that almost anything I have read about Bill contains it, really—that he even sought to make himself such a center, that that's how he heard Valery Larbaud advise him to go back to America. But I am in this position: I'd like you to hear it from me in particular that in the emotion of learning last night he had died, and in the desire to speak to you in particular—to hope to console you and at the same time wipe away a sense I have that you don't trust me—I don't know that Bill did either! that this at least get said, and for the record, that I did love him, and this is the way, and that if I don't say it now, to you, it might not get said. And I want to say it. And I hope I hope and hope it will mean something to you.

This letter with its repetitions has dug a firm post-hole for Olson's flag of affection for WCW.

There had been squabbles, though the only face-to-face one was that mentioned in the letter. Olson in *Mayan Letters* had tried to pit his newly acquired vision of the archaic postmodern against the limited viewpoints of both Pound and WCW:

> date 1917, not only did Yurrup (West, Cento, Renaissance) go, but such blueberry America as Bill presents (Jersey dump-smoke covering same) also WENT (that is, Bill, with all respect, don't know fr nothing abt what a city is) (*Selected Writings* p. 84)

I suppose Olson meant by this that there was a range of polis that was outside Williams's ken, and that Williams should have known something was up when the power company had the right to put a street light in front of their window.

Clark brings up another squabble. Williams had written to Cid Corman about *Origin* 2 when it came out, saying he liked Creeley very much but that "he's very unformed … It depends on his intelligence, what that finally comes to find." Williams then adds a comment on Olson (as found in Butterick's notes in *CO/RC* 7.260):

> The intelligence is the crux of the matter in Olson's case also. What will he find. He's searching and he's making notes. He's got some good thoughts too, valuable thoughts, some of which I have already used but I'd like to see them a little more pulled together in firmer terms. I acknowledge that we're all searching, it's our present status in America. But we're the ones who've been destined to FIND.

This comment was passed on to Olson, who didn't rise to the bait in any extant letters to Corman, but made a very full response in his next letter to Creeley, 10 August 1951 (*CO/RC* 7.82), saying in part:

> GODDAMN IT—I wish the christ he hadn't written that letter. It sounds so fucking far back: all that goddamn close going on— apparently so discriminating—by the local of the instant he writes—and yet, who has been the most valueless enthusiast of our time but Bill? so much so, that when he did praise so extravagantly the PV thing, I had no final pleasure in it, because, he has praised too much.

There is more, much more, in this letter to Creeley, but we must stop and point out that Clark takes out of context the phrase "the most valueless enthusiast of our time," saying that it "shocked Creeley" (p. 208). Olson is not saying that Williams has no value. That would indeed be quite a shock. No, it's simply that Williams "has praised too much," too widely. Thus, even the "extravagant" praise of "Projective Verse" (and it certainly was extravagant, Williams putting the whole of the first part of the essay en bloc into his *Autobiography*) gave Olson no pleasure finally. In other words, Williams's enthusiasms, after so many of them, do not confer the value they would have if there were fewer of them. In that sense, and that sense only, he is a "valueless" enthusiast. Of all the ten important pages in this letter to Creeley, Clark picks on this one easily misunderstood phrase, implying that Olson reacts to criticism in a petty way.

Creeley's eight-page response of 16 August 1951, according to Clark, brought Olson to self-realization:

> Anger fading, he sheepishly acknowledged his reversion to an old bad habit, setting up a dispute with a father-surrogate merely to rouse his own oppositional energies. The Williams he was using to rev up his creative tensions was not a real person but a projective figment. "I honestly don't know *how to act* toward anyone," he admitted in some embarrassment. "What a goddamned little baby the Strong Man comes out!" (p. 208)

It is in a 23 August letter that we find the final two quotes of Clark's paragraph, but they are more than a page apart; Clark has conflated them to try to make plausible his idea that Olson is embarrassed.

True, Olson says that he was "using Bill ... just to find out how better how to use myself" (*CO/RC* 7.122), but he never says that he had reverted in his criticism of Williams to the old habit of setting up "a father-surrogate" just to oppose him. That's Clark's addition. And the bit about not knowing how to act with anyone is in a quite general passage, off to one side of the WCW discussion:

> It completely buggers me—always has. I honestly don't know how to act, toward any one, or any thing, except, to *shoot* myself—the only law I know is, that, energy, provokes, what I am interested in—what I *have* to do. And it has forever got me into nothing but confusion, & disappointment: bewilderment, as to what happens, what the response is, of persons, or things, how suddenly, usually, they are scared—wrongly charged—or repelled. (*CO/RC* 7.121)

What Clark picks out of this, i.e. that Olson doesn't "know how to act toward anyone," is quoted without the telling proviso: "except, to shoot myself" (i.e. to come on to people with maximum force). Olson is explaining why he is often bewildered in his dealings with people. But it is not, as Clark tries to say, a specific expression of embarrassment at having said things about Williams.

The second thing quoted by Clark as supposedly showing Olson's embarrassment is "What a goddamned little baby the Strong Man comes out!" This is not Olson talking about himself but about Hercules. He's remembering what WCW said of Creeley, that he was "unformed," and responds this way:

> The trouble is, I don't know when one ceases to be unformed (again, the peril, the damned business, in saying that, that, my mind knows, it surely is a sign—given our present premises—that I, myself, stay, unformed! Which is a risk (the risk of innocence, least of all!) I have, now, age 40, no alternative but to take! (I am thinking, knowing, what knocks, in the cellar, of a passage in Herodotus which has stirred me, keeps stirring me, of Herakles, in the arms of, some goddess—& how silly, & little & what a god-damned little baby the Strong Man comes out!) (*CO/RC* 7.122)

Of course, the analogy with Hercules is meant to reflect back on himself. But it cannot be (as Clark wants it to be) a *mea culpa* about WCW. It is part of a serious discussion about maturity, prompted by Williams's remark.

Further on the subject of Olson's attitude to WCW, we have to take up here the *contretemps* of Marjorie Perloff's article, "Charles Olson and the 'Inferior Predecessors': 'Projective Verse' Revisited" in *ELH* 40 (1973) pp. 285–306. It is strange that Clark makes no effort to deal with this attempt to undermine Olson's originality in "Projective Verse." The gist of Perloff's complaint is that Olson takes most of the essay from the ideas of William Carlos Williams and Ezra Pound, and then tries vainly to assert his independence by calling them "inferior predecessors." However, when we look at the phrase in context what appears to be insulting is discovered to be a very neutral attribution.

The phrase occurs in an Olson letter to Cid Corman of 23 November 1953. It occurs twice; the second occurrence helps us to see how it should be taken in the first. Olson is saying that he has chastised Corman before over his conduct as the editor of *Origin* magazine.

> I am not one to keep after a man. But you will recognize this letter as having inferior predecessors—at least two, one last year on Origin, a penny postcard; and another, three years ago, on the whole biz of how such a mag might live. (*CO/CC* 1.102)

It seems clear that here Olson has gone back to the root meaning of "inferior." He obviously does not mean that his previous two letters of complaint were of lesser quality. They stand below or underneath this latest one, as a scaffold; they give backing from the past, which can be considered a layer under the present.

Perloff does not quote in her article this paragraph with its neutral use of the adjective "inferior." It would certainly have blunted the effect. In the passage she quotes, Olson is made to seem arrogant and ungrateful in applying the adjective to Pound and Williams when talking about his own verse:

> I know what's missing in the music. But it's olson which ain't there, not Williams or Pound. And you shld know that's who is missing. Not these two inferior predecessors ... (p. 298 [Perloff's dots])

Christopher Beach in his *ABC of Influence* (California 1992) p. 117 has done useful service in pointing out that Perloff does not quote to the end of Olson's sentence, and that, if she had, the effect would have been quite different. Olson is saying that whatever his verse at present lacks it is because he has not risen up to his own potential self:

> ... it's olson which ain't there, not Williams or Pound. Not these two inferior predecessors—just as I am inferior, to myself! and predecessor, of myself! (*CO/CC* 1.102).

The complete quotation, as Beach says, "puts Olson's seemingly arrogant comment in perspective" (p. 117). Again Olson is using that neutral, non-judgmental "inferior." It indicates position. In the "Paris Review Interview" Olson talks of Pound and Williams as "vanes to my propeller who were about two inches astern of the vanes on my propeller" (*Muthologos* II.121). Olson's "inferior" self is a former self that he has climbed on top of, just as one climbs on top of any predecessor. Olson is not scorning Pound and Williams.

Christopher Beach does not suggest that Perloff has deliberately used the old debater's trick of quoting out of context to win a point. It seems to me that she has, displaying an animus that betrays itself in several other picayune ways. Olson occasionally uses a swear word in his letter to Corman; she talks of "a series of nasty expletives" (p. 298). She thinks that Olson's real "hurt" is due to Corman's putting a Williams poem first in *Origin* #10 and leaving Olson's poem to last (p. 297). I don't believe it.

To handle the more substantive question of plagiarism, Perloff splits the page into two columns and puts on the left-hand side a string of quotations from "Projective Verse" and on the other side quotations from Pound and Williams which are given the heading "Sources." This is what the *New Yorker* used to do when it had caught someone red-handed. Unfortunately in this case, with Clouseau-like finesse, Perloff gives as sources for "Projective Verse," finished in July 1950, passages that Olson could not possibly have seen at that time. Williams's letters to Kay Boyle (1932) and to James Laughlin (1940) could not have been known to Olson before *Selected Letters of William Carlos Williams* was published in 1957; nor were Pound's letters to W.H.D. Rouse (1932) and to Hubert Creekmore (1939) available until his *Selected Letters, 1907–41* appeared in October 1950. Another "source," Williams's essay "The Poem as a Field of Action," is dated 1948 by Perloff because it was given as a lecture then at the University of Washington; but Olson was not there on that occasion and would not have known it before 1954 when Williams's *Selected Essays* was published. This takes care of six of Perloff's nine supposed sources: Olson could not have known them.

Another "source" cited twice in these double columns is Williams's introduction to *The Wedge*, a collection of poems published in Cummington, Massachusetts, September 1944 in a run of 380 copies. There is no evidence the author sent Olson a copy. They didn't really correspond until 1949. Olson might have seen it before "Projective Verse," but it is unlikely: he never mentioned it anywhere, nor was there a copy in his library.

Neither did Olson own a copy of Pound's *Gaudier-Brzeska*. The 1916 first edition (200 copies in the U.S.) was not reprinted until 1961. If Olson saw it, it must have been in a library. Perloff cites four passages that Olson is supposed to have remembered when writing "Projective Verse." I consider it most unlikely that he did. Similar arguments apply to Pound's *ABC of Reading*, which Yale published in 1934. Olson did not own a copy. The reprint by New Directions was not till 1951, after the essay it is supposed to have influenced.

This leaves only two items in the "Source" columns that Olson could have read and was likely to have read. Olson had a copy of *The Harvard Wake* No. 5 (Spring 1946), but was it a source for "Projective Verse"? Perloff quotes from it part of one sentence from Williams's "Lower Case Cummings": "With cummings every syllable has a conscience and a specific impact." This is put alongside the following from "Projective Verse": "Let's start from the smallest particle of all, the syllable. It is the king and pin of versification, what rules and holds together the lines, and larger forms, of a poem." Is Perloff saying that if Olson hadn't come across Williams on Cummings he wouldn't have thought about the importance of syllables in poetry? She cannot be suggesting that Olson took his precise formulation from Williams, for their imagery is quite different. Williams talks about the "conscience" of syllables (whatever that is) and their "impact" as Cummings uses them self-consciously. Olson, on the other hand, sees syllables as a usually unconscious cohesive governing force in every line, "king" and "pin."

There remains Pound's *Guide to Kulchur*. Olson owned the Faber & Faber 1938 edition, which Pound had inscribed to him in January 1946. Let us present in the manner Perloff does the quotation from "Projective Verse" and the passages from *Guide to Kulchur* from which it is supposed to be "derived" (Perloff pp. 289–90):

OLSON	SOURCE
"Now (3) the process of the thing, how the principle can be made so to shape the energies that the form is accomplished. And I think it can be boiled down to one statement (first pounded into my head by Edward Dahlberg): ONE PERCEPTION MUST IMMEDIATELY AND DIRECTLY LEAD TO A FURTHER PERCEPTION … get on with it, keep moving, keep in, speed … USE USE USE the process at all points, in any given poem always, always one perception must must must MOVE, INSTANTER, ON ANOTHER!"	"At this point we must make a clean cut between two kinds of 'ideas.' Ideas which exist and/or are discussed in a species of vacuum, which are as it were toys of the intellect, and ideas which are intended to 'go into action' …" *Guide to Kulchur* (1938) p. 34. "The ideogrammatic method consists of presenting one facet and then another until at some point one gets off the dead and desensitized surface of the reader's mind, onto a part that will register." *Guide to Kulchur* p. 51.

As to the first quotation in the "source" column, Pound favors ideas which lead to action in the world of conduct rather than ideas that are the playthings of philosophers. Pound is probably thinking of Mussolini. Olson, on the other hand, is entirely concerned with what is useful within a poem.

Likewise, the "ideogrammatic method" of presenting different glimpses or images of a thing is quite removed, I believe, from Olson's kinetic, where a poem moves from one thing to another linearly and with the energy of discovery. In any case, this "source," like the other Perloffisms, can be dealt with very simply. The passage in "Projective Verse" did not come from Pound; it came from Edward Dahlberg. Olson says so. Perloff does not follow up on this acknowledged source.

More important as a general source for "Projective Verse," Olson brings in Keats. In his campaign against the lyric ego in poetry Olson claims Keats as an ally, and refers to Keats's discriminating epithet "the Egotistical Sublime." Perloff says Olson "is, of course, simply paraphrasing Pound, who insisted on this distinction as early as 1914" (p. 288). We are supposed to believe that Olson couldn't read Keats for himself? Very obtuse. And to support her claim, Perloff again cites Pound pieces that Olson would not have seen, published in the *Literary Essays of Ezra Pound* four years after "Projective Verse." The particular quotations she uses as evidence, which do not, by the way, include any mention of the "Egotistical Sublime," are from reviews of A.E. Housman's *The Name and Nature of Poetry in Criterion* (January 1934) and of a Swinburne biography in *Poetry* (March 1918), both of which reviews are guaranteed not to have attracted Olson's attention, nor would they, by any stretch of the imagination, have contributed to the notion of "projective verse" even if they had.

Further obtuseness is Perloff's discounting Olson's acknowledgment of H.M.S. Coxeter, whose work was brought to Olson's attention by Corrado Cagli when they were working together on Olson's first poems, *y & x* (1948). Both *Non-Euclidean Geometry* (1942) and *Regular Polytopes* (1948) were keenly explored by Olson before his "Projective Verse" essay; they contain discussions of "projective" geometry. Instead of exploring this lead, Perloff says, "Olson had to go no further than his own backyard to find this vocabulary" (Perloff p. 287). Well, Coxeter happens to have been as much Olson's backyard as *Antheil and the Treatise on Harmony* by Pound, suggested as the source for the term "projective verse," a "source" that does not include the word "projective" at all.

Perloff avoids using the word "plagiarism," but plagiarism is what we think of when we see those accusatory double-columns. That closer examination reveals only slap-dash scholarship on the part of the critic may never, alas, dislodge the first impression that her "plausible" article establishes.

25
"I'm a perfect father, until I'm not"

Early February 1956 was the moment of decision, described so dramatically in Jane Atherton's account in *Minutes* #31/32:

> As I was sitting at the dining room table writing to Connie to inquire why I had not heard from her, I heard a car drive up to the door. Looking out the window I saw an old beat-up Ford convertible coupe with three figures bundled up with blankets against the bitter cold. My stomach knotted. I knew who it was immediately and ran out to the car. Charles was disentangling himself from behind the driver's wheel, grabbing his many shawls. I opened the passenger door and lifted out a small blanketed figure that struggled in my arms to get to the ground. It was Kate, who had been sitting on Connie's lap. Wearily Connie attempted to climb out. She too was wrapped in many shawls and sweaters, for the car heater did not work. I half-lifted her from the car and the four of us, the weary Connie, the gamboling child, tall stooped Charles and the apprehensive sister went wordlessly into the house.
>
> I nervously welcomed them, removing Kate's coat and hat, and helping Connie with her garments. I made hot coffee and some sandwiches. My children were all in school. There was almost no conversation. I made some chit-chat. There was no response except an occasional sigh from Charles as he drank his coffee and ate his sandwich. Connie said nothing and ate nothing. She ignored her coffee cup. Kate aimlessly wandered about asking for the children and poking at toys that lay about.
>
> Soon Connie and Charles excused themselves and went into the living room, closing the door behind them. They remained there for an hour. I could hear voices rising and falling, not in argument but in some kind of earnest discussion. When they returned to the dining room, Connie sank into an old rocking chair as Charles began putting on his many sweaters, jacket and shawls. He said nothing as he meticulously arranged layer after layer of clothing. I

looked at Connie. Tears were rolling down her cheeks. Charles went over to her and kissed her.

"I don't want you to go. I don't want you to go," she said, raising her arms and struggling to speak.

"Baby, I must go," he said.

He slowly put her arms down. "I must go," he repeated.

He turned and went out the door towards the automobile. I, stunned, ran after him. I knew some great emotion was churning within him, but all I could say was "Be careful driving, Charles, that car....that car...." My words died away as I saw he could not hear me and I stood as he backed the Ford out and turned it into the road ... (pp. 31–32)

Slowly Connie began to tell her sister Jane what happened during the past few months at Black Mountain. She had discovered that Charles had had a serious love affair during the summer with one of the students. The girl was pregnant. Connie with Kate had followed them to New York and found Charles; he refused to consider a reconciliation. He told Connie he had to stay with his new love and see her through her pregnancy and the birth of their child.

We have just one glimpse of Charles and Betty's New York situation from Betty's sister, Jean Kaiser. When she was asked on a public occasion in 1995 (see *Minutes* #10 p. 7) what it felt like meeting Olson for the first time, she laughed: "Well, actually, I brought my mother to meet Charles Olson, and it was very quick and very abrupt, and we were there about a half hour, and my mother told Charles off like I think very few people ever did. He never got a word in edgewise." This would be at the time of Betty's pregnancy, I presume, and something of this pressure lies behind Olson's "I must go."

And what about Kate? Jane Atherton continues her account:

I took Kate upstairs to the small room she would later share with her mother. While the other children were getting ready for bed I sang some songs to Kate. She seemed to like that, and soon was drowsy. She wanted to see her mother, but by that time Connie was asleep and I did not want to wake her. I told Kate her mother was sleeping, that she was very tired from her long trip, but all would be well in the morning. That explanation seemed to satisfy her, and she let me tuck her in bed and put out the light. I tiptoed out of the room and silently closed the door, hoping the child would soon be in a really sound sleep. Within a minute the door was flung open and Kate stood there shouting, "Leave the God damned door OPEN!"

Kate was three years old. She was tiny. She was dressed in a pink pajama suit, her curly hair tousled. Yet the little figure had an imperiousness that reminded me of her father.

I assured her the door would remain open.

Obviously a "perfect father" does not desert a young daughter. But there was some communication by mail, drawings from Kate and a valentine in February 1956. Storrs has a letter of 31 January 1957 from Connie in Boston to Olson who was still doing the last chores at Black Mountain. She thanks him for sending "several cartons" of clothing and other possessions. Then she tells him an anecdote: "Kate said yesterday, musingly, looking out of the window, do you think Pappa is dead by now, ma ma. I roared, her tone and expression were so speculative, and wistful."

Olson was very busy at this time, delivering the "Special View of History" lectures in San Francisco, February 1957, then returning to face the complicated legal business of closing the college and also the physical task of disposing of the property, including the books of the library. Very soon after Olson got his new family settled in Gloucester, however, he made a day trip down to the Athertons just south of Boston. Jane Atherton does not give a date to the following events; it must have been mid-August 1957:

> One summer Sunday at our house the telephone rang in the late afternoon. It was Charles. I answered the phone and he said he was at North Scituate village, had just arrived by train, and wanted to come to visit and see Kate.
>
> Connie had told me she was perfectly willing to have Charles see Kate, but she also had said she would not see him herself. I stammered some kind of greeting into the telephone, knowing that Connie was nearby. I was amazed that Charles had come to Scituate. Somehow I thought he would make formal arrangements to see his daughter prior to the actual visit. Instead, here he was within a mile of the house and asking to visit! I said that would be impossible. My answer seemed to astonish him. He was speechless for a couple of seconds and then asked me if that was what Connie wished. I told him that she had left instructions that we were not to welcome him and that she did not want to see him. I did not want to see him either. I did not want to face that conflict, liking him, despising him, feeling that I had to help him over his hurdle of making friends with his daughter again.
>
> The matter was resolved when Mel took over the telephone. He told Charles he would be right down to meet him in the village. He

departed, taking not only Kate, but Paula, Janet and young Mel. His solution was so simple! With so many kids clamoring around there was no opportunity for an emotional scene. Charles picked up his daughter, gave her a kiss and a hug, and told her she was beautiful. Then he greeted his nieces and nephew and asked them if they were hungry. Of course they were. Putting Kate on his shoulder and followed by Mel and the three Atherton kids, Charles strode down the road to the little general store. There he bought boloney, bread, mustard, cheese and cake plus some soft drinks. He carried the food outside and promptly spread it out under a nearby tree. The kids made sandwiches, using Mel's jackknife to cut the cheese and spread the mustard. Charles was oblivious to the passing traffic and the stares from those who entered and left the store. With miles of sandy beaches and groves of pine trees nearby it must have seemed strange to see the alfresco picnickers sitting crosslegged by the side the road near the general store and two gas stations.

They all had a marvelous time. Mel returned with the children about two hours later and regaled Connie and me with a description of the picnic. The children loved it. Janet returned wide-eyed and told us how Charles had picked her up and held her "way, way up in the air!" She said he told them all kinds of stories and that he was always laughing—laughing.

Clark describes this visit erroneously as an unhappy affair:

> To test things, he made a surprise visit to Scituate; Connie herself refused to see him and permitted him only a few hours with Kate, who was deposited by Mel Atherton outside the town's general store for a forlorn picnic with her father. (p. 274)

What possible intention could a biographer have for changing the facts of Jane Atherton's account so that this first meeting with Kate in their new situation is made to seem "forlorn" instead of the uproarious party it was? It is in keeping with Clark's continuing attempt to have the father–daughter relationship seem pathetic throughout the remaining years to Olson's death:

> Kate would come to Gloucester to stay a few times a year, during school holidays. In the actual event, however, he often found these scheduled visits occurring in the midst of work drives. When that happened, he either canceled out or showed up woefully late to pick up the girl at South Station in Boston. The experience of waiting for hours in a crowd of strangers for him to appear became a particularly traumatic chapter in the prolonged disappointment of

> Kate's relations with her father, "one repeated broken-heart story"
> to unfold over the decade to come. From his point of view as well,
> there was much heartache in the situation. (pp. 274–75)

This exaggerated tale of woe is nothing like the picture revealed in the many letters that went back and forth between father and daughter, and Olson's caring letters to Connie from time to time. The Kate Olson Archive (at the moment in the possession of the author) indicates that in the years 1956 to Olson's death in 1970, beginning with notes and valentines to a five-year-old, Olson sent 513 missives to his daughter and thirty-four to Connie. There is also a later letter from Panna Grady to Kate (26 December 1976) which puts a different light on Clark's "repeated broken-heart" theme: "Yes, I remember well indeed the day we picked you up from school, and Charles' care and concern for you, almost solicitude, from not having occasion enough to show you."

On the question of Kate's adoption by George Bunker, Clark reports:

> When in September 1959 Connie married George Bunker, an independently wealthy Philadelphia art teacher, and Kate thereby acquired a stepfather, Olson ruefully reported the news to friends: "Kate now Katherine Mary Bunker, to my dismay." Lacking the ability to provide child support himself, however, he had no choice but to surrender control of his daughter's future. (p. 275)

I'm not sure Olson ever surrendered anything. He comes out well in this situation, stubborn and loving, witness the letter to Kate in *Selected Letters* (#161):

> I feel like your father, my nature has no recognition of any accommodations, realistic or otherwise, of such primary things—and I fear my belief here is of such proportions that I'm going to be, if that's what it comes out as, a lot of trouble ...
>
> I can only say this—that I've never known any of these real things to be anything but just this way, and if, in the end, I come out without having been able to agree to lessen or remove my relationship to you as father no more nor less & solely only as per se, I pray God it may life-wise both a true thing to do—and a real one, in the end for your own life.

And he signs the letter "your own Father for better or for worse."

Clark even puts a damper on Kate's graduation day, "a bittersweet occasion for Olson":

He had reason both to glory in the sight of the poised, grown-up-looking young woman he had somehow managed to father … and to mourn her childhood, which seemed to have gone by while he was looking away. (p. 344)

I prefer Jane Atherton's description in *Minutes* #31/32:

Mel and I arrived at Weston early in the day and we began taking pictures of Kate. She was stunningly beautiful in a long white Victorian gown, her hair tied up with fresh flowers.

As we moved about with the camera there was a sudden stir among a group of persons nearby. Putting the camera down I looked around and saw Charles, the center of attention, shaking hands and beaming as he met members of the faculty. Kate joined her father and began introducing him to her friends. Charles greeted us with enthusiasm, embracing both Mel and me. Connie, seemingly annoyed, stood aside, merely nodding to Charles, although she had confided to me not long before that Charles had been very sweet in recent telephone calls regarding Kate.

This day Connie did not consider him sweet.

"Look at him, he loves being lionized," she said. "He could have let us know he was coming. George is responsible for Kate's education and you would think it was all Charles's idea!" (pp. 37–38)

This was only a few weeks before Olson left Gloucester to teach at the University of Connecticut until the pain from liver cancer was such that he had to go to the local hospital. Clark does not tell the whole story of Kate's insistence on being with her ailing father, though again his source, Jane Atherton, does:

I had to tell Kate that her father was ill. I did not say what the trouble was but Kate guessed immediately.

"I'm going with you," she said.

I repeated that the doctor and her father both had said the children should not go.

"I'm going with you and I'm going to call Charles Peter too!"

I tried to explain as gently as I could that she would see her father later, that only I was to make this trip.

She pulled herself up to her full height. Though she was now several inches taller than me, she reminded me of the little three year old who had yelled, "Leave the God damned door OPEN."

"I said I'm going," she shouted, "and you can't stop me. I'll go and get Charles Peter if I have to do it all by bus!"

I became angry and said she could go to her room and plan

Kate's high school graduation, June 1969.
Kate Olson Archive.

anything she wanted. She left and I sank into a chair wondering what to do. I thought about my sister charging me with her daughter's care. I thought about all the years of ups and downs with Charles, his loveable qualities, his exasperating ways, his indecisions, his exciting visits, his verse that set the mind to thinking, and then I knew what I had to do.

I went upstairs. Kate was crying. I put my arms around her and said I was sorry. I said we would all go. I told her to make arrangements over the telephone to have Charles Peter's aunt put him on the Boston train from Gloucester and we would meet him at the North Station, leaving immediately from there for Connecticut.

The next morning snow was falling, but by 9 A.M. we were in Boston and at the North Station where Kate found Charles Peter. Greetings said, I turned the car to the expressway and in silence began the three-hour drive to Connecticut in steadily falling snow. The ground was well-covered when we reached the university around one o'clock. We got directions to the hospital and still silent the three of us found our way to Charles's room.

He was half lying, half-sitting in his hospital bed, and he was talking! Two visitors were in the room and he was carrying on a discourse with that old animation I remembered so well. He turned toward us when he saw us at the door.

"Jane, how delightful. You're looking great—wonderful. Here, meet my friends."

He introduced me to the two men. (As I recall they were Charles Boer and Harvey Brown, but I cannot be sure.)

He then reached his arms to his children and embraced each one as well as he could from the hospital bed. I heard myself saying some inane remark, I think it was "What are they doing to you, Charlie?" He kept up the bantering conversation for a couple of minutes, then seemed to tire. He sank back on his pillow. He turned to his other visitors and picked up the conversation that had been interrupted by our arrival.

I felt uncomfortable. I had been told not to bring the children. I felt that Charles was showing his displeasure.

I said that I would leave for a few minutes so the children could speak to their father in private. The two other visitors did not leave the room with me as I expected they would. Instead they continued to sit, leaving only when a nurse came in to announce that Mr. Olson would soon be taking the ambulance to New York City and the Cornell Medical Center.

Soon the small room was full of bustle. The two visitors left. Kate and I stood aside, as did Charles Peter, as Charles was lifted to a stretcher and wheeled into the corridor. We walked along beside him, Kate holding his hand and talking softly to him. She was brave and strong and very concerned that her father be handled carefully. Charles Peter seemed shy and uncomfortable.

We continued to walk beside the rolling cot. We found ourselves in an elevator and then were lowered to the ground floor. An ambulance was backed up to the door. The nurses had covered Charles with blankets, and his own shawl was draped around his shoulders, but his head was bare. When the doors opened and Kate realized that the snow was still falling, she shrieked,

"Stop that bed! Wait! Put his hat on!"

The same command was in her voice.

She found his hat somehow and pulled it down carefully over her father's head. (p. 40)

Clark finishes the story:

The eighteen-year-old Kate, matured by grief, remained constantly at her father's side, often staying on when other guests were gone, soothing him with quiet conversation: visitors sometimes found them lying side by side, a "royal pair," the loving, fiercely loyal Cordelia and the dwindled, suffering Lear. She was with him to the end. (p. 350)

This is a moving scene, but there has been little or nothing in Clark's account previously to acquaint us with this eighteen-year-old who had developed such a fondness for her father.

26
"Human Universe"

Clark has a fairly extended discussion of the "Human Universe" essay with ample quotations of Olson's view that the Greek philosophers introduced a discourse which has been debilitating and that we must find an alternative discourse that can give us the kinetics of reality in its particulars (the following quoted by Clark):

> There must be a way of expression ... a way which is not divisive as all the tag ends and upendings of the Greek way are. There must be a way which bears in instead of away, which meets head on what goes on each split second, a way which does not—in order to define—prevent, deter, distract, and so cease the act of, discovering. (p. 200)

But then Clark gets a clever idea: the "Human Universe" essay itself is "curiously" an example of exactly the new discourse sought, in that its "intensive unfolding" (Clark's phrase, not Olson's) is as much as "anything Olson had yet attempted in open-field verse" (p. 200). He explains the notion:

> Stripped of all mechanics save those hidden in the nature of his subject, Olson's scattershot argument came out curiously true to its intent: "A thing ... impinges on us by ... its self-existence." His serial, accumulative style in the essay served to accent that point, highlighting the individuating, anti-identifying quality of his thought. The rhetorical form employed was one of simple parataxis—or as he would later define it, the placement of "words or actions ... side by side in the order of their occurrence in nature, instead of by an order of discourse or 'grammar.'" This appositional or "dream syntax" would dictate the internal ordering of much of his major work to come. (p. 201)

The phrases quoted here by Clark are from Olson's review of Eric Havelock's *Preface to Plato*. Clark is proposing that Olson in this review of

1963 had at last found the words to express what he had been doing in the "Human Universe" essay of 1951.

A plausible idea, but wrong. The "Human Universe" essay, or "The Gate and the Center," or any published prose Olson wrote up to the "Proprioception" essay of October 1959, is good old-fashioned exposition. It could perhaps be mistaken for something new because of its singular lilt and raciness, but it is essentially hard-nosed argumentation. Clark will have it that the method is presentational. Not true. Olson argues his points like the old debater he was all through college and national politics:

> I have found, for example, that the hieroglyphs of the Maya disclose a placement of themselves toward nature of enormous contradiction to ourselves, and yet I am not aware that any of the possible usages of this difference have been allowed to seep out into present society. (*Selected Writings* p. 63)

If this isn't a formally stated comparison and a damn good topic sentence I'll eat my *Harbrace College Handbook*. And when at the end of the essay Olson gives us a Mayan myth, he carefully makes it part of a syllogism:

> Man has made himself an ugliness and a bore. It was better to be a bird, as these Maya seem to have been, they kept moving their heads so nervously to stay alive, to keep alerted to what they were surrounded by. (p. 64)

It is only after the formal comparison of the present with the mythic past that the retelling of the Mayan story is allowed to proceed.

> Or to be a man and a woman as Sun was, the way he had to put up with Moon, from start to finish, the way she behaved, and he up against it. (p. 64)

The myth is a two-and-a-half page exemplum designed to clinch the argument in the way any persuasive preacher might use a parable. Olson in his own voice comes out at the end to comment:

> O, they were hot for the world they lived in, these Maya, hot to get it down the way it was—the way it is, my fellow citizens. (p. 66)

The final terms of address give it away—the essay is a political pitch from beginning to end!

Clark would have us believe an anachronism: that Olson's parataxis of the '60s was not something he had earned by intelligent effort but that he had already stumbled into it somehow in the '50s without really knowing what he was doing until he read Havelock:

> His delighted discovery, in a book read a decade after the writing of
> "Human Universe" (Eric Havelock's *Preface to Plato*), that a parat-
> actic method not unlike his own, uniquely suitable for containing
> "an experience of experience, vision dream seeming," had actually
> reigned supreme in the poetic expression of pre-Socratic times,
> would strike him as the ultimate confirmation of the legitimacy of
> his entire approach in writing. (p. 201)

Olson's achievement was much greater than herein implied. In the '50s he
had some idea of where Western thought was letting us down, and his
equating the future postmodern with the archaic was a stroke of genius;
but it was only with the opening of the new decade of the '60s that Olson
found himself able to step into the world he had foreseen, "Maximus from
Dogtown—I" and especially "Maximus from Dogtown—II" breaking open
the old syntax and bewildering us with an entirely new regimen. This was
new; it was not something he had been doing all the time.

And it was no reversion to the pre-Socratic parataxis of epic narrative.
What Olson managed to do was to utilize the Homeric way of reifying
knowledge, what Havelock neatly called "the Homeric encyclopedia," the
body of what was then known expressed as a series of events, paratactic in
the sense that each event in turn is experienced for itself before the next
event occurs—Olson carried this over into the reflective epic of daily experienced history, psyche, or myth which we know as *Maximus IV, V, VI* and
The Maximus Poems Volume Three. He called his *Maximus Poems* "dailies."
These journal poems, along with the ongoing letter-writing, are Olson's
bid to be "equal to the real itself," a modern parataxis as the instants of the
real are paratactic.

The way Clark talks about the revisions Olson made to the "Human
Universe" essay seems quite damning:

> On June 17, copies of the essay's first draft were sent to Cid
> Corman, for submission to his magazine, and Robert Creeley, for
> editorial comment. Both recipients cautioned Olson about an
> occasional overaggressiveness of tone, especially in a passage
> attacking the "collectivists," "existentialists" and "homosexuals"
> who were his fellow contributors to the latest New Directions
> annual. Heeding their politic advice, he deleted the potentially
> embarrassing sections ... (p. 201)

Olson wrote about the *New Directions* annual #12 because, as a contri-
butor, it had been sent to him and he received it in Yucatan at the moment
he wanted to say something about the laws of a new humanism. What had

just fallen into his lap, Olson thought, was symptomatic of how lost contemporary writing had become, and he used it to make that point. Within a month he was at Black Mountain College and the first thing he did straight off the bus was read in a public session the first draft of "Human Universe," and on the basis of hearing it through his own voice he started revising it, throwing out the New Directions passage (CO/RC 6.136). In saying that Olson heeded Corman's and Creeley's "politic advice" on this, Clark is far from the mark. It is true that in sending Corman the final typescript Olson wrote: "I found your letter, by the way, on it of considerable help … I do hope I have taken care of the things which balked you, in the original version" (CO/CC 1.199), but this gives no clue to what it was Corman balked at and Corman's letter on the subject is not extant. Clark's guesswork as to the various motivations involved is quite without foundation. We do have Creeley's response to the New Directions section (CO/RC 6.84). He is supportive of what Olson is saying, but believes that the passage in question is on a level of argumentation beneath the rest of the essay. Only with grave distortion can Creeley be said to be cautioning Olson against "attacking the 'collectivists,' 'existentialists' and 'homosexuals'" (Clark, in the quotation above).

One should add—though here one enters the realm of the incredible— that the three words Clark puts into quotes (i.e. "collectivists," "existentialists" and "homosexuals") do not appear in Olson's essay at all. (The pertinent paragraph is quoted below from Albert Glover's transcription of the draft "Human Universe" essay in his Ph.D. dissertation, "Charles Olson: Letters for Origin," SUNY Buffalo 1968):

> What makes such writing unsatisfactory is, that each thing is allowed to present itself on one face only. These writers satisfy themselves that they can only make a form by selecting one place of content, the psychological, say, or the psychic, or that third which overtakes the other two more and more, the plane of social reality, whether it is collectivism straight on (ah! but tomorrow!) or that escape from same, from its fatherism into a kafka kafka land or from its motherism into existenz or American sonism—superman, or his backward brother, who is also such a performer these days, the homosexual writer.
>
> The laws are larger and more durable than these sad modern and personal solutions. (p. 159)

We have "collectivism" and "existenz" not "collectivists" and "existentialists": these misquotations we can disregard because of the minimal damage involved; but Clark was most careless to report that Olson was using a broad and loaded word "homosexuals" when he was actually speaking of "the homosexual writer," a phrase with a much less harsh sound to it, and in this instance quite specifically referring to Tennessee Williams, Gore Vidal and others who would answer to the name of "homosexual writer," in that particular issue of *New Directions*. But, as the passage shows, Olson did not name anybody, and didn't make a big thing of it.

The paragraph is part of what Creeley criticized, but not because it was potentially politically embarrassing. In any case, Olson had already cut it out before receiving Creeley's letter. That Olson heeded "politic advice" is something Clark dredged up out of his own sense of how ambitious people would behave in the bog of literary politics.

It is also important to rectify the notion that Havelock was a sort of postmodern prophet for Olson. An editorial note in the *Collected Prose* exaggerates things in saying that Olson "brought Havelock to Buffalo from Yale in December 1964" (p. 456). This makes it seem that Havelock left Yale to teach at Buffalo because Olson had both the desire that he should and the power to effect it. No, the invitation was only for a single lecture, and the chance to have a chat.

This was a lecture and meeting that I did not want to witness—for good reason. I knew enough to make me sure that Havelock's view was quite contrary to Olson's. He was a Platonist and would not at all assent to Olson's confident statement in "Human Universe" that Plato's "world of Ideas, of forms as extricable from content, is as much and as dangerous an issue as are logic and classification, and they need to be seen as such if we are to get on to some alternative to the whole Greek system" (*Selected Writings* p. 55). Olson sought for that alternative by going back *before* Plato, to Homer and before that, where he felt better human values lay. He appreciated *Preface to Plato* because it showed in exact detail what those earlier values and techniques of education were that Plato would banish (and which Olson would want to reinstate in some way as the post-modern). To Havelock the Pre-Socratics signified no more than what was implied in his title; they were a preface to the real beginning of culture with Plato. Olson had got caught up in admiration of Havelock's clarity and accuracy, and had not caught on—or refused to catch on—to the general drift of the book. I was fearful of an inevitable clash between them when they met.

I had taken Havelock's course in Virgil in 1952 when I was an under-graduate at Harvard (he had not yet left for Yale). I felt a special relationship with him, his having come from a town in Yorkshire about ten miles from where I was as a schoolboy. He also had the reputation of radical political leanings, and was said to have been a candidate for the CCF in Ontario, Canada. However, whatever high deeds Havelock may have done in Ontario, he was a grey enough full professor by the time I took a front row seat and listened to him read his lectures. For he was no more an Olson in this than anything else: he read his lectures.

There was one particular class I remember that bears out the distinction. Havelock was half way through a lecture when a window cleaner's ladder appeared at the window ledge outside, then a head, and then a shoulder and arms that began to work on the window. This was a few feet directly to the left of the lectern. Havelock gave no indication of being disturbed, but after a few moments began to sidle sideways towards the window, carrying his notes and continuing to read from them. He pulled down on the cord of the window blind intending to blot out this competing image of a man working. Unfortunately, when he had pulled the blind down it wouldn't stay down. He gave those little tugs that normally get a blind to catch and stay, but it wouldn't. There he was, holding the blind cord and continuing his lecture in the same calm reading manner, which with every instant became more and more unendurable. This was existentialist dignity threatened by an unfair universe. I leapt up from the first row. I couldn't restrain myself. From the professor's hand I took the fateful blind-cord. Did I hear titters from somewhere in the class? It was unmistakably comic. But worse was to come. I saw that if I attached the cord to a spare chair, that would hold it down. Unhappily the cord wouldn't reach the chair unless I stuck the chair legs down the side of the old fashioned radiator at the window. (Meanwhile, the window cleaner, an unnatural perfectionist, was continuing his arm strokes long past the time when a normal mortal would have desisted.) I got the cord fastened and the chair in place, but as I resumed my seat the chair slowly tipped forward into the room and stopped at an angle determined by its pull on the cord. Should I get up and readjust my contrivance? I saw with great clarity that if I tried to do anything the chair would simply subside again to that position of stability. I sat petrified that I might get up again. Havelock continued lecturing with the window cleaner in full view of the class. *Arma virumque cano.* Know ye now why I might, in all timidity, absent myself from any encounter between Olson and Havelock, two men I in different ways admired, in Buffalo on the 10 December 1963?

27
Background to Berkeley

Clark has the following to say about Olson's scheduled poetry reading of 23 July 1965 at the Berkeley Poetry Conference. I have a feeling that Robert Creeley and Edward Dorn agreed with this assessment and this is why statements from them appeared as blurbs on the back cover of *Charles Olson: The Allegory of a Poet's Life*.

> His drunken performance that night offended a few older friends— especially Robert Duncan, who as master of ceremonies felt personally insulted and walked out in protest at the first available break, some hours into things—but left most of the younger spectators in Wheeler Hall merely puzzled. Few understood the real pathos of the spectacle—the lonely, aging and insecure man, desperately running for the offices of President of Poetry and Great Lover at once. Loaded on Dexedrine and gulping liberally from a fresh fifth of Cutty Sark, Olson managed only two poems before the "reading" degenerated into a wandering, confused monologue on politics and poetry. Only intermittently coherent, laced with personal references that were largely obscure to his present audience, the long, swaggering confessional speech was actually more like a filibuster. He bragged that he belonged "where I have been, in Madison Square Garden," and only half playfully proposed appointments to his poetry cabinet: Allen Ginsberg, for instance, was "going to be my Secretary of State for Love." One impatient audience member, poet Lew Welch, called out for poems to be read. Olson overruled the suggestion, claiming he was "addressing the convention floor. The only convention I care of in the whole earth is occurring tonight." When Welch repeated his request, Olson shot back that there was plenty of time: he'd made it clear, hadn't he, that "we stay here all night." As the odd evening wore on and defectors began to file out, his tone took on an edge of challenge. "If you don't know, brother, that poetics is politics, poets are political leaders today, and the only ones," he jeered at the back of

Olson on the platform, Berkeley, 1965.
Photo: Jim Hatch.

one escaping spectator, "you shouldn't have come." The "nonread-ing," conference co-organizer Professor Thomas Parkinson noted, had turned into a painful "loyalty test" for those who'd respected Olson's work: Duncan left at the Moscow trials, I left at the Finnish War." Finally even the poet's close friends were squirming. "Is this the Charles Olson we all know and love?" Creeley asked Ed Dorn. (pp. 324–25)

Creeley has confirmed in *Minutes* #4 that he "felt a lot of bleak dismay" (p. 2). I have to confess I left Berkeley for family reasons before that evening and cannot say how I would have felt had I been present; but listening to the full tape of the occasion (as I presume neither Creeley nor Clark have done) gives an entirely positive feeling, attested to by all those I know who have ever listened to it, without exception. Olson did not ignore dissension, but he handled it with off-the-cuff remarks that are honest, self-assured and usually funny in a bemused sort of way, e.g. "You know, this is the greatest thing, and if you'll endure it, babies ... You know, every time I ever read before, the awful thing is that I might talk, instead" (*Mythologos* I.134). Or again, recognizing he was talking about poems instead of doing a poetry reading, he asked, along with the good-humored laughter of the audience, "Would you read the poems I mention. I mean, literally?" (p. 119). There is lots of this good-humored laughter through-out the evening, Olson functioning remarkably as a public poet, a poet thinking on his feet, and being absolutely delightful. Creeley says it was not a pleasure for him. I, however, can say categorically that I have never had as much sustained pleasure from any other occupation to compare with the many hours, hundreds of hours, I have spent listening to the Berkeley Reading tape, alone and with students, and preparing the transcription which is printed in *Mythologos* volume I.

Students, in my experience, have always responded to the tape with eager curiosity—which belies Clark's remark that Olson "left most of the younger spectators in Wheeler Hall merely puzzled." This is one of those comments that a plausible fellow like Clark seems to be able to get away with in spite of having not the slightest evidence to back it up. Was he there? Did he take a poll? No, he's just writing fiction. As he is when he calls the chief (fictional) character of his book a "lonely, aging and insecure man, desperately running etc., etc." On one level, Clark can be contra-dicted on any of those words, "lonely," "aging," "insecure," "desperate"; but on another level all that one really wants to contradict is Clark's appalling tone. "Pathos" is a beautiful thing, and all the above words

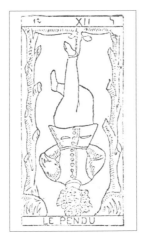

Tarot card of "The Hanged Man."

applied lovingly to Olson would be true and would make him infinitely admirable for presenting us with an image of the active, willful man publicly taking the risk of tragedy. Olson's victory here is to offer a totality, not just the selected attractivenesses one calls one's personality.

In fact, there was a conscious recognition on Olson's part of the internal struggle between two aspects of himself: was he going to wield once more his enormous powers of expression, or was he going to stumble? And thereby stumble on a rarely exposed image of man? On the platform, feeling the microphone cord around his neck, Olson became the trussed Hanged Man of the Tarot. "And that's the image I want to end with," he said (*Muthologos* I.132), "no matter how few of you stay, is that poem of Maximus with his feet in the air. Maybe tonight is the night I alter myself." When he read the lines from *Maximus* "Letter 9"

> measure me, measure
> my forces

he said, "Wish I could abandon them tonight" (p. 135). Apropos of this internal struggle, Jack Clarke quoted D.H. Lawrence's poem "To Let Go Or To Hold On—?" with its question

> Must we hold on?
> Or can we now let go?
> Or is it even possible we must do both?

and said: "To do both, as Charles Olson did, required an ordering of experience of the antithetical influx of our time" (*intent*. Vol. 3 Nos. 2 & 3 Summer/Fall 1991 p. 16). Olson's image of this synthesis is a domestic one: "To my mind, it's like a table service, with good linen and silver and plate or something, without servants, and without really having the stuff that ought to make a meal work, except that the stuff that's on the plates is what I was able to cook or something" (*Muthologos* I.134). This is another way of stating the postmodern possibility of home.

I first heard the Berkeley tape in June 1966 at Jack Clarke's house in Buffalo. He had listened to it a number of times, but was glad to put it on for me and a student of his, and to sit with us for a while. It was on that occasion that Jack confirmed with me the opinion that something truly remarkable had entered the twentieth century with Charles Olson, something really extraordinary, a genius that might appear once in a generation, if that. After the tape was over, we sat there in the twilight feeling very, very lucky.

All this is manifest on the tape. Olson is in close-up, with all the *sotto voce* in high fidelity. Unfortunately, this clarity was lost in the Zoe Brown transcription, which has so many errors that the whole thing feels disjointed. If Tom Clark read only this version he might be forgiven for considering Olson's performance "intermittently coherent." When Zoe Brown's *Reading at Berkeley* reached me from Oyez in late 1967 I saw my duty clearly. I had missed the event itself; I would recreate it accurately on paper for myself and others. I bought the tape from the Language Laboratory at Berkeley and started annotating corrections in the Oyez edition. In summer 1968 and spring 1969 I had students in my Modern American Literature classes follow the tape and help decipher some of the cruxes. Many ears and much library research had gone into the new typed transcription sent to George Butterick and left with Olson himself when I visited Gloucester on 6 June 1969. Olson mentioned it in a telephone conversation with Butterick on 11 July 1969. "Charles equally and especially pleased with it," Butterick wrote me the next day, "though he did wax somewhat and grow dark about your 'accuracy' to the point of including every 'er' and other such stutters, noting the wastefulness of same, how boring and distracting." Butterick added, "I must completely agree."

I didn't completely agree, and left in a good many 'ers' when I retyped it with footnotes as what I called a "triptite" edition—voice, text, and annotations—for use in English 414 in the Spring Semester of 1970 at Simon Fraser University. (This is the edition that Butterick dignified with a bibliographical entry in the list of Olson posthumous publications in *OLSON* #7 p. 43.) By the time this triptite edition reached Olson he was in Connecticut and became terminally ill before he could write to me. I did however, receive the following letter through a Gloucester poet acting as Olson's amanuensis:

28 Fort Square
Gloucester, Massachusetts 01930
December 15, 1969

Dear Ralph Maud,

    Charles is currently ill in the hospital and unable to get word to you himself he has asked me to tell you how very happy he is with your publishing of the Berkeley Lecture. He says of the index of references: "one of the most successful evidences of the lecture itself!!!!!". He's also pleased with the letter to Leroi.

    I tried to reach you by phone but find you are in Salt Lake City. I hope you are home to read this in good time.

Linda Parker
(for Charles Olson)

(This might conceivably count as the last letter Charles Olson sent in his lifetime.)

Olson didn't mention the remaining "ers," but when I came to prepare a "definitive" text for Butterick to include in *Muthologos,* I remembered the previously stated opinions and tempered my enthusiasm for such stutterings, and have now become resigned to the comparative smoothness of the *Muthologos* version.

In the recently published *The Letters of Robert Duncan and Denise Levertov,* ed. Robert J. Bertholf and Albert Gelpi (Stanford University Press, 2004), there is surprisingly little useful new information on Olson. Below is an excerpt from a Duncan letter of 9 August 1965 which is so not useful that it has to be challenged. Duncan is opining that at the Berkeley Poetry Conference Olson made his reading "an occasion for the emotion's display" and an exercise of "personality" in a disparaging sense:

> Charles … arrived drunk and drinking, Barbara Joseph in some stupid sympathy having given him two dexamils to lift him out of his actual depresst pre-reading temper. After forty-five minutes or so of Charles emoting and throwing up chunks of what he does not like about himself, I calld an intermission from the floor, shouting out "Charles. Give us a break to go pee." But it was a break too to leave without making a scene of it; as it certainly wld have been had I expresst my disgust. He had begun reading very badly (too drunk to get thru) his "Ode On Nativity," then he announced he was going to talk, and (belligerently) that "talk was poetry"; O.K., but nothing was moving anywhere but up and at 'em in the first part. After the break when I left, he talkt on "out of his head" until first the janitors and then the campus police arrived at midnight to

remove him and the remaining audience from the building. At dinner last night, Paul Sawyer a Unitarian minister who stayd for the whole thing and went then to the party afterwards recalld an interesting episode. During the second section Bob calld out for Charles to read some poems. Olson stopt in tracks and tried, reading with distaste an opening stanza, and then came over to Bob's side of the platform and said: "This is the last time you are going to correct me Robert Creeley!" At the party Bob confronted Charles and askt him what he had meant, but Charles could not remember saying that and denied it of course. (pp. 499ff)

One factual matter should be cleared up before we go on to the general interpretation. Duncan has forgotten that Olson first read the short poem "The Ring of" and read it very well indeed. Olson then went on to "An Ode on Nativity," which he interrupted for extensive explications from life experience, but he did in fact complete it in its full-bodied entirety.

Duncan's call for an intermission took advantage of some people leaving the hall:

> Olson: Isn't it wonderful. People cannot wait for poetry. Ha, ha! The activity has to be produced in a time schedule. You remember how we write these things? The same way I'm behaving. I'm a Professor of Posture, and I'm proving it.

> Duncan: Charles, can you give us time to go pee?

> Olson: Oh, my god, I forgot about that intermission. You mean, in a political convention, you think the heat and the stuff inside yourself has to be relieved?

> Duncan: Five minutes.

> Olson: You're ... I mean, "Teacher." [Laughter. Trouble with microphone cord.] That's called "recall." I'm either going to lose my position or I won't, that's all.

Duncan's calling for "five minutes" implied he wanted only a short break and would return, but according to the above letter to Levertov he was really intending to leave altogether out of "disgust." He compliments himself on this device to avoid "a scene." Since, on resuming, Olson called out several times for the absent Duncan, the "scene" was not avoided, nor can I believe Duncan thought it would be.

After his leaving, of course, Duncan's account in the letter relies on third-party reportage. Duncan is happy to pass on to Levertov hearsay from a source who, strangely, stayed on in the hall for a further two hours even while supposedly considering Olson "out of his head." As for the gossip about Robert Creeley trying to get Olson to read poems instead of talking, and Olson's supposed overreaction: "This is the last time you are going to correct me, Robert Creeley," because of the tape transcription we can safely say that such a remark was never uttered. It's true that Creeley interrupted Olson, but it was in the form of aiding someone who was certainly sinking at that moment, and one detects a touch of gratitude in Olson's voice:

> Olson: Isn't it nice, really. This is the private soul at the public wall. Charlie Olson. Closed verse. Not even bothering to play music. I got the music. I mean, it's like scores, Beethoven and all those things, John Keats's letters in Harvard's library. I read 'em. In fact, I wrote a fourteen-line sonnet. You know, it's powerful. I was talking to Ed Dorn recently. Probably I shouldn't have eaten supper, but ...

> Creeley: Please read the poems.

> Olson: All right, Bob, I heard you. I'll continue 5, goddamn it. I stopped there. I will see if it can ...

> (Saint Santa
Claus!

> [Slaps table.] You son of a bitch! Raymond Weaver, my ass, Allen! You are my instructor. I am not a professor. And I've been instructed. And if you don't graduate me tonight on this platform at the University of California. Ha ha ha!

Whether or not Olson's turning on Ginsberg (in a mock aggressive manner) was misunderstood by Duncan's informant as a chiding of Creeley we cannot know, nor can we know the nature of Creeley's raising a point at the party (if it actually happened). We can certainly understand Olson's denial. The tape punctures a big hole in this disparaging anecdote.

Why would Duncan want to listen to such defamation of Olson and pass it on? Why, indeed, did he have such a strong reaction to the reading itself, so that he had to leave? There may be deeper reasons, but I suggest that one answer lies in what turns out to be another error of fact in his account. He says that it was "after forty-five minutes or so" that he called for the break. The fact is that Olson had held the stage for a full hour and twenty-three minutes, and I am sure that that is the longest period of time in Duncan's life when he had not heard the sound of his own voice.

I would like, in rebuttal of the "older friends," as Clark calls them, to present testimony from one of the so-called "younger spectators," Anna

Waldman, from *Fast Speaking Woman* (City Lights, expanded edition, 1996):

> I date my empowerment or confirmation of a life in poetry, not simply my own, to Charles Olson's reading in 1965 at the famous Berkeley Poetry conference. At one point Olson says:
>
>> No, I wanna talk, I mean, you want to listen to a poet. You know, a poet, when he's alive, whether he talks or reads you his poems is the same thing. Dig that! and when he is made of three parts—his life, his mouth, and his poem—then, by god, the earth belongs to us! And what I think has happened is that that's—wow, gee, one doesn't like to claim things, but god, isn't it exciting. I mean, I feel like a kid, I'm in the presence of an event, which I don't believe, myself.
>
> "In the presence of an event" was the illuminating phrase for me. He gave a brilliant talk/reading: fragmented, disturbed, and chaotic on one level, but completely lucid on another. He kept the audience there for more than four hours. Robert Duncan kept begging him to take a break so everyone could "go pee." Olson said perceptive things like: "You need to know that experience and society is a complex occasion, which requires as much wit and power as only poets have." I remember having an intuitive sense of the man's mind-weave, of catching the grammar of his thinking, of his synaptical leaps of thought and insight.
>
> I wrote the poem "Eyes In All The Heads To be Looked Out Of" to finally honor my connection to the poet Charles Olson and that particular occasion in Berkeley and to express my "birth" as a poet. (pp. 145–46).

28
The "Christine Kerrigan" Affair

Clark used the pseudonym "Christine Kerrigan" to speak of that most eminent among patronesses, Panna Grady. Such a disguise implied that there was something in her behavior that could not be talked about using her real name. Panna Grady is, to my certain knowledge, a very straight person who has high standards for herself and the company she keeps. I remember her saying, as though to establish this, that "the only true men" in New York City were Norman Mailer and Allen Ginsberg, whom she was satisfied to have had at her dinner table together. Her circle in the early '60s, maintained by what seemed magical wealth in such a young person, was wide and appreciative. Ed Sanders in the June/July 1965 edition of *Fuck You / a magazine of the arts* (#5 vol. 9) began "Notes from Editor" with:

> Great pleasure it is to announce the FIRST ANNUAL FUCK YOU PRESS AWARD FOR DISTINGUISHED SERVICE TO THE ARTS. This year the award goes to Panna Grady for incredible generosity, kindness, tenderness, and benevolence in dealing with many freaky neurasthenic artists, poets, moviemakers, magicians, etc. on the N.Y. scene. It often takes great patience in aiding writers, but her grace and squack-vectors have been fantastic.

A few pages later in the same issue of this magazine is John Wieners's poem "Memories of You," which includes the lines:

> And I have known women, too, laid beside them in the dawn—
> but never balled them. Tho I want to.
> Would some woman come up and give me enough of her flesh ...
> ... inwardly I scream and dream of the day
> when I will be free
> to marry

By the time of my visit to Gloucester on 29 June 1966 that seemingly unlikely dream of Wieners's had, up to a point, happened. I know few details. Jack Clarke in refuting Tom Clark on various points (his review in *intent.* 2:4/3:1 Winter/Spring 1991 p. 19) says that the conception occurred at the University Manor Motel, Buffalo, not at the Dennison house in Annisquam. That fits the chronology as I know it. The principals in this drama may some day tell their story, but as a bit player I would like to add now what I know in order to correct erroneous impressions in Tom Clark's biography, which are damaging to others besides Olson.

Clark: "Olson, as Wieners' fatherly spiritual adviser, did some heavy hanging-out at the Riverdale manse, whose woodsy setting provided landscape inspiration for a June *Maximus* poem on pathfinding as a way of knowledge ..." (p. 330).

John Wieners and Panna Grady took up residence in Annisquam (adjacent to Gloucester) on 17 May 1966. Writing to Edward Dorn a month later on 11 June 1966, Olson said: "Haven't seen John or Panna yet." We know of a visit Friday to Sunday 17–19 June 1966 because Olson shares the memory of it in a letter to David Haselwood, who with a friend had also been a guest then. There had probably been a brief visit a few days prior to this, as mentioned in the poem "AN ART CALLED GOTHONIC." But this hardly constitutes "heavy hanging-out" with the intimation of incipient ménage a trois. Clark says Olson "hinted mysteriously of sudden dramatic complications in his emotional life, with Christine Kerrigan at 'the center of the web.'" This is a misreading of a letter to Ed Dorn where Olson is saying no more than that there have been a great many visitors to Gloucester because of the presence of John Wieners and Panna Grady: "Panna (Grady) was in & *out of* the center of so much of the web." So this is not "mysterious" at all, especially since the letter is not dated May or June or July or August, but 27 September 1966, and Olson is summarizing the whole summer, not "sudden dramatic complications," as Clark would have us think, in a "three-way romantic entanglement" (p. 331).

Clark: "Learning upon Christine Kerrigan's return that she'd become pregnant with Wieners' child, Olson counseled an abortion (an action that would be regarded as a serious betrayal—leading to a tragic loss of 'good blood'—by the prospective father, once he found out about it)" (p. 332).

This is all fiction. Panna Grady did not need anyone's counseling in coming to her decision. As she said to me at the time, "Would you want

John Wieners' child?" I couldn't answer in the affirmative. The end of the Wieners poem quoted above is:

> when I will be free
> to marry
> and breed more children
> so I can seduce them
> and they be seduced by
> saintly motorcyclists in the dawn

This is not to discount John's feelings of fatherhood, which I saw to be very real. But the decision had been made irrevocably as soon as there was a decision to be made. That was what I gathered from being there. As I remember it, there wasn't any time for Olson to be a significant participant in the decision. We get the detailed chronology in Olson's own notebook entry (notebook 19 at Storrs):

> Wed Thurs June 29th 30th at John and Panna's with Ralph Maud also as guest—John and I starting out Tuesday, & Maud running into us at Little Pond & taking them through Long Cove to Richard Window house & the Surf then to John's & talking until—?
> & Wednesday Panna & Ella return & Thursday Ralph & they ship & dinner & I came home at 3:00AM (Friday Jly 1st.

After the all-night talk with me, Olson slept most of the day Wednesday. By the time he got up I'm pretty sure I had already been asked by Panna if I could take her along with me to Long Island the next day.

Which I did. I was an innocent functionary in all this, but I shall never forget the look on John Wieners's face as we were getting into the car that would take his fatherhood away from him. I had agreed to do what I thought was a convenient favor, but it turned out to be much more momentous. I have always felt that John thought of me as the fatal surgeon.

But, in any case, Olson's role was far different from what Clark implies. From the poet's diary quoted above it is clear that, after our departure, Olson stayed in the house with John alone for the whole of Thursday and into the early hours of Friday, as an act of friendship.

Clark: "Soon afterward, in a strained telephone call between Gloucester and the Chelsea Hotel in New York—where Kerrigan herself, Creeley and several other witnesses stood by the phone—he [Olson] broke the news to his fellow poet [Wieners] that he himself was about to sail off with their mutual paramour to England" (p. 332).

However little is known at present about how Olson and Panna Grady came to embark on a European jaunt, we do know that it was not "soon after" the events just discussed. It was not until six weeks after my visit and some time after Panna had returned to reside in Annisquam again that Olson reported to me, in a letter of 11 August 1966, that he had been with the couple again—"the single time since you were here":

> in fact made Panna pop her eyes, and John as usual grin when I suddenly screamed at them twice, in the middle of a lovely night around the Cafe Table (d'Hotestesse), on two counts—immense countries I accused them of impossible ignorance of:
>
> > the Unconscious; and
> > econometrics!

Clearly "it" had not happened yet. Nor by the end of the following month, though Olson does report in a letter of 27 September 1966 to Ed Dorn, then in England, that Wieners is "becoming more and more edgy, with the threat of fall coming," It is in a letter of 4 October 1966 that he expects to be "happy now *soon* to be cleared out ... which I hope means—say via Reykjavik or Montreal—to approach yours and Jeremy's *shores*!" (letters at Storrs). We can be very precise as to when things did finally break: Olson tells Dorn that "Panna or Mrs Grady ... will be travelling with me from 1:30AM tonight onward" (letter 27 October 1966). With Panna's daughter Ella they embarked on the *Empress of London* on 29 October from Montreal.

It was for five months, then, that Olson had given Wieners his space. Some might suggest, I suppose, that talking econometrics once every few weeks was Olson's way of stealing a woman away from his friend. There may be some truth in that, for compatibility is rare and irresistible. I saw for myself the great rapport there was between Panna and Charles in the conversation that Wednesday evening in the Dennison house. (Hitler's sex life I remember as one of the topics!) The phrase "mutual paramour" (Clark p. 332) belittles the growing relationship; there are enough signs that the trip to England came about through a genuine joie de vivre.

Clark: "The discovery [now in London] that Raworth's wife, Val, was Welsh prompted an Olson monologue on the previously unremarked correspondences between the Welsh and the Mandan Indians that went on until the break of dawn" (pp. 332–33).

This is somewhat off the subject, but it is something I have unique knowledge of; for it was I who was responsible for Olson's "monologue" in that I brought him from Aberystwyth (where I was spending a research year) a series of clippings from the Welsh daily newspaper *The Western Mail* in which Richard Deakin was reviewing the evidence for the long-standing supposition that prince Madoc had in prehistoric times sailed across the Atlantic and up the Mississippi, reaching the Mandan Indians with an influence that is said to be detectable today. Olson wrote to me from 22 Mount Street, London, on 4 December 1966, the day after my visit, that he had already passed the clippings on to "a Welsh lady patriot." I am gratified to learn via Tom Clark's account that Olson thoroughly digested the contents before doing so! This was interesting stuff at the time, and if this sort of talk "bored" some individual, as Clark chooses to state (p. 335), I think a biographer could, for an alternative view, have consulted many another whom Olson did not so offend.

Clark: "For some days after the cardiac episode [during a trip to Berlin for a reading] he lay abed in the Hotel Steinplatz, meditating upon his life and writing letters to women he knew in a new effort to recruit someone to care for him in his 'protectionless' remaining days. The list of candidates, however, was now sadly short. Joyce Benson was sounded out about a rendezvous on the isle of Crete" (p. 333).

Let's stop right there. Olson's letter to Joyce Benson about Crete was sent on 27 November 1966, long before he set off for Berlin. It had nothing to do with his heart attack, which as a matter of fact was of a mild sort, where the doctor ended up giving him a clean bill of health. And "protectionless" was a word used not at this time but a year before, in a notebook entry of 18 January 1966. Certainly, the time alone in a hotel room in Berlin was one of self-reflection—and respite from the social life Panna created in London. Yes, Olson was looking around him again, but the short "list of candidates," as Clark scornfully phrases it, was actually a list of one, and that of long acquaintance: Frances Boldereff. She had sent him a gift which had only just reached him, forwarded to Germany. That would seem to deserve a letter, would it not? Since Clark garbles the letter in quoting from it, the full text (at Storrs) is presented below:

December 30th (1966)

Frances love,
          Simply to tell you. And that your Maenad (with double flute) came into my hands, with its endearing message, only yesterday—even too late, for my 56th birthday!
          I am poised here on the tilt (of the East) only

to gather strength (I hope) to go into those places my mind has fed on, as has yours. And which now lie open before me—casements, wasn't it, Keats called magic casements opening on seas forlorn (?)—

      In any case
my heart lies at your feet—And I wish you shared my bed. And life. Happily, & Eternally Yours

If you wld ever write you can reach me for at least another fortnight [indicates hotel address on letterhead]

Unfortunately for Clark's portrait of a downcast invalid, Olson is here rallying to follow an old urge to go to the Middle East. He doesn't even mention his heart attack, never mind needing a nurse.

Olson in Germany, 1966.
Photo: Renate Gerhardt. Kate Olson Archive.

Clark: "His relations with Kerrigan were meanwhile rapidly deteriorating. 'I'm here with a human vampire from Transylvania,' he complained in a letter to his daughter" (p. 335).

Such a letter is not to be found in the Kate Olson archive. Olson put it rather more moderately in a letter to Robert Creeley from his "hiding" place, the May Fair Hotel, Berkeley St., London W.1, on 26 March 1967, after ten days of enjoying London alone (letter at Stanford):

> after 6 months with Panna—& a 10 day visit with the Dorns (who *also* don't know where I am nor does Panna—I have allowed myself to "disappear," between Colchester & London, in order actually to recover freedom of all or any movement. Everything had gotten too conversational for the likes of an old winter bear; and equally—as still the earth seems to me—overpopulated.

Oblivious to Olson's disappearance, I myself turned up at 17 Hanover Terrace, London, on 2 April. Panna put me in the guest house in the garden that she was preparing for Allen Ginsberg to enjoy on a proposed visit. She had to go out to a restaurant dinner she had arranged for the purpose of introducing William Burroughs to Tom Driberg, M.P., socialist journalist and, at that time, secret homosexual. She returned at midnight full of stories about the evening, interspersed with reiterated worry and puzzlement over Charles's disappearance. This went on into the early hours, and I realized again the attraction in the fiery wit but also the tax on one's energies which acquaintance with Panna might involve.

Clark: "On May 8 he reached Dorchester and booked into the Antelope Hotel. The next month or so he spent lying low in Dorset, poking halfheartedly through local port records and rummaging idly in antiquarian bookshops" (p. 335).

"Halfheartedly" and "rummaging idly" are figments of the imagination of someone trying, for unknown reasons, to make the subject of his biography look pathetic. I went down to Dorchester some time in the '70s and found R.N.R. Peers, who had been the assistant curator at the Museum at the time (and was now the Director). He had the fondest memories of Olson, whose digging into the records he was daily in awe of. There never was (contra Clark) such a vital presence in that museum. He made a point of recalling for me the day he took Olson out in his little Morris Minor to an archaeological site, where they "heard a lark sing."

Clark: "Another unsettling reunion awaited Olson in October [1967] at Cortland, New York, where he addressed a state university poetry convocation and encountered his estranged comrade John Wieners, whom he hadn't been able to face since the previous summer's indelicate double cross. Obviously intent on peacemaking, he gave over his keynote talk before the big banquet crowd to a lavish if rambling tribute to Wieners and Ed Sanders. By the end of the convocation he had managed by old-fashioned charm and wooing, to patch things up sufficiently with his wounded fellow poet to appease his own conscience on at least that one touchy point" (p. 337).

What a shabby fellow this Olson must be, methinks! I was glad to see that Jack Clarke in his review in *intent.* objected to the biography's interpretation of these events, declaring that in his view there had been no "betrayal," and pointing out that he had heard that Wieners's only accusation to Olson at Cortland was, "You lost my scarf." We can fill out a few further facts. Olson struck a carefree tone in a letter to Harvey Brown on 20 October 1967 (letter at Buffalo): "Off today to do that stunt before New York State College I suppose poets—including I hear one John Wieners. So hold your breath—I'm not sure I shldn't have you along as my bodyguard, at least to frisk him unnoticeably!" A perusal of Olson's "Talk at Cortland" (printed in *Muthologos* II and, revised, in *Minutes #4*) reveals that, beyond singling out Wieners as "responsible for this thing that I'm calling 'affect,'" he did not flatter him with a lavish tribute, as Clark states. Maybe what Olson did was just about right. Duncan McNaughton in the pages of *Minutes #4* gave a full account of the social gathering afterwards, when Olson asked Wieners something pointblank, giving him a chance to have his say:

> I do not remember John's words exactly, but it was something like: "But I trusted you, and you abandoned me ... without a penny ... I had to ask So-and-so to give (or send) me enough money for a train ticket back to Boston!" You know, it stopped Olson cold. Perfectly direct poignant emotional honesty of Wieners which at that time nobody could touch—so the room went dead, didn't matter how much or little one knew of the details behind the reply. The boom got lowered, John had said what he had to say, he then departed to his room.

Olson did not, according to McNaughton, follow Wieners, but got the conversation going again in the room, "got on with it." The real reconciliation was at the poetry reading when Wieners read his poem "What Happened":

he read it just right. Which so delighted Olson he actually leapt from the sofa, really tickled—and very probably thrilled, more than the rest of us, because John may have prefaced the poem by saying that his reading it was in honor of Mr. Olson's presence. At any rate that poem broke the ice between the two men.

Olson wrote to Harvey Brown on 26 October 1967: "Saw John and he was just as usual too much. Read marvelously—& was more than ever my Admired One! ... He *is* sharp-tongued and swollen with hurt-pain and feeling, but anybody who can't see he is quicker and more profound than ever are themselves fools!"

Epilogue

A couple of times in the spring of 1965 I found Olson in the café across from the main gates of the State University of New York at Buffalo, and asked him a few direct questions about the earlier *Maximus* poems, such as, "How can you draw a map in spelt?" (I.77), "Who is the 'grey-eyed one' who makes 'a man's chest shine'?" (I.21), "Who is Helen Stein?" (I.18). Obvious things once you knew the answers, but Butterick's *Guide to the Maximus Poems* hadn't yet come out. After the second session, Olson leaned across the booth table, his eyes round in his glasses, and said, "How would you like to be my scholar?" Each participant at the coming Berkeley Poetry Conference had been given a free pass to hand out to his or her "scholar." I accepted the title and turned up in Berkeley in July.

The position of "scholar" was, as it turned out for the next forty-some years, no sinecure. In my first semester at Simon Fraser University that fall I used the 1960 Totem/Corinth edition of *The Maximus Poems* as a required text, and then the New Directions *Selected Writings* regularly after it came out the following year. In fact, I taught Olson at least one semester every year from 1965 to 1994. I mention this for only one reason: to substantiate my authority for saying what I said earlier when I insisted that young people take to Olson's work. And I think I know why. Because he is an optimist. He believes in something, something that poetry can effect in the real world. His subject is

> how to dance
> sitting down

—how to dance with pen in hand. Methodology.

> Eyes
> & polis,
> fishermen
> & poets

                    or in every human head I've known is
                    busy
              both
              the attention, and
              the care

"Every human head"—my students thought about it and said, "That's me. I must get busy." It's what we mean by "inspirational," a word that has been debased but can be used of Olson in its best original meaning.

I do not think it is the role of the critic to prove that a poet is inspirational. I assert it and ask you to believe me and to gain your own experience of it, if you have not already. What a critic has a right to do is the other job: to prove that the poet is not a dead log in the water and, if someone says he is, prove them wrong. This corrective work is what I have been about in this volume.

Maybe, after all, in the suitably limited space of a brief epilogue, I should make a try at the other, impossible job, to convince you of Olson's readiness and responsiveness as he stands at the harbor—by which we mean "at the ready" and, more than that, "at command." Let's play it this way: that he is the Man of Good Voyage whom we see as we look back from the harbor mouth, and he is holding us, holding us to the promise that we be the best we can imagine we should be.

                    the demand
              will arouse
              some of these men and women

There is that moment when Olson knew that that must be his role, when he was very young, being given his model for life in the way a young person could feel it, if he had the sensibility. As Olson tells it (in *Muthologos* II.165) referring to a fisherman friend Louis Douglas, eighty-five years old as Olson commemorates him to his interviewer, Herbert Kenny:

> I can tell you just as many stories of great men who came in from the sea and raised families and even to this day are of such dignity and shape that I don't know their equal in other forms of life or business or profession in the rest of the world. I can take you, introduce you to them on the streets of Gloucester right now. In fact, there's one man I see taking a bus back over the Cut that I consider the man who made me a poet simply because of the nature of his language when I listened behind a stone wall to him and his brother from Newfoundland talk when I was four years old.

Louis Douglas and Charles Olson, c. 1969.
Kate Olson Archive.

And I just want to add, in this particular context, as my last chastisement of Tom Clark, that it was not that the young Olson's imagination was "captured by the high romance of oceangoing" (pp. 9–10). Olson refutes that in the passage above. It was the "nature of his [Louis Douglas's] language" that caused Olson to be a poet, and you can bet it was not just his Newfoundland accent. I'm sure it was, as Olson put it in "Projective Verse," his "stance toward reality." The proof is that, when Douglas came over to Fort Point some fifty years later, Olson particularly described him in terms of his caring:

> when he walked in he wasn't going to stop, but then he saw my windows and he said, "My lord, Charlie, you do have, you have some, you have a lot of windows looking out!" I say, "Yes." So I said, "Come through the house and see it." Sat down and talked for three hours, identified everything that ever was on the Fort! He has that fantastic condition of the human race when everything mattered. Today, nothing does, and that's what's so poor. And I know men for whom everything matters. Still! Who see, feel, and know that everything that they run into does matter. Hah! And then they retain it. And then they have it. And they have it forever. And when they're buried they're bigger than those people who don't. Even if they look the same and fit the same box. (*Mythologos* II.166)

Winter view from 28 Fort Square.
Kate Olson Archive.

After this peroration, Herb Kenny can't help but ask the obvious question which we all want to ask: Is it because Douglas was a Gloucester fisherman? "No," replies Olson, but even so, "the container had a better chance to have a content." In this, Olson was very lucky. His father, who was no slouch in the "stance toward reality" department, chose Gloucester, and Olson early came to know its special qualities. And it isn't that he hankered after being a fisherman. That was one of the "false" lines in "Maximus, to himself": "The sea was not finally my trade." "Finally?" It never was his trade, nor could it have been, and the "high romance of oceangoing" could not possibly be part of this. But the town of Gloucester and the harbor itself that sheltered this life of courage and care were a gauge of the real, and gave Olson his polis and his discriminations.

It is, in a word, the affirmation of the authentic. And I have my exemplum ready; "Maximus, to himself," which is Olson's anthology piece, everybody's favorite, right? Well, here I can for once commend Tom Clark because he does not get sucked into this poem at all, in spite of its being so very available. As one might expect, it's the poem that Gerard Malanga, interviewing Olson for the *Paris Review* in April 1969, requested that Olson read on the tape. What happened then was one of the most amazing deconstructions imaginable, for instead of performing the poem as a well-behaved poet would do, Olson took it almost line by line and shook it to see what value was left when the falsities fell out. The result is still on tape, and transcribed in *Muthologos* II.118ff.

> I can assure you, fifteen years later, don't listen to me. "I have had to learn the simplest things last." I mean, the simplest thing is going to occur tomorrow! What am I going to do?

Olson gets through four lines and then says, "This is boring," and asks to read instead a "brand new" poem on the same theme of his incompetence at sea, and does so. Olson wants to be with the new, the instant, the now. But Malanga gets him back to "Maximus, to himself" (*Muthologos* II.151):

                I have made dialogues

(That's true.)

                I have discussed ancient texts

(To my pride.)

                have thrown what light I could.

Olson interrupts himself again to say, "I think that's a little bit special pleading. It's begging your sympathy …'Please …'."

Then, as the most amazing of this amazing thing he does, Olson starts to re-write these lines to cut out the pleading:

But I'd thought, like, I'd change the syntax, it would be OK.

> I've discussed ancient texts;
> on some things have been original, innate, inertial,
> never to be forgotten.
> Fuck you.
> Can't do it again.
> Somebody can.

I don't know how the above words come over on the page to someone who has not had the chance to hear Olson say them, but I find this intrusion of bedrock personal truth into a most romantic poem one of the great acts of moral rectitude. It is especially moving because Olson, here in his last year, is handing the baton to us, somebody, anybody who is running alongside.

There's more. Always with Olson there's more. That's what this great man has to offer, not only more than we can handle, but more than he can get out at any one time. There is never the sense that "this wraps it up." Olson talked all night, as not a few of us can attest to, and this *Paris Review* tape itself attests to, but always with surprises and laughter—as here when Olson says it took him "all these years" to find out how bad "Maximus, to himself" was: "But I knew it instantly, by the way. There's that point. I knew this poem was no good from the moment that I wrote it." Which remark, of course, produced laughter. Olson has to repeat: "It's absolutely true. Hear me. If you don't hear this, I haven't got anything at all." He stakes everything on our agreeing with his sense of the poem's inauthenticity. As he had said earlier, to indicate the kind of discrimination of value he was demanding of us: "If we don't get that straight, we ain't got but 98 percent of everything, and ... if you don't get a hundred today you're just killing time" (*Muthologos* II.148).

The gist of Olson's complaint seems to be that "Maximus, to himself" is a soliloquy that pretends the subjective is of valid concern:

> it is undone business I speak of
> this morning
> with the sea stretching out
> from my feet

It smacks too much of personal angst, whereas Olson has to be "an image of man," to quote his poem, "Maximus of Gloucester" (III.101):

> It is not I
> even if the life appeared
> biographical. The only interesting thing
> is if one can be
> an image
> of man, "the nobleness, and the arete"

Olson is thinking here of the ideal hero presented in Werner Jaeger's *Paidea* or, by this time, specifically Havelock's definition of the Homeric heroes as "conspicuous" and "public," and therefore of use, like Olson's fishermen.

Then, what about "Maximus, at the Harbor," the poem of this book's title? Olson startlingly calls it "equally weak ... a sucker poem, if I may tell the world" (*Muthologos* II.148). Olson lumps the two poems together as having "the lesion of talking about myself, which I permit myself at this one point to let the leak in ... Otherwise, the boundaries have to be as tight as our moral structure." This will be a nice conundrum to take with us on our travels. "Maximus, at the Harbor" is a poem that definitely seems as though it should pass muster. It has at the back of it Henry Corbin's "Cyclical Time in Mazdaism and Ismailism" from *Man and Time* (Eranos Yearbook 1957). It has the kind of objectivity given to a poem by mythology. And, on the other hand, it has a realistic storm crashing on known places, the waves breaking on Norman's Woe rocks like the "bone" of foam made by the prow of a ship. There are bits that Olson might know are personal sex-writing, but they are covered by the powerful line: "Encircling Okeanos tears upon the earth to get love loose." And, needless to say, the "Perfect Child" of the last line is not biographical; it's from Henry Corbin again, "a celestial archetype."

So, is Olson kidding us? He's certainly not making it easy. These are two of his most likeable poems, and he is asking us to suspect them as not truly authentic. What a task, then, to sort it all out. He does not say to dismiss them. On the tape, he says anyone who gets "caught" by "Maximus, at the Harbor" is being "caught on my treadle," which doesn't sound so good. "But," he continues:

> you don't think I put it in there without meaning that I should comb my hair with every one of them things, uh? Otherwise, what's the excuse for a comb? I mean, I'm only giving you value in that devaluated sense, the depression with which we exist at all. But that's part of it too, god damn the present, because it doesn't understand the bum trip or bad trip is where there's as much to be found as …

And Olson leaves the sentence unfinished. We will follow him in this regard and end with that unfinished sentence, whose reverberations extend back through the whole of this volume.

I find it only invigorating that Olson has left us so much to do, with the added reassurance that we are not supposed to finish things. Especially we are not to rush to untie the Hanged Man, if we are lucky enough to get that card. With Olson, we get that card, which is not the Tower of a different assertiveness, nor even the "Perfect Child." It's the state of being buffeted by the wave that presents itself (*apophainesthai*) at the harbor mouth.

Olson with scholar George Butterick on the beach at Gloucester.
Photo: Ann Charters. Kate Olson Archive.

28 Fort Square, Gloucester, as it was at the time of Olson's death, 1970.
Photo: Charles Olson Society.

Afterword

I realize that I have shied away from saying much about Betty Olson. The topic is difficult for me for reasons that will become apparent.

Michael Rumaker was there when Olson first began wooing Betty at Black Mountain. He was living in quarters immediately below Betty's, and tells all in his *Black Mountain Days*. I cannot add to his account, nor to Clark's in general. His description of Olson's first meeting with Betty's family is revealing: "All but Jean gave him a chilly reception" (p. 251). Clearly Olson and Betty were setting themselves up for a fairly isolated existence.

They were never more isolated than in Wyoming, New York. I went with my wife and son the hour's drive out of Buffalo on a Sunday afternoon on 30 October 1963, thinking that 2:30 in the afternoon would be a reasonable time to drop in. And we were lucky. Olson and Betty were up and about, and Donald Allen was also there. That could have been a problem because, in a previous life as editor of *Audit* I had assigned John Simon to review Allen's *The New American Poetry: 1945–1960* in his predictably sarcastic way. But, though Don would not forget such a thing, he was invariably polite. I was not quite sure, for he immediately announced he would retire. However, when I looked at the old-fashioned large country fireplace, I knew why. The fire had an old look, sagging in on itself, and the amount of ashes piled in the grate indicated only one thing: that Olson and Don Allen had been up all night and hadn't stopped talking until we arrived in mid-afternoon.

But Olson was not about to ignore his new guests, and I found myself walking with him across the fields of upstate New York, with talk that was so much of that particular time and place that I do not remember any of it—except for one thing: Olson dug the toe of his boot into a loose sod of earth as though discovering an old arrowhead (which he said he had several times done), and he raised his head to the skies to announce, "Injuns! They are my people!" (It was the result of this one remark that, when settled in British Columbia after 1965, I myself dug into the ethnographic history of my landscape.)

Betty I remember only as a slim shadow of a figure in the kitchen offering us some tea and saying very little, as though accustomed to being self-effacing. Carol Cook, the wife of the English Department Chairman Al Cook, who had brought Olson to SUNY Buffalo with an offer he couldn't refuse, called her "shy, quiet, polite" (Clark p. 304). It is sad to report that the next time I saw her she was quiet indeed, for she was in her coffin. Carol Cook in her account describes receiving the phone call one day in late March of 1964 from the "incredulous" Charles that Betty, driving alone, had skidded on the icy roads and was killed. In a section of her unpublished memoir, Carol describes the day of the funeral:

> We drove out early, my younger son in the back seat with the comestibles and flowers. Charles met us at the door. And Betty met us at the door, in her open casket a few feet inside the living room. Her stockinged feet peeping out from the long black skirt lent an air of innocent naturalness to her stilled figure. Why did Charles want an open casket? I guess I knew. It prolonged her presence among us, it gave at least a brief illusion that she was back from that fateful ride. I took it as a measure of his reluctance to give her up. But it was unbearable somehow to see in her face the features inherited by Charles Peter. He seemed to be floating about, my son at his side, neither of them seeming to know what to do with themselves.

Today, at the time of my writing this, I know that Charles Peter Olson is a happy family man plying his trade of carpenter in Gloucester, and I feel he understands that his father's fame imposes on us who knew him the duty to say what is vital to be said though it may trespass on what otherwise would be privacies.

It was your father's genius for life and poetry that asks you, Charlie, to excuse my adding my own experience to the above description; for it was you as a waif of nine years old that I saw first as I entered that same door as Carol did—except I was terribly late. Ed Budowski and I had driven to the Catholic Church some miles away, having been told it was to be a proper Catholic service, but not told the priest was to come to the house rather than the mourners to the church. The Mass with the holy water and the priest in full robes was all over by the time I got there. Carol Cook in her account said it struck her as odd: "I never thought of Charles and Betty as Catholics, certainly not as believers. But all wish to bury the dead decently and ritual makes things easier. And ritual was respected by Charles."

All the old friends and visitors had repaired to the nearby big house for the wake by the time Ed Budowski and I burst through the door into the room where I had previously been with Don Allen and the overflowing ashes of the fireplace. Young Charles Peter had his back to the door and did not turn around. Olson leaning over the coffin was pitifully engrossed in his lamentation. Two funeral attendants were trying to close the coffin's lid while Olson was physically holding it open, delaying. I stood transfixed. No non-participant should be witness to such a tableau. Our lateness had put us in a frightfully intrusive position. However, nobody noticed us, it seemed, so I pulled myself away from the scene and went through a door on the immediate left, which was to the downstairs bathroom, and waited breathlessly while the morticians prevailed upon the audibly stricken Olson to allow the coffin to be closed. Then, more frightful still, through the other door of the bathroom, which was open to the living room, I saw the figure of the bereaved widower slump face-down on the sofa. I tensed up even more, for he was literally not more than six feet from me and his contorted face was turned in my direction. I was terrified that he might open his closed eyes and see me and have to recognize me and acknowledge me. I was frozen because I thought that if I moved he would open his eyes at the movement. But he didn't. He was sobbing into himself. He was indeed the true picture of one wracked by grief and loss, oblivious to all but that personal momentousness. Finally, I turned slowly and went across the hallway in the opposite direction, into the kitchen where I had last seen Betty. Vincent Ferrini was there, preparing a whiskey for his friend Charles. I did not stay, but rushed out into the cold air and walked somnambulistically on the frozen snow's surface into an area away from the house where there were no other footprints.

Some who were there told me afterwards that I should not have got in the car and had Ed Budowski drive me back to Buffalo. They said Olson joined the group eventually and was all right. Carol Cook says differently in her unpublished piece: "It was a wake. Charles was grieving as he drank. He seemed a lonely and blinded giant in the crowd, feeling and hearing everything, seeing nothing. My son says he remembers Charles sitting backwards on a high-backed chair, leaning his head on his arms which he had draped over the top rung, and sobbing."

Olson was in hospital for a while, but he stayed at Buffalo to finish the academic year, and then another year; but knowing there was no happiness in it, in the third week of the third year, he left—left his courses to Jack Clarke and the explanations for Al Cook to make (who organized sick leave). He went back to 28 Fort Square, Gloucester, his eyrie by the harbor. When I saw him there four years later he said, "Wasn't I right to get home?" I can answer that more confidently now, knowing how much he accomplished in those years, the absolute newness of the quality of it as it appeared concurrently in letters to the *Gloucester Daily Times*, posthumously in *The Maximus Poems Volume Three*, and in letters to a wide range of correspondents that it has been my privilege to peruse as editor of *The Selected Letter of Charles Olson*. His work and my work took us far away from the funeral room with the coffin and the ashes, but not unaffected by it.

I tell in my Introduction to *The Selected Letters* of being on Fort Point one time during those later years, returning to Gloucester town center after having found Olson not at home. I saw an automobile coming up the empty street, very slowly, meandering from one side to the other. It stopped when it reached me and the driver leaned over to open the passenger door and wave me in. "I bet you think I'm drunk." It was Olson, beaming as was his wont. "No, I've eaten, and I'm just exhausted." And he added by way of explanation: "Today I wrote eight letters, all of them of some consequence." I had encountered Olson at the end of his work-day.

In the Introduction I dwell on the word "consequence" in terms of how it was always by letters that Olson pushed forward the boundaries, for himself as well as the recipient. He sometimes asked for his holograph letters back to see what he had said that he remembered as important; just as the only time I was in Olson's classroom in Buffalo—it was long after the students had left—and he was sitting in the front row surveying the blackboards that he had filled during class time. He was fixing in his mind where the journey that day had taken him: the consequences.

The consequence of that encounter with Olson in the street was remarkable—but not atypical for him. He parked the car and we started walking along Pavilion Beach. He brightened up as we walked the harbor's sandy verge and talked, rallying in such a remarkable way I had to blurt out, "Charles, two hours ago you were exhausted, and now ..." He straightened his back and said, "That's the nature of the thing." To a world which in the twenty-first century seems in a hopelessly exhausted state, I offer this picture of a refreshed Charles Olson at the harbor, with his shoulders back.

Index

Abbreviations (Library Sources)

Archives of American Art = Archives of American Art, Smithsonian Institution, Washington, D.C.

Berkeley = Bancroft Library, University of California, Berkeley

Buffalo = Poetry/Rare Books Collection, University Libraries, State University of New York at Buffalo

Harvard = Houghton Library, Harvard University, Cambridge, Massachusetts

Indiana = Lilly Library, Indiana University, Bloomington

Kate Olson Archive = In possession of Ralph Maud via Ken Stuart

Minnesota = Manuscript Division, University of Minnesota Libraries, St. Paul

New York Public Library = Henry W. and Albert A. Berg Collection, New York Public Library, New York

Raleigh = North Carolina State Archives, Raleigh

Simon Fraser = Contemporary Literature Collection, Bennett Library, Simon Fraser University, Burnaby, British Columbia

Southern Illinois = Morris Library, Southern Illinois University, Carbondale

Stanford = Stanford University Libraries, Stanford, California

Storrs = Special Collections Department of the Thomas J. Dodd Research Center, University of Connecticut, Storrs

Texas = Harry Ransom Humanities Research Center, University of Texas, Austin

UCLA = University Research Library, University of California, Los Angeles

Utah State = Special Collections and Archives, Merrill Library, Utah State University, Logan

Wesleyan = Olin Library, Wesleyan University, Middletown, Connecticut

Yale = Beinecke Library, Yale University, New Haven, Connecticut

Abbreviations
(published works of Charles Olson)

Call Me Ishmael = *Call Me Ishmael* (New York: Reynal & Hitchcock, 1947; London: Cape, 1967).

y & x = *y & x* (Washington, D.C.: Black Sun Press, 1948).

Maximus 1–10 = *The Maximus Poems / 1–10* (Stuttgart: Jonathan Williams, 1953).

Mayan Letters = *Mayan Letters*, ed. Robert Creeley (Palma de Mallorca: Divers Press, 1953; London: Cape, 1968).

Maximus Poems (1960) = *The Maximus Poems* (New York: Jargon/Corinth, 1960; London: Cape Goliard, 1970).

Selected Writings = *Selected Writings*, ed. Robert Creeley (New York: New Directions, 1966).

Maximus IV, V, VI = *Maximus Poems IV, V, VI* (London: Cape Goliard, 1968; New York: Grossman, 1968).

The Post Office = *The Post Office* (Bolinas, California: Grey Fox Press, 1975).

Maximus Volume Three = *The Maximus Poems: Volume Three*, ed. Charles Boer and George F. Butterick (New York: Grossman, 1975).

Seelye = *Charles Olson and Ezra Pound: An Encounter at St. Elizabeths*, ed. Catherine Seelye (New York: Grossman, 1975).

Fiery Hunt = *The Fiery Hunt and Other Plays* (Bolinas, California: Four Seasons, 1977).

Mythologos = *Mythologos: The Collected Lectures and Interviews*, ed. George F. Butterick (Bolinas, California: Four Seasons, 1978–79).

CO/RC = *Charles Olson & Robert Creeley: The Complete Correspondence*, ed. George F. Butterick, later Richard Blevins, vols 1–10 (Santa Barbara: Black Sparrow Press, 1980–96).

Maximus Poems = *The Maximus Poems*, ed. F. Butterick (Berkeley: University of California Press, 1983).

Collected Poems = *The Collected Poems of Charles Olson Excluding the Maximus Poems*, ed. George F. Butterick (Berkeley: University of California Press, 1987).

In Love, In Sorrow = *In Love, In Sorrow: The Complete Correspondence of Charles Olson and Edward Dahlberg*, ed. Paul Christensen (New York: Paragon House, 1990).

Collected Prose = *Collected Prose,* eds. Donald Allen and Benjamin Friedlander (Berkeley: University of California Press, 1997).

CO/CC = *Charles Olson & Cid Corman: Complete Correspondence 1950–1964*, ed. George Evans, 2 vols. (Orono: National Poetry Foundation, 1987, 1991).

CO/FB = *Charles Olson & Frances Boldereff: A Modern Correspondence* (Middleton: Wesleyan University Press, 1999).

Selected Letters = *Selected Letters*, ed. Ralph Maud (Berkeley: University of California Press, 2000).

CO/DA = *Poet to Publisher: Charles Olson's Correspondence with Donald Allen*, ed. Ralph Maud (Vancouver: Talonbooks, 2003).